Lists Of Chapels Belonging To The Church Of England ... Of Places Of Public Worship, Registered For Solemnization Of Marriages, Also Of All Superintendent Registrars, And Deputy Superintendent Registrars

L I S T S

OF

CHAPELS BELONGING TO THE CHURCH OF ENGLAND,

From Returns made to the Registrar General of Births, Deaths, and Marriages,
by Registrars of Dioceses in England and Wales;

OF

PLACES OF PUBLIC WORSHIP,

Registered for Solemnization of Marriages under the Provisions of the Acts of 6 and 7
William IV., c. 85, and 1 Victoriæ, c. 22;

ALSO OF ALL

SUPERINTENDENT REGISTRARS,

AND

DEPUTY SUPERINTENDENT REGISTRARS;

REGISTRARS OF MARRIAGES,

AND OF

REGISTRARS OF BIRTHS AND DEATHS,

AND

DEPUTY REGISTRARS;

WITH THEIR PLACES OF ABODE, AND THE DISTRICTS FOR WHICH THEY RESPECTIVELY SERVE.

1840.

LONDON:
PRINTED BY W. CLOWES AND SONS, 14, CHARING CROSS,
FOR THE REGISTRAR GENERAL OF BIRTHS, DEATHS, AND MARRIAGES.

LIST

OF

CHAPELS BELONGING TO THE CHURCH OF ENGLAND,

FROM

*Returns made to the Registrar General of Births, Deaths, and Marriages,
by Registrars of Dioceses in England and Wales.*

DIOCESE OF ST. ASAPH.

St. Asaph.

A List made by the Registrars of the Diocese of St. Asaph, within fifteendays after the 1st day of January, 1840, in pursuance of the Provisions of the Acts of 6 and 7 Wm. IV., c. 85, and 7 Wm. IV., c. 1 ; being a List of all Chapels belonging to the Church of England within that Diocese wherein Marriages may lawfully be solemnized according to the Rites and Ceremonies of the Church of England—distinguishing which have a Parish, Chapelry, or other recognized Ecclesiastical Division annexed to them, and which are Chapels licensed by the Bishop under the Act of 6 and 7 Wm. IV., c. 85, and stating the Districts for which each of such Chapels is licensed, according to the description thereof in the License.

Name of Chapel.	Name or Description of Parish, Chapelry, or other recognized Ecclesiastical Division thereunto annexed.	Whether licensed under the Act of 6 and 7 Wm. IV., c. 85.	Description of District for which it is so Licensed.
Treyddyn . .	Mold	No.	
Nerquis . .	Mold	No.	
St. German's .	Llanwrst	No.	
Foelas . . .	Llanufydd . . .	No.	
Gwernafield .	Mold	Yes . . .	The whole of the township of Hendre Byffd, and the whole of Gwernafield township, with the exception of Rhual, Rhual-issa, Maesgarmon, and Croesonnen.
Brymbo . .	Wrexham. . . .	Yes . . .	The township of Brymbo.
Pontbleiddyn .	Mold	Yes . . .	The whole of the township of Hartsheath, the whole of the township of Leeswood, with the exception of the houses and farms of Pentrehobin and Tynewydd, and that part of the township of Biatre which lies on the south of the Mold and Broughton turnpike road.
St. Mark's . .	Northop	Yes . . .	The whole of the townships of Golftyn, Wepre, Kelsterton, Leadbrooke Major, and Leadbrooke Minor.
Rhosygwalie .	Llanfawr	Yes . . .	The township of Rhywedog.

(Signed)   E. and C. W. WYATT,
Deputy Registrars of the Diocese of St. Asaph.

DIOCESE OF BANGOR.

Bangor.

A Return of the several Chapels belonging to the Church of England, within the Diocese of Bangor, wherein Marriages may be lawfully solemnized according to the Rites and Ceremonies of the Church of England, distinguishing the Rectory or Vicarage to which such Chapels are respectively annexed.

Carnarvonshire.

Llanfaelrhus	A distinct parish annexed to the Vicarage of Aberdaron.
Cappel Cerrig	A Chapel of Ease annexed to the perpetual Curacy of Llandegai.
Ynyseynhaiarn and Treflys	Two distinct parishes annexed to the Rectory of Criccieth.
Penmorfa	A distinct parish annexed to the Rectory of Dolbennan.
Carngiwch and Pistill	Two distinct parishes annexed to the Rectory of Edern.
Llangian and Llanfihangel-Cachelleth .	Two distinct parishes annexed to Llanbedrog Rectory.
Llanarmon	A distinct parish annexed to Llangybi Rectory.
Penllech and Llandegwning. . . .	Two distinct parishes annexed to Llaniestyn Rectory.
Llanfagdalan	A distinct parish annexed to Llanwuda Vicarage.
Bottwnog.	A distinct parish annexed to Meyllityrne Rectory.
Llandudwen	A distinct parish annexed to Rhiw Rectory.
Llanrhochwyn	A distinct parish annexed to Trefriw Rectory.

County of Anglesey.

Llanwenllwyfo	A distinct parish annexed to Amlwch perpetual Curacy.
Trewalchmai	A distinct parish annexed to Heneglwys Rectory.
Llanfaelog, Ceirchiog, and Llechylched.	Three distinct parishes annexed to Llanbeulan Rectory.
Llanerchymedd	A Chapel of Ease annexed to Llanbeulan Rectory.
Llanbabo and Llanfairynghornwy . .	Two distinct parishes annexed to Llanddausaint Rectory.
Bodwrog	A distinct parish annexed to Llandrygarn perpetual Curacy.
Llanfihangel-trerbeirdd	A distinct parish annexed to Llandyfrydog Rectory.
Coedana . . . . :	A distinct parish annexed to Llaneilian Rectory.
Llanallgo	A distinct parish annexed to Llaneugrad Rectory.
Llanfigael and Llanynghenedl . . .	Two distinct parishes annexed to Llanfachreth Rectory.
Llanfwrog	A distinct parish annexed to Llanfaethelu Rectory.
Llandisilio	A distinct parish annexed to Llanfairpwllgwyngill Rectory.
Llanffinan	A distinct parish annexed to Llanfihangel Esgeifiog Rectory.
Llangaffo.	A distinct parish annexed to Llangeinwen Rectory.
Tregaian	A distinct parish annexed to Llangefui Rectory.

DIOCESE OF BANGOR.—*continued.*

Llaniestyn and Llanfihangel-tinsilwry .	Two distinct parishes annexed to Llangoed perpetual Curacy.
Cerrigceinweg	A distinct parish annexed to Llangristiolus Rectory.
Llanedwan and Llanddaniel . . .	Two distinct parishes annexed to Llanidan Vicarage.
Llanfflewin and Llanrhwydrys . . .	Two distinct parishes annexed to Llanrhyddlad Rectory.
Llechcynfarwydd and Rhodogeidio . .	Two distinct parishes annexed to Llantrisaint Rectory.
Llanfairyneubwll & Llanfihangel-yuhowyn	Two distinct parishes annexed to Rhoscolyn Rectory.
Llangwyfan	A distinct parish annexed to Treffdaeth Rectory.
Denbighshire.	
Gyffylliog.	A distinct parish annexed to Llanynys Vicarage.
Merionethshire.	
Maentwrog	A distinct parish annexed to Ffestiniog Rectory.
Llanbeder	A distinct parish annexed to Llandanwg Rectory.
Llanfihangel-y Traethan.	A distinct parish annexed to Llandecwyn perpetual Curacy.
Llanddwywe	A distinct parish annexed to Llaneuddwyn Rectory.
Montgomeryshire.	
Benhaglog Chapel	Licensed under 6 & 7 Wm. IV., cap. 85, sec. 26 ; being a Chapel of Ease within the parish, and forming part of the Vicarage of Llandinam.

Bangor, 20th June, 1840.   (Signed)   JOHN HUGHES,
Deputy Registrar.

DIOCESE OF BATH AND WELLS.

A List made by the Deputy Registrar of the Diocese of Bath and Wells, within fifteen days after the 1st day of January, 1840, in pursuance of the Provisions of the Acts of 6 and 7 Wm. IV., c. 85, and 7 Wm. IV., c. 1 ; being a List of all Chapels belonging to the Church of England within that Diocese wherein Marriages may be lawfully solemnized according to the Rites and Ceremonies of the Church of England—distinguishing which have a Parish, Chapelry, or other recognized Ecclesiastical Division annexed to them, and which are Chapels licensed by the Bishop under the Act of 6 and 7 Wm. IV., c. 85, and stating the District for which each of such Chapels is licensed according to the description thereof in the License.

Name of Chapel.	Name or Description of Parish, Chapelry, or other recognized Ecclesiastical Division thereunto annexed.	Whether Licensed under the Act of 6 and 7 Wm. IV., c. 85.	Description of District for which it is so Licensed.
Ashcot	Ashcot	No.	
Baltonsborough . . .	Baltonsborough . . .	No.	
Bath, St. James . . .	St. James in Bath . . .	No.	
Bath, St. Michael . .	St. Michael in Bath . .	No.	
Bicknell or Bickenhall .	Bicknell or Bickenhall .	No.	
Bourton	Bourton	No.	
Bradley, West . . .	West Bradley . . .	No.	
Buckland, West . . .	West Buckland . . .	No.	
Catherine.	Catherine	No.	
Chinnock, West . . .	West Chinnock . . .	No.	
Cranmore, East . . .	East Cranmore . . .	No.	
Cranmore, West . . .	West Cranmore . . .	No.	
Dinnington	Dinnington	No.	
Dundry	Dundry	No.	
Emborough	Emborough	No.	
Farrington	Farrington. . . .	No.	
Glastonbury, St. Benedict	St. Benedict in Glastonbury	No.	
Hatch, West	West Hatch	No.	
Kenn.	Kenn	No.	
Langford Budville . .	Langford Budville . .	No.	
Langport	Langport	No.	
Lawrence, St. in Week .	Week St. Lawrence . .	No.	
Load	Load	No.	
Luxborough	Luxborough	No.	
Leigh-upon-Mendip . .	Leigh-upon-Mendip . .	No.	
Monkton Combe. . .	Monkton Combe . . .	No.	
Nempnett	Nempnett	No.	
Paulton	Paulton	No.	
Preston	Preston	No.	
Priddy	Priddy	No.	
Road Huish	Road Huish	No.	
Ston Easton	Ston Easton	No.	
Williton	Williton	No.	
Withypoole	Withypoole	No.	
Woolley	Woolley	No.	
Wootton, North . . .	North Wootton . . .	No.	

(Signed)   EDWARD PARFITT, *Deputy Registrar.*

DIOCESE OF CANTERBURY.

Canterbury.

A List made by the Registrars of the Diocese of Canterbury, within fifteen days after the 1st day of January, 1840, in pursuance of the Provisions of the Acts of 6 and 7 Wm. IV., c. 85, and 7 Wm. IV., c. 1; being a List of all Chapels belonging to the Church of England within that Diocese, wherein Marriages may lawfully be solemnized according to the Rites and Ceremonies of the Church of England—distinguishing which have a Parish, Chapelry, or other recognized Ecclesiastical Division annexed to them, and which are Chapels licensed by the Bishop under the Act of 6 and 7 Wm. IV., c. 85, and stating the District for which each of such Chapels is licensed, according to the description thereof in the License.

We have no Chapels of the above description within the Diocese of Canterbury.

Wm. ABBOT, and W. H. CULLEN,

Canterbury, 14th January, 1840.   *Deputy Registrars.*

DIOCESE OF CARLISLE.

Carlisle, April 23rd, 1840.

SIR,

     I send a Return of the Chapels in the Diocese of Carlisle, wherein Marriages may be celebrated.

And am,

Your most obedient Servant,

G. G. MOUNSEY.

Carlisle.

A List of all Chapels belonging to the Church of England within the Diocese of Carlisle, wherein Marriages may be lawfully solemnized according to the Rites and Ceremonies of the Church of England—distinguishing which have a Parish, Chapelry, or other recognized Ecclesiastical Division annexed to them, and which are Chapels licensed by the Bishop under the Statute of the 6 and 7 Wm. IV., c. 85.

Name of Chapel.	Parish in which situate.	County.	Ecclesiastical Division annexed.	Whether licensed under the Statute or not.
Bolton . . .	Morland . . .	Westmorland	Chapelry of Bolton . .	Not licensed under the Statute.
Mardale . .	Shap	Westmorland	Chapelry of Mardale . .	Ditto.
Matterdale .	Greystoke . . .	Cumberland	Chapelry of Matterdale .	Ditto.
Milburne . .	Kirkbythore . .	Westmorland	Chapelry of Milburne . .	Ditto.
Nicholforest .	Kirkandrews-on-Esk	Cumberland	Chapelry of Nicholforest .	Ditto.
Patterdale . .	Barton	Westmorland	Chapelry of Patterdale .	Ditto.
Raughtonhead .	Castlesowerby . .	Cumberland	Chapelry of Raughtonhead	Ditto.
Threlkeld . .	Greystoke . . .	Cumberland	Chapelry of Threlkeld. .	Ditto.
Templesowerby	Kirkbythore . .	Westmorland	Chapelry of Templesowerby	Ditto.
Watermillock .	Greystoke . . .	Cumberland	Chapelry of Watermillock	Ditto.

R. and G. G. MOUNSEY,

Carlisle.   *Deputy Registrars.*

DIOCESE OF CHESTER.

Chester

A List of all Chapels within the several Deaneries of Amounderness, Lonsdale, Kendal, Furness, and Copeland, in the Archdeaconry of Richmond, and Diocese of Chester, in the Counties of Lancaster, Westmorland, and Cumberland, where Marriages may be solemnized according to the Rites and Ceremonies of the Church of England, returned to the Office of the Registrar-General of Births, Deaths, and Marriages, by virtue of, and in compliance with, an Act of Parliament made and passed in the 7th year of the reign of His late Majesty, King William the Fourth, this 15th day of January, 1840.

Name of Chapel.	Name or Description of Parish, Chapelry, or other recognized Ecclesiastical Division thereunto annexed.		Whether licensed under the Act of 6 and 7 Wm. IV., c. 85.	Description of District for which it is so Licensed.
Deanery of Amounderness.				
Chapels where Marriages are solemnized.				
Broughton	Chapelry in the Parish of Preston . .		Not.	
Goosnaigh	Ditto	Kirkham .	Ditto.	
Woodplumpton	Ditto	St. Michael's .	Ditto.	
Pilling	Ditto	Garstang .	Ditto.	
Overton	Ditto	Lancaster .	Ditto.	
Stidd	Ditto	Ribchester .	Ditto.	

DIOCESE OF CHESTER—(*continued*).

Name of Chapel.	Name or Description of Parish, Chapelry, or other recognized Ecclesiastical Division thereunto annexed.		Whether licensed under the Act of 6 and 7 Wm. IV., c. 85.	Description of District for which it is so Licensed.
Deanery of Amounderness.				
Chapels where Marriages were formerly solemnized, but not recently.				
Ellel	Chapelry in the Parish of Cockerham .		Not.	
Poulton	Ditto	Lancaster .	Ditto.	
Warton	Ditto	Kirkham .	Ditto.	
Wyersdale	Ditto	Lancaster .	Ditto.	
Deanery of Lonsdale.				
Chapels where Marriages are solemnized.				
Caton	Chapelry in the Parish of Lancaster .		Not.	
Gressingham	Ditto	Ditto . . .	Ditto.	
Firbank	Ditto	Kirkby Lonsdale	Ditto.	
Hutton Roof . . .	Ditto	Ditto . . .	Ditto.	
Killington	Ditto	Ditto . . .	Ditto.	
Middleton	Ditto	Ditto . . .	Ditto.	
Hornby, *Marriages formerly solemnized—not recently.*	Ditto	Melling . .	Ditto.	
Deanery of Kendal.				
Chapels where Marriages are solemnized.				
Over Kellett	Chapelry in the Parish of Bolton-by-the-Sands.		Not.	
Ambleside	Ditto　　Grassmere and Windermere.		Ditto.	
Burnside	Ditto	Kendal	Ditto.	
Crook	Ditto	Ditto	Ditto.	
Crossthwaite	Ditto	Heversham . . .	Ditto.	
Grayrigg	Ditto	Kendal	Ditto.	
Rydal	Ditto	Grassmere . . .	Ditto.	
Hugil, or Jugs	Ditto	Kendal	Ditto.	
Helsington	Ditto	Ditto	Ditto.	
Natland	Ditto	Ditto	Ditto.	
New Hutton	Ditto	Ditto	Ditto.	
Kentmore	Ditto	Ditto	Ditto.	
Langdale	Ditto	Grassmere . . .	Ditto.	
Longsleddale	Ditto	Kendal	Ditto.	
Old Hutton	Ditto	Ditto	Ditto.	
Preston Patrick . . .	Ditto	Burton-in-Kendal .	Ditto.	
Selside	Ditto	Kendal	Ditto.	
Staveley	Ditto	Ditto	Ditto.	
Troutbeck	Ditto	Windermere . .	Ditto.	
Underbarron	Ditto	Kendal	Ditto.	
Winster	Ditto	Ditto	Ditto.	
Witherslack	Ditto	Beetham . . .	Ditto.	
Holme	Ditto	Burton	Ditto.	
Deanery of Furness.				
Chapels where Marriages are solemnized.				
Blawith	Chapelry in the parish of Ulverstone .		Not.	
Conistone	Ditto	Ditto	Ditto.	
Lowick	Ditto	Ditto	Ditto.	
Tower	Ditto	Ditto	Ditto.	
Broughton	Ditto	Kirkby Ireleth . .	Ditto.	
Finsthwaite	Ditto	Colton	Ditto.	
Holy Trinity, Ulverston	Ditto	Ulverstone . . .	Ditto.	
Deanery of Copeland.				
Chapels where Marriages are solemnized.				
Clifton	Chapelry in the Parish of Workington		Not.	
Cockermouth	Ditto	Brigham . . .	Ditto.	
Ennerdale	Ditto	St. Bees . . .	Ditto.	
Embleton	Ditto	Brigham . . .	Ditto.	
Lorton	Ditto	Ditto	Ditto.	
Loweswater	Ditto	St. Bees . . .	Ditto.	
St. Nicholas, Whitehaven .				
Holy Trinity,　　ditto .	The Town and Chapelry of Whitehaven		Ditto.	
St. James,　　ditto .				
Eskdale	Parish and Chapelry of St. Bees . .		Ditto.	
Netherwasdale . . .	Ditto	Ditto . . .	Ditto.	
Thwaites	Ditto	Millom	Ditto.	
Ulpha	Ditto	Ditto	Ditto.	
Wasdalehead	Ditto	St. Bees . . .	Ditto.	
Hensingham	Ditto	Ditto	Ditto.	
St. John's, Workington .	Ditto	Workington . . .	Ditto.	

Chester ;
continued.

Consistory Court,
Lancaster, 15th January, 1840.

SIR,

    In compliance with the Act of His late Majesty, I beg to transmit to you the annexed List of Chapels in the several Deaneries of Amounderness, Lonsdale, Kendal, Furness, and Copeland, in the Archdeaconry of Richmond, and Diocese of Chester, in the several Counties of Lancaster, Westmorland, and Cumberland.

I have the honour to be,

Your obedient Servant,

(Signed)   WILLIAM SHARPE,

Deputy Registrar, Lancaster.

A List made by the Registrar of the Diocese of Chester, in pursuance of the provisions of the Acts of 6 and 7 Wm. IV., cap. 85, and 7 Wm. IV., cap. 1, being a List of all Chapels belonging to the Church of England within that Diocese, wherein Marriages may lawfully be solemnized, according to the Rites and Ceremonies of the Church of England, distinguishing which have a Parish, Chapelry, or other recognized Ecclesiastical Division annexed to them, and which are Chapels licensed by the Bishop, under the Act of 6 and 7 Wm. IV., cap. 85, and stating the District for which each of such Chapels is licensed, according to the description thereof in the License.

Name of Chapel.	Name or Description of Parish, Chapelry, or other recognized Ecclesiastical Division thereunto annexed.	Whether Licensed under the Act of 6 & 7 Wm. IV., c. 85.	Description of District for which it is so Licensed.
Bruera	Parish of St. Oswald.		
Hargreaves . . .	Parish of Tarvin.		
Isycoed	Parish of Holt.		
Threapwood . . .	Extra Parochial Chapel.		
Birkenhead . . .	Parish of Bidston.		
Nether Peover . .	Chapelry of Nether Peover, in the parish of Budworth.		
Latchford . . .	Chapelry of Latchford, parish of Grappenhall.		
Daresbury . . .	Parochial chapel of Daresbury, parish of Runcorn.		
Aston	Parochial chapel of Aston, parish of Runcorn.		
Disley	Parish of Stockport.		
Marple	Ditto.		
Macclesfield . . .	Parish of Astbury.		
Poynton	Parish of Prestbury.		
Ashworth . . .	Parish of Middleton.		
Cockey	Ditto.		
Hollingwood . .	Parish of Prestwich.		
Billinge	Wigan.		
Hindley	Parish of Wigan.		
Farnworth . . .	Parish of Prescot.		
Hale.	Parish of Childwall.		
Melling	Parish of Halsall.		
Maghull	Ditto.		
Witton	Parish of Great Budworth.		
Saddleworth . . .	Parish of Rochdale.		
St. George's . . .	Parish of Liverpool.		
St. Thomas . . .	Ditto.		
St. Ann	Ditto.		
St. Martin's . . .	Ditto.		
St. Mark's . . .	Ditto.		
St. Bridget's . . .	Ditto.		
St. Philip's . . .	Ditto.		
St. Michael's . .	Ditto.		
West Derby . . .	Toxteth Park.		
Accrington . . .	Parish of Whalley.		
Oldham	Parish of Prestwich		
St. Peter's, Oldham .	Ditto.		
St. James, Oldham .	Ditto.		
All Saints, Oldham .	Ditto.		
Shaw	Ditto.		
St. James . . .	Parish of Rochdale.		
Upholland . . .	Parish of Wigan.		
St. Helen's . . .	Prescot.		
Rainford . . .	Ditto.		

DIOCESE OF CHESTER—*(continued.)*

Name of Chapel.	Name or Description of Parish, Chapelry, or other recognized Ecclesiastical Division thereunto annexed.	Whether Licensed under the Act of 6 & 7 Wm. IV., c. 85.	Description of District for which it is so Licensed.
St. James, Toxteth Park . . .	Parish of Walton.		
St. Michael's . .	Ditto.		
Samlesbury . . .	Parish of Blackburn.		
Altham	Parish of Whalley.		
Whitewell . . .	Ditto.		
Tarleton	Parish of Croxton.		
Wettenhall . . .	Parish of Over.		
Tyldesley . . .	Parish of Leigh.		
Clitheroe . . .	Parish of Whalley.		
Colne	Ditto.		
Churchkirk . . .	Ditto.		
Downham . . .	Ditto.		
Haslingden . . .	Ditto.		
New Church, Pendle	Ditto.		
Over Peover . .	Parish of Rosthorne.		
Milne Row . . .	Parish of Rochdale.		
Christ Church . .	Liverpool.		
St. Luke's . . .	Ditto.		
St. John's . . .	Ditto.		
St. Paul's . . .	Ditto.		
Holy Trinity . .	Ditto.		
St. Catherine . .	Ditto.		
St. David . . .	Ditto.		
Bootle	Ditto.		
St. Augustine . .	Parish of Everton.		
Formby	Parish of Walton.		
Kirkby	Ditto.		
St. Jude's . . .	Toxteth Park, parish of Walton		
Todmorden . . .	Parish of Rochdale.		
Edge Hill . . .	Toxteth Park.		
Burnley	Parish of Whalley.		
Rochdale . . .	Parish of Rochdale.		
Walton	Parish of Blackburn.		
Darwen	Ditto.		
Harwood . . .	Ditto.		
Burnley	Parish of Whalley.		
Newchurch-in-Rossendale	Ditto.		
Padiham . . .	Ditto.		
Beeconsall . . .	Parish of Croston.		
Haslington . .	Parish of Barthomley.		
Marbury	Parish of Whitchurch.		
Goostrey . . .	Parish of Sandbach.		
Church Hulme . .	Ditto.		
St. John's, Blackpool	Parish of Bispham .	Licensed under 6 & 7 Wm. IV., c. 85.	Township of Layton-cum-Warbreck
St. Paul, Warrington	Parish of Warrington	Ditto . .	Township of Warrington.
St. Stephen's, Tockholes	Parish of Blackburn .	Ditto . .	Township of Tockholes.
Immanuel, Feniscoles	Ditto	Ditto . .	Townships of Livesey and Pleasington.
Balderston . . .	Ditto	Ditto . .	Township of Balderston.
St. Mary, Mellor .	Ditto	Ditto . .	Townships of Mellor and Ramsgrave.
Salesbury . . .	Ditto	Ditto . .	Townships of Duckley, Wilpshire, Osbalderston, Salesbury, and Clayton-le-dale.
Lango	Ditto	Ditto . .	Township of Billington.
St. Ann's, West Derby	Parish of West Derby	Ditto . .	Township of West Derby.
Wavertree . . .	Chapelry of Wavertree	Ditto . .	Township of Wavertree.
Newchurch . . .	Parish of Winwick .	Ditto . .	Township of Culcheth (except the Lordship of Risley).
Walney	Parish of Dalton . .	Ditto . .	Township of Walney.
Langton	Parish of Penwortham	Ditto . .	Township of Langton.
St. Peter's, in Woolton	Parish of Childwall .	Ditto . .	Chapelry of Woolton.
Christ Church, Salford	Parish of Manchester .	Ditto . .	That part of the division between the township of Pendleton, in the parish of Eccles; and the township of Salford aforesaid, which is intersected by the high-road from Liverpool to Manchester; and from thence passing along and

B

DIOCESE OF CHESTER—(*continued.*)

Name of Chapel.	Name or Description of Parish, Chapelry, or other recognized Ecclesiastical Division thereunto annexed	Whether Licensed under the Act of 6 & 7 Wm. IV., c. 85.	Description of District for which it is so Licensed.
Christ Church, Salford (*continued.*)	Parish of Manchester	Licensed under 6 & 7 Wm. IV., c. 85.	including the south side of the said high-road, and the street called Crescent, to Hulme-place; and then diverging southward so as to include the westward side thereof; then passing along and including the south side of Hulme-street; then passing along and including the west side of part of the street called Gaythorne-street; then crossing a wooden bridge over the Bolton canal to Oldfield-road; passing along and including the westerley side thereof to Regent's-road; passing along and including the southwardly side thereof to the toll-bridge over the river Irwell; and then following the banks of that river to the division between the parishes of Manchester and Eccles; and from thence proceeding along that division to the commencement of the said district first hereinbefore mentioned.
St. Philip, Salford .	Ditto	Ditto . .	Such part of the district assigned to St. Philip's by Her Majesty's Commissioners, as is not included in the district assigned by the Bishop to Christ Church.
St. Stephen, Salford .	Ditto	Ditto . .	Bounded by the east side of St. Stephen-street and Pleasant-street; south side of Broughton-road; and west side of Paradise-street and Garden-lane; south side of Foundry-street and of Chapel-street, as far as St. Stephen-street south.
Holy Trinity, Salford	Ditto	Ditto . .	Bounded on the north side of Foundry-street; east side of Garden-lane and Paradise-street; north side of Broughton-road, river Irwell; north side of New Bailey-street; east side of Chapel-street, back to Foundry-street.
St. George's, Manchester	Ditto	Ditto . .	Bounded by the east side of Swan-street; south side of St. George's-road up to the township of Harpurhey; the boundary between that township and Newton, up to the Rochdale canal; the Rochdale canal, up to Great Ancoates-street; east side of Ancoates-street, back to Swan-street.
St. Peter's, Manchester	Ditto	Ditto . .	Within Moseley-street, south side; Oxford-street, east side of river Medlock; along the river Medlock to Brook-street, north side; thence to Rochdale canal; along Rochdale canal, to west side of Sackville-street, Portland-street, west, Nicholas-street; thence to Moseley-street again.
St. Michael's, in Manchester	Ditto	Ditto . .	Bounded by the east side of Mellors-street, north side of St. George's-road up to the road bounding the Hendam-hall Estate, on south; such road up to the wood bridge over the Irk near Smedley old hall, and from that point back to Mellors-street, by the boundary between the townships of Manchester and Chatham.
St. John's, in Manchester	Ditto	Ditto . .	Within the west side of Bridge-street, north side of Deansgate; west side of Brazennose-street, Poole-street, and Princess-street; north side of Bond-street, and Moseley-street; east side of Peter-street; south side of Deansgate, to east side of Camp-street and Charles-street, and back to Bridge-street, along the river Irwell.
St. Ann's, Manchester	Ditto	Ditto . .	Bounded by the west side of Market-street; south side of Deansgate; east side of Brazennose-street, Poole-street, and Princess-street; north side of Moseley-street, back to Market-street.
St. Mary's, Manchester	Ditto	Ditto . .	Within the east side of Bridge-street; the river Irwell to Blackfriars-bridge, Blackfriars-street, and north side of Deansgate-street, back to Bridge-street.
St. Andrew's, Manchester	Ditto	Ditto . .	Bounded by the boundary between Manchester and Newton, commencing at the point where the Rochdale canal enters Newton, up to the river Medlock; by the river Medlock to London-road; east side along Travis-street; south side of Great Ancoats-street; east side of Rochdale canal; along the Rochdale canal to the point where it enters the township of Newton.
St. Matthew's, Manchester	Ditto	Ditto . .	Within the river Medlock where it crosses Oxford-road to its junction with the Irwell; along the river Irwell to west side of Charles-street, Camp-street; thence along south side of Deansgate, to south side of Peter-street and Oxford-road, to the river Medlock.
St. Paul's, Manchester	Ditto	Ditto . .	Bounded by south side of High-street; west side of Thomas-street, and Hilton-street; north side of Lever-street; west side of Great Ancoats-street to Travis-street; north side of Travis-street to east side of London-road, Piccadilly, and Market-street, to High-street.

DIOCESE OF CHESTER—(*continued.*)

Name of Chapel.	Name or Description of Parish, Chapelry, or other recognised Ecclesiastical Division thereunto annexed.	Whether Licensed under the Act of 6 & 7 Wm. IV., c. 85.	Description of District for which it is so Licensed.
St. James, Manchester	Parish of Manchester	Licensed under 6 & 7 Wm. IV., c. 85.	Within the south side of Moseley-street, east side of Nicholas-street, and Sackville-street, to the Rochdale-canal; along Rochdale-canal to south side of Brook-street, by the Medlock to Ardwick-bridge; west side of London-road and Piccadilly, back to Moseley-street.
Birch Chapel . .	Ditto	Ditto . .	Township of Rusholme, and such part of the township of Moss-side, as is contiguous to that township on the north, and is not included in district assigned to St. Saviour's.
Ardwick. . . .	Ditto	Ditto . .	Township of Ardwick, together with such portion of the township of Chorlton-upon-Medlock as is not included in the district assigned to St. Saviour's or All Saints.
All Saints, Chorlton-upon-Medlock	Ditto	Ditto . .	Such portion of the township of Chorlton-upon-Medlock as is bounded by the Parliamentary district of Hulme, and by the district assigned by the Bishop to St. Saviour's, and is not included within either.
St. George, Hulme .	Ditto	Ditto . .	Township of Hulme.
St. Saviour, Chorlton-upon-Medlock	Ditto	Ditto . .	Such part of the township of Chorlton-upon-Medlock as is comprised within the boundaries hereinafter mentioned, namely, that part bounded on the east by the township of Ardwick and Gorton; on the south by the township of Rusholme; on the west by Oxford-road; and on the north by Bootle-street, and Rusholme-road; and that part of Upper Brook-street that runs from Bootle-street to Rusholme-road.
Stretford . . .	Ditto	Ditto . .	Township of Stretford.
Chorlton-cum-Hardy	Ditto	Ditto . .	Township of Chorlton-cum-Hardy.
Gorton	Ditto	Ditto . .	Township of Gorton.
Blakeley . . .	Ditto	Ditto . .	Township of Blakeley.
Newton	Ditto	Ditto . .	Townships of Newton, Failsworth, and Droylesden.
Didsbury . . .	Ditto	Ditto . .	Townships of Didsbury, Withington, and Burnage.
Heaton Norris . .	Ditto	Ditto . .	Townships of Heaton Norris, Levenshulme, and Reddish.
Denton	Ditto	Ditto . .	Townships of Denton and Houghton.
St. James, Lower Darwen	Parish of Blackburn .	Ditto . .	Bounded by the townships of Eccles-hill, Yate, and Pickup-bank, and part of the township of Entwistle on the north and east; and on the west and south by a line drawn athwart the township of Over Darwen, in manner following; (viz.), from Baring-mill on the river Darwen, where Over Darwen and Eccles-hill march, to Dobhole-bridge, and thence to Shorey-bank, the river Darwen being thus far the boundary; from Shorey-bank-bridge up the course of a small rivulet called Norris-brook, which runs at the bottom of Shorey-bank-wood to March-house Occupation-road; pursuing the said Occupation-road till it terminates in Pole-lane; and ascending the said Pole-lane until it meets the old road from Manchester to Blackburn, which is now called the Old Bury-road; and thence pursuing the said Old Bury-road and the parish of Blackburn at Grimes-mill-bridge, and enters the township of Entwistle.
Holy Trinity, Over Darwen	Ditto	Ditto . .	Bounded on the south-east, south, and west, by the township of Entwistle, and other parts of the parish of Bolton-le-Moors, and by the townships of Tockholes and Lower Darwen; where the last of these marches on Eccles-hill, at Barings-mill, and bounded on the north and east, by a line drawn athwart the township of Over Darwen in manner following; (viz.), from Baring-mill on the river Darwen, where Over Darwen and Eccles-hill march to Dobhole-bridge, and thence to Shorey-bank, the river Darwen being thus far the boundary; from Shorey-bank-bridge, up the course of a small rivulet called Norris-brook, which runs at the bottom of Shorey-bank-wood, to March-house Occupation-road; pursuing the said Occupation-road till it terminates in Pole-lane, and ascending the said Pole-lane until it meets the old road from Manchester to Blackburn, which is now called the Old Bury-road; and thence pursuing the said Old Bury-road, until it leaves the township of Over Darwen, and the parish of Blackburn at Grimes-mill-bridge, and enters the township of Entwistle.
St. Thomas, Norbury	Parish of Stockport .	Ditto . .	Townships of Norbury and Bosden.
Trinity Chapel, Habergham Eaves	Parish of Whalley .	Ditto . .	Township of Habergham Eaves.
St. John's, Worsthorne	Ditto	Ditto . .	Township of Worsthorne.
Holme	Ditto	Ditto . .	Township of Cliviger, Chapelry of Holme.

B 2

DIOCESE OF CHESTER—*(continued.)*

Name of Chapel.	Name or Description of Parish, Chapelry, or other recognised Ecclesiastical Division thereunto annexed.	Whether Licensed under the Act of 6 & 7 Wm. IV., c. 85.	Description of District for which it is so Licensed.
Goodshaw . . .	Parish of Whalley .	Licensed under 6 & 7 Wm. IV., c. 85.	Township of Higher Booths and Dunnockshaw.
Marsden . . .	Ditto	Ditto . .	Township of Little Marsden.
St. John, Bacup .	Ditto	Ditto . .	Hamlet or district of Brandwood, comprising the upper and lower, and within the parish of Rochdale.
St. Anne's, Fence .	Chapelry of Newchurch	Ditto . .	Of the district of Fence, comprising the whole of the township of Old Laund Booth, and that part of the township of Goldshaw Booth, which lies south of the estate called Height, situate in the parochial Chapelry of Newchurch in Pendle; that part of the township of Higham Booth which lies east of the road leading from Ighton-hill-park, to Pendle-hall, Foxendale-lane, and Higham-rough, to its junction with the highway from Newchurch to Whalley in the parochial Chapelry of Padiham; that part of the township of Barrowford Booth which lies west of the horseway leading from Marsden to Wheatley-lane, in the parochial Chapelry of Cole, the whole of the extra-parochial township of Wheatley Carr, and that part of the extra-parochial township of Reedly-hollows, Filly-close, and New-maund, which lies north of the river called Pendle-water.
St. Anne, Aigburth .	Parish of Childwall .	Ditto	
Birch	Parish of Middleton .	Ditto . .	Township of Hopwood.
Thornton, Christ Church	Parish of Poulton .	Ditto . .	Township of Thornton.
Marton, St. Paul's Church	Ditto	Ditto . .	Township of Marton, except such parts of said township or district which have been assigned to Trinity Church, South-Shore.
Ringley	Parish of Prestwich-cum-Oldham	Ditto . .	The hamlet or district of Outwood.
Mansergh . . .	Parish of Kirkby Lonsdale	Ditto . .	Township of Mansergh.
Barbon	Ditto	Ditto . .	Township of Barbon.
Hambleton . . .	Parish of Kirkham .	Ditto . .	Chapelry of Hambleton.
Disley	Parish of Stockport .	Ditto . .	Township of Disley.
Southshore . . .	Parish of Bispham .	Ditto . .	District known by the name of Layton Hawes.
Milnthorpe, St. Thomas	Parish of Heversham	Ditto . .	That part of the parish of Heversham which lies north of the turn on the Kendal-turnpike-road, at Watery-lane end, and Haverflat-lane, to the turn of Woodhouse-lane end on the north-east; on the east by that part of the said parish which lies north-east of the end of the lanes (nearest to Arkenthwaite) leading to Woodhouse, and to Rowet, and by the boundary line on the east, between the parishes of Heversham and Beetham; on the south by the river Beeta, from Paradise-lane to Dallam-tower-bridge, at the boundary of the parishes of Heversham and Beetham, on the south and south-west; on the west by that part of the parish of Heversham which lies west of Dallam-tower-bridge, Scout bank, and north-west of the tower at Grisley-mire-lane, on the Kendal and Lancaster turnpike-road.
Norley	Parish of Frodsham .	Ditto . .	Townships of Norley and Kingsley.
Crossons . . .	Parish of North Meols	Ditto . .	That part of the parish of North Meols known by the names of Crossons and the Banks.
Southport . . .	Ditto	Ditto . .	That part of the parish of North Meols known by the names of Birkdale, Southport, South Hawes, Little London, Cop End, Higher Blowick, Trap-lane, Smittering-lane, and the western part of the Row-lane, terminating at Row-lane academy.
Little Lever. . .	Parish of Bolton-le-Moors	Ditto . .	Township or district of Little Lever, Darcy Lever, and Great Lever.
Bollington . . .	Parish of Prestbury .	Ditto . .	Township of Bollington.
Chatburne . . .	Parochial Chapelry of Clitheroe, in the parish of Whalley	Ditto . .	Township of Chatburne and Worston.
Padgate	Parish of Warrington	Ditto . .	Township or district of Poulton-cum-Fearnhead, Woolston-cum-Martinscroft, and the hamlet of Orford.
Garston	Parish of Childwall .	Ditto . .	Township of Spoke, and all such parts of the township of Garston, as are not included in the district of St. Ann, Aigburth.
Tintwistle . . .	Parish of Mottram .	Ditto . .	That part of the township of Tintwistle, which lies west of the Brook running into the Mersey, on the eastern side of Vale-house, and called Rowton's-brook, excepting the district called Ricklehurst, and that part of the township of Hollingworth which lies eastward of the Brook, called Clay-lands, or Wednesbough-brook, which runs into the Mersey, near the Gun-inn, in the said township of Hollingworth.

DIOCESE OF CHESTER—(*continued.*)

Name of Chapel.	Name or Description of Parish, Chapelry, or other recognised Ecclesiastical Division thereunto annexed.	Whether Licensed under the Act of 6 & 7 Wm, IV., c. 85.	Description of District for which it is so Licensed.
Ashton, Holy Trinity Church	Parish of Winwick .	Licensed under 6 & 7 Wm. IV. c. 85.	In respect of the inhabitants of the chapelry of Ashton.
Bamber Bridge, St. Saviour's	Parochial Chapel of Walton-le-Dale, parish of Blackburn	Ditto . .	Shall consist of, and comprise that part of the township of Walton-le-Dale, which lies south and south-west of the line drawn athwart the said township, commencing at Tardy-gate, and running along what is called Back-lane, to the Preston and Chorley turnpike-road, the crown of the said Back-lane being the boundary; thence taking in the house adjoining both sides of the turnpike-road, to School-lane, along which it runs to what is called the Back-lane, through which it pursues its course, till having passed through Seed-lee-lane, it terminates and enters the township of Brindle, the crown of the said School-lane, Back-lane, and Seed-lee-lane, being the boundary.
Swinton	Parish of Eccles . .	Ditto . .	In respect of persons residing within the chapelry of Swinton, but not further or otherwise.
Pendleton . . .	Ditto	Ditto . .	In respect of persons residing within the chapelry of Pendleton.
Congleton . . .	Parish of Astbury .	Ditto . .	In respect of the townships of Congleton, Buglawton, Eaton, and Hulme Wallfield, in the said parish, but no further or otherwise.
Cheetham, St. Mark's	Parish of Manchester	Ditto . .	To consist of, and comprise the township of Crumpsall, and that part of the township of Cheetham, which is next adjacent to the township of Cheetham by Smedley-road, Smedley-lane, the Old Bury-road, Halliwell-lane.
Harpurhey, Christ Church	Ditto	Ditto . .	To comprise and consist of the township of Harpurhey and Morton, together with that part of the northern extremity of the township of Manchester which is separated from the rest of that township, by the lane which bounds the Endham-hall estate, to the south; commencing at the wooden-bridge over the river Irk, near Smedley old hall, and terminating at its intersection with St. George's-road, a line from that point across St. George's, to a lane called Lamb-lane, and that lane to the boundary between Manchester and Newton.
Stockton Heath, St. Thomas's	Parish of Great Budworth	Ditto . .	In respect of the inhabitants of the township of Walton Inferior, in the parochial chapelry of Daresbury, and parish of Runcorn, and of such portion of the township of Appleton as shall lie on the north side of a line to be drawn on the south side of, and parallel with the end of the Duke of Bridgewater's canal, in the said township of Appleton, at a distance of three hundred yards from the said canal.
Little Marsden . .	In the parochial Chapelry of Colne, parish of Whalley	Ditto . .	The township of Little Marsden.
Colne, Christ Church	Ditto	Ditto . .	The whole of the township of Trawden, and those portions of Colne and Foubridge which lie to the east of Carry-lane, and the turnpike-road leading to Skipton, through the village of Foubridge.

(Signed)　　H. RAIKES, *Registrar.*

DIOCESE OF CHICHESTER.

Chichester, June 17th, 1840.

Sir,

In reply to your letter of the 17th instant, reminding me of the Provisions of the 34th sec. of the 6 and 7 Wm. IV., I beg leave to inform you that there is no Chapel belonging to the Church of England within the Archdeaconry of Chichester for which I act as Deputy Registrar, wherein Marriages may be lawfully solemnised according to the Rites and Ceremonies of the Church of England.

Chichester

I am sorry I gave you the trouble of writing to me.

I am, Sir,

Your very obedient Servant,

J. B. FREELAND.

DIOCESE OF ST. DAVID'S.

St. David's.

A List of the Number of Chapels belonging to the Church of England within the said Diocese, wherein Marriages may be lawfully solemnized according to the Rites and Ceremonies of the Church of England.

Name of Chapel.	County.	Deanery.	Post Town.
Brongwin	Cardigan	Lower Sub-Ayron.	Newcastle Emlyn.
Castellan	Pembroke	Emlyn.	Newcastle Emlyn.
Coedcenlas	Pembroke	Narberth	Haverfordwest.
Colva	Radnor	Elwell	Builth.
Crickadarn	Brecon	West Hay	Builth.
Cynon	Cardigan	Lower Sub-Ayron.	Cardigan.
Kilgwyn	Pembroke	Upper Kemis	Cardigan.
Llanbardarn-y-Garreg	Radnor	Elwell	Builth.
Llandyry	Carmarthen	Kidwelly	Llanelly.
Llanelly	Brecon	Third Part Brecon, North	Abergavenny.
Llangenny	Brecon	Ditto South.	Crickhowell.
Llanina	Cardigan	Upper Sub-Ayron	Lampeter.
Llansaint	Carmarthen	Kidwelly	Kidwelly.
Llanthoysaint and Llangadock	Carmarthen	Llangadock	Llangadock.
Llanfihangel-rhosy.corn	Carmarthen	Llandilo	Carmarthen.
Llanwida and Llansadwrn	Carmarthen	Llangadock	Llandovery.
Llanyrnewydd	Glamorgan	East Gower	Swansea.
Newcastle Emlyn	Carmarthen	Emlyn	Newcastle Emlyn.
Penpont	Brecon	Brecon, First Part	Brecon.
Rhydbert	Pembroke	Castlemartin	Pembroke.
Robeston, East	Pembroke	Narberth	Narberth.
Rulen	Radnor	Elwell	Builth.
Spytty-ystwith	Cardigan	Lower Ultra-Ayron	Lampeter.
St. Mary's, Brecon	Brecon	Brecon, First Part.	Brecon.
Taff Fechan	Brecon	Third Part Brecon, South	Brecon.
Tretower	Brecon	Ditto	Crickhowell.
Williamston	Pembroke	Narberth	Pembroke.
Ystrad, *alias* Spytty Ystwyth	Cardigan	Upper Sub-Ayron.	Lampeter.
Ystrad Gynllais	Brecon	Second Part, Brecon	Neath.

A List of the Number of Chapels belonging to the Church of England, within the Diocese aforesaid, wherein Marriages may be lawfully solemnized according to the Rites and Ceremonies of the Church of England, and which have been licensed for that purpose under the Provisions of 6 and 7 Wm. IV., c. 85.

Name of Chapel.	District.	County.	Deanery.	Post Town.
Gwynfe	Chapelry of Gwynfe	Carmarthen	Llangadock	Llandilo. ;
St. John, *otherwise* Capel Juan	Chapelry of St. John, *otherwise* Capel Juan.	Carmarthen	Kidwelly	Llanelly.
Trinity Chapel, Newcastle Emlyn	The hamlet of Emlyn, part of the hamlet of Dolbryn, containing the following farms, Penybyarth, Blainfoes, Blaengwydder, Llwynygog, Bleandyffrin, Ffollfach, and Dolbryn.	Carmarthen	Emlyn	Newcastle Emlyn.

These I certify,

(Signed)   VALENTINE DAVIS,

Registry, Carmarthen, 27th June, 1840.   *N. P. Deputy Registrar,*

P.S.—I have no means of setting forth the Districts of the Chapels mentioned in the first List.

V. D.

DIOCESE OF DURHAM.

A List made by the Registrar of the Diocese of Durham within fifteen days after the 1st day of January, 1840, in pursuance of the Provisions of the Acts of 6 and 7 Wm. IV., c. 85, and 7 Wm. IV., c. 1, being a List of all Chapels belonging to the Church of England within that Diocese, wherein Marriages may lawfully be solemnized according to the Rites and Ceremonies of the Church of England—distinguishing which have a Parish, Chapelry, or other recognized Ecclesiastical Division annexed to them, and which are Chapels licensed by the Bishop under the Act of 6 and 7 Wm. IV., c. 85, and stating the District for which each of such Chapels is licensed, according to the Description thereof in the License.

Name of Chapel.	Name or Description of Parish, Chapelry, or other recognized Ecclesiastical Division thereunto annexed.	Whether licensed under the Act of 6 and 7 Wm. IV., c. 85.	Description of District for which it is so Licensed.
Painshaw	Chapelry of Painshaw annexed.		
West Rainton . . .	Chapelry of West Rainton.		
Hetton-le-Hole . .	Chapelry of Hetton-le-Hole.		
St. Nicholas, Durham .	Parish of St. Nicholas.		
Trimdon	Chapelry of Trimdon.		
St. Giles, Durham . .	Parish of St. Giles.		
Castle Eden . . .	Chapelry of Castle Eden.		
Lanchester . . .	Parish of Lanchester.		
Chester-le-Street . .	Parish of Chester-le-Street.		
Croxdale	Chapelry of Croxdale.		
Satley	Chapelry of Satley.		
Esh	Chapelry of Esh.		
Ebchester	Chapelry of Ebchester.		
Medomsley . . .	Chapelry of Medomsley.		
Jarrow	Parish of Jarrow.		
Muggleswick . . .	Chapelry of Muggleswick.		
Heworth	Chapelry of Heworth.		
Tanfield	Chapelry of Tanfield.		
Wilton Gilbert . . .	Chapelry of Wilton Gilbert.		
Lamesley	Chapelry of Lamesley.		
St. Hild's	Chapelry of St. Hild's.		
St. Margaret's, Durham	Chapelry of St. Margaret's.		
Monkwearmouth . .	Chapelry of Monkwearmouth.		
Hunstanworth . . .	Chapelry of Hunstanworth.		
Shincliffe	Chapelry of Shincliffe.		
Darlington	Chapelry of Darlington.		
Heathery Cleugh . .	Chapelry of Heathery Cleugh.		
St. John's, Weardale .	Chapelry of St. John's, Weardale.		
Sadbergh	Chapelry of Sadbergh.		
Eggleston	Chapelry of Eggleston.		
Cockfield	Chapelry of Cockfield.		
St. Andrew, Auckland	Chapelry of St. Andrew, Auckland.		
Escomb	Chapelry of Escomb.		
Shildon	Chapelry of Shildon.		
St. Helen's, Auckland	Chapelry of St. Helen's, Auckland.		
Witton-le-Wear . .	Chapelry of Witton-le-Wear.		
Whitworth . . .	Chapelry of Whitworth.		
Hamsterley . . .	Chapelry of Hamsterley.		
Barnard Castle . .	Chapelry of Barnard Castle.		
Whorleton	Chapelry of Whorleton.		
Denton	Chapelry of Denton.		
Etherley	Chapelry of Etherley.		
Hartlepool	Chapelry of Hartlepool.		
Wolviston	Chapelry of Wolviston.		
All Saints, Newcastle .	Chapelry of All Saints, Newcastle.		
St. John's, ditto . .	Chapelry of St. John's, Newcastle.		
St. Andrew, ditto . .	Chapelry of St. Andrew, Newcastle.		
Dinnington . . .	Chapelry of Dinnington.		
Gosforth	Chapelry of Gosforth.		
Cramlington . . .	Chapelry of Cramlington.		
Earsdon	Chapelry of Earsdon.		
Wallsend	Chapelry of Wallsend.		
Hamshaugh . . .	Chapelry of Hamshaugh.		
Haydon	Chapelry of Haydon.		
Garrigill	Chapelry of Garrigill.		
Birtley	Chapelry of Birtley.		
Slaley	Chapelry of Slaley.		
Ovingham	Chapelry of Ovingham.		
Shotley	Shotley.		
Blanchland . . .	Chapelry of Blanchland.		
Whittenstall . . .	Chapelry of Whittenstall.		
Netherwitton . . .	Chapelry of Netherwitton.		
Hebburn	Chapelry of Hebburn.		
Ulgham	Chapelry of Ulgham.		
Byrness	Chapelry of Byrness.		
Widdrington . . .	Chapelry of Widdrington.		

DIOCESE OF DURHAM—(*continued.*)

Name of Chapel.	Name or Description of Parish, Chapelry, or other recognized Ecclesiastical Division thereunto annexed.	Whether licensed under the Act of 6 and 7 Wm. IV., c. 85.	Description of District for which it is so Licensed.
Horton	Chapelry of Horton.		
Newbiggin . . .	Chapelry of Newbiggin.		
Alnwick	Chapelry of Alnwick.		
Framlington . . .	Chapelry of Framlington.		
Rennington . . .	Chapelry of Rennington.		
Rock	Chapelry of Rock.		
Doddington . . .	Chapelry of Doddington.		
Cornhill	Chapelry of Cornhill.		
Holy Island . . .	Chapelry of Holy Island.		
Bamburgh . . .	Chapelry of Bamburgh.		
Tweedmouth . . .	Chapelry of Tweedmouth.		
Ancroft	Chapelry of Ancroft.		
Carham	Chapelry of Carham.		
Lowick	Chapelry of Lowick.		
Belford	Chapelry of Belford.		
Kyloe	Chapelry of Kyloe.		
North Sunderland . .	Chapelry of North Sunderland.		
Beadnall	Chapelry of Beadnall.		
Lucker	Chapelry of Lucker.		
Cresswell	Chapelry of Cresswell.		
Mickley	Chapelry of Mickley.		
Newbrough . . .	Chapelry of Newbrough.		
Alnham	Chapelry of Alnham.		
Holy Trinity, Stockton	Chapelry of Holy Trinity . . .	Licensed by Bishop under 6 and 7 Wm. IV. 3rd Oct. 1838.	Holy Trinity District commences at the centre of the river Tees, opposite to the centre of Finkle-street, and proceeds in a southwardly and westwardly direction, in the centre of the said river, to where the parish of Egglescliffe joins the parish of Stockton; thence following in a westwardly and northwardly direction, the boundary line that divides the last mentioned two parishes, to where the same meet the parish of Elton; thence in a northerly and north-westwardly direction, along the boundary line that divides the parish of Stockton from the parish of Elton, to where those parishes meet the parish of Norton; thence in an eastwardly direction, following the boundary line that divides the township of Hartburn, in the parish of Stockton, from the parish of Norton, as far as the township of Stockton. Thence, following the boundary in a southwardly and eastwardly direction that divides the township of Hartburn from the township of Stockton, to the point where it crosses the lane or road called Oxbridge-lane, and so along the centre of that road eastwardly, including all the south side thereof, to the point where it forms a junction with the occupation-lane leading to Light-pipe-hall; thence, along the centre of the said lane and the footpath, in a northerly and easterly direction, to an occupation road leading from Stockton to the windmill, continuing along the centre of the same to Dovecot-street; then, east, down the centre of Dovecot-street, crossing the high-street south of the towns-house, and down the centre of Finkle-street, including all the houses on the south side thereof, to the centre of the river Tees, where the boundary commenced.

(Signed)   JOSEPH DAVISON,

Deputy Registrar of the Consistory Court of Durham.

DIOCESE OF ELY.

A List made by the Registrar of the Diocese of Ely, within fifteen days from the 1st day of January, 1840, in pursuance of the Provisions of the Acts of 6 and 7 Wm. IV., c. 85, and 7 Wm. IV., c. 1, being a List of all Chapels belonging to the Church of England within that Diocese, wherein Marriages may lawfully be solemnized according to the Rites and Ceremonies of the Church of England—distinguishing which have a Parish, Chapelry, or other recognized Ecclesiastical Division annexed to them, and which are Chapels licensed by the Bishop under the Act of 6 and 7 Wm. IV., c. 85, and stating the District for which each of such Chapels is licensed, according to the Description thereof in the License.

Name of Chapel.	Name or Description of Parish, Chapelry, or other recognised Ecclesiastical Division thereunto annexed.	Whether licensed under the Act of 6 and 7 Wm. IV., c. 85.	Description of District for which it is so Licensed.
Chettisham . .	Ely, St. Mary	No.	Each of these places exercise all the rights of distinct parishes, having separate Churchwardens and Overseers, as they have indeed for several hundred years.
Huntney. . .	Ely, Trinity	No.	
Thetford . .	Stretham	No.	
Parson Drove .	Township of Leverington .	No.	

Cambridge, 17th June, 1840.

GEORGE J. TWISS,
Deputy Registrar.

DIOCESE OF EXETER.

A List made by the Registrar of the Diocese of Exeter, in the year 1840, in pursuance of the provisions of the Acts of 6 and 7 Wm. IV., c. 85, and 7 Wm. IV., c. 1, being a List of all Chapels belonging to the Church of England, within that Diocese, wherein Marriages may lawfully be solemnized according to the Rites and Ceremonies of the Church of England, distinguishing which have a Parish, Chapelry, or other recognized Ecclesiastical Division annexed to them, and which are Chapels licensed by the Bishop under the Act of 6 and 7 Wm. IV., c. 85, and stating the District for which each of such Chapels is licensed, according to the description thereof in the License.

(Signed) RALPH BARNES,
Deputy Registrar.

There are in the Diocese of Exeter many Chapels, with Chapelries thereunto belonging (called Daughter Churches), belonging to a Mother Church, and constituting together one benefice, each Chapel being esteemed, for all civil and ecclesiastical purposes, a distinct parish.

In all these Chapels Marriages have been accustomed to be solemnized, and may be lawfully solemnized for the Chapelry or Parish thereto belonging.

A List of these Chapels is subjoined:—

Mother Church.	Chapel.	Mother Church.	Chapel.
Devon.		Harberton	Halwell.
West Allington . .	Marlborough.	Heavitree	St. Sidwell.
	South Huish.		St. David.
	South Milton.	Kingsteignton . . .	Highweek.
Ashburton	Buckland.	Paignton	Marldon.
	Bickington.	Maristowe	Thrushelton.
Axminster	Kilmington.	Northmolton . . .	Hoitchen.
	Membury.	Stoke Fleming . . .	St. Petrox, Dartmouth.
Bickleigh	Sheepston.	Yealmpton	Revelstoke.
Bradworthy . . .	Pancras Week.	Townstall	St.Saviour's,Dartmouth.
Bridestowe . . .	Sourton.	Shebbear	Sheepwash.
Brixham	Churston Ferrers.	Stokenham	Sherford.
	Kingswear.		Chivelstone.
Broadwoodwidger .	Week, St. Germans.	Dawlish	East Teignmouth.
Buckland Brewer .	Bulkworthy.	Bishopsteignton . .	West Teignmouth.
Loddiswell	Buckland-tout-Saint.	Harpford	Venn Ottery.
Plymouth, St. Andrew	Stonehouse.	Ipplepen	Woodland.
	St. Budeaux.	Tormoham	Cockington.
Budleigh, East . .	Withycombe Rawleigh.		
Church Stowe . .	Kingsbridge.		
St. Mary Church . .	Kingskerswill.	*Cornwall.*	
	Coffin's Well.	Lanteglos	Advent.
Colyton	Shute.	Perranzabuloe . . .	St. Agnes.
	Moukton.	St. Austel	St. Blazey.
Milton Damerell . .	Cookbury.	Boconnock	Broadoak (Union).
Linton	Countisbury.	Breage	Cury.
Dunchideock . . .	Shillinford Union.		Germoe.
Ermington	Kingstown.		Gunwalloe.
Great Torrington . .	St. Giles.	South Hill	Callington (Borough).

C

DIOCESE OF EXETER—*(continued)*.

Mother Church.	Chapel.	Mother Church.	Chapel.
St. Michael, Caphays .	St. Dennis.	Landrake	St Erney.
	St. Stephen's.	Myler	Mable.
Egloskerry. . . .	Tremain.	Madron	Morva.
Ewny Lelant . . .	Toednack.	Stythians . . .	Perranarworthal.
	St. Ives (Borough).	South Petherwin . .	Trewen.
St. Gurgras . . .	Badock.	Trenecloss	Warbstowe.
Phillack	Gwythian.	Mawgan	Martin.
Kenwen	Kea.	Tywardwreath . . .	St. Sampson's.

Ancient Chapels, with a Chapelry, Township, or other recognized Ecclesiastical Division belonging thereto, such not being esteemed a distinct Parish, wherein Marriages have been accustomed to be solemnized :—

Name of Chapel.	Chapelry, Township, or other recognized Ecclesiastical Division.
Newton Abbott, in the parish of Woolborough.	The township of Newton Abbott.
Helston, in the parish of Madron	The borough or chapelry of Helston.

Ancient Chapels, with Chapelries, Townships, or other recognized Ecclesiastical Division belonging thereto, such not being esteemed distinct Parishes, licensed by the Bishop for the solemnization of Marriages, under the Act of 6 and 7 Wm. IV., c. 85.

Name of Chapel.	Name or Description of Parish, Chapelry, Township, or other recognized Ecclesiastical Division.	Description of District.
Marazion .	The township or Chapelry of Marazion.	The limits of the town and chapelry of Marazion.
Penzance, in the parish of Madron.	The township or Chapelry of Penzance.	The limits of the town and chapelry of Penzance.
The Church or Chapel of Lower Brixham, in the parish of Brixham.	Part of the parish of Brixham.	The boundary-line commences on the east at the Sea at Man Sands, and proceeds westward to Bowling-green Cross, from thence it passes northward through Bowling-green-lane to Yard's-lane, Castor's-lane, and Doctor's-lane to Burton-street ; it then turns southward up Burton-street, proceeds through it and Mathill-lane to Mathill-gate ; from thence it passes along the southern boundary-hedge of Lower and Higher Mathill-fields, the western boundary-hedge of Broadpark and Great Broadpark, the northern boundary-hedge of Mill Meadow, as far as Lower Churston Mill ; it there meets the boundary-line between the parishes of Brixham and Churston Ferrers, which it follows till it touches the sea at Fishcombe Cove ; the sea continues the boundary from thence to Man Sands again.—Under the Act 58 Geo. III., c. 45.
The Church or Chapel of Starcross, in the parish of Kenton.	Part of the several parishes of Kenton and Dawlish.	The boundary-line to commence due north at the Lower Marsh-gate, situated on the road leading from the village of Starcross, in the parish of Kenton, to Powderham church, and proceeding from thence in a south-west direction to Westcombe Cross-roads, thence south-west to Black Ditch Cross, and proceeding south-west by west to the road leading from Cosford to Mawlish, all which said places are in the parish of Dawlish, to the parish of Mamhead, and continuing to the southward, and bounding on Lane End, in the parish of Dawlish ; and from thence to the southward, and adjoining the Cliffs on the sea-shore, in the parish of Kenton, and along the sea-side to the south-east, and to Langston Point, in the parish of Kenton; and from thence proceeding to the north, and to the Saltworks in the parish of Kenton, and including the Rabbit Warrens situate north-easterly or northerly from Langston Point, and to Cockwood, in the parish of Dawlish ; and from thence to the north, and to the village of Starcross, and along the bank of the Exe river to Lower Marsh-gate, from which the boundary commenced.—Under the Act 58 Geo. III., c. 45.

DIOCESE OF EXETER—*(continued).*

Name of Chapel.	Name or Description of Parish, Chapelry, Township, or other recognized Ecclesiastical Division.	Description of District.
The Church or Chapel of St. Day, in the parish of Gwennap.	Part of the parish of Gwennap.	The boundary of the district to be that of the parish of Gwennap north of the following line, (viz.), commencing at Hayle Mills, and proceeding through the stream up the valley between Wheal Jewell and Wheal Damsel, to Lower Trevethan, along the left or south side of the road to High Trevethan, including the houses in both those villages, and from thence keeping the boundary of the manor of Tollcarne, till it meets the boundary of the parish on the Redruth side.—Under an Order in Council, dated 6th August, 1835.
The Church or Chapel of St. Paul Chasewater, in the parish of Kenwyn.	Part of the several parishes of Kenwyn and Kea.	Bounded on the north-west by St. Agnes parish, on the north-east by the turnpike-road from St. Agnes to Truro, on the south-west by the parishes of Gwennap and St. Feock, and on the east by the road from Bizza Bridge to Kirley Barrow, until it meets the road passing through Seveock Town place ; and thence by the said road to its junction with the turnpike-road from Chasewater to Truro.—Under an Order in Council, dated 19th April, 1837.

Chapel built under the Provisions of the several Acts of Parliament for building Churches and Chapels in populous Parishes, and to which a District is intended to be assigned:—

Name of Chapel.	Parish, Chapelry, or other recognised Ecclesiastical Division.	Description of District.
St. John, Ivybridge, in the parish of Cornwood.	Part of the several parishes of Cornwood, Ermington, and Ugborough.	Part of the said three several parishes of Cornwood, Ermington, and Ugborough.

Licensed under Act 4 Geo. IV., c. 76 :—

Name of Chapel.	Parish, Chapelry, or other recognised Ecclesiastical Division.	Description of District.
The Chapel of Bedford, in the City of Exeter.	The precinct or extra-parochial place of Bedford, in the City of Exeter.	The precinct of Bedford, an extra-parochial place, in the City of Exeter.

DIOCESE OF GLOUCESTER.

A List made by the Registrar of the Consistory Court of Gloucester, within fifteen days after the 1st day of January, 1840, in pursuance of the provisions of the Acts of 6 and 7 Wm. IV., c. 85, and 7 Wm. IV., c. 1, being a List of all Chapels belonging to the Church of England within that part of the Diocese of Gloucester and Bristol which, before the union of the Sees of Gloucester and Bristol, formed the Diocese of Gloucester, wherein Marriages may lawfully be solemnized according to the Rites and Ceremonies of the Church of England—distinguishing which have a Parish, Chapelry, or other recognized Ecclesiastical Division annexed to them, and which are Chapels Licensed by the Bishop under the Act of 6 and 7 Wm. IV., c. 85, and stating the District for which each of such Chapels is Licensed according to the description thereof in the License.

Name of Chapel.	Name or Description of Parish, Chapelry, or other recognized Ecclesiastical Division thereunto annexed.	Whether Licensed under the Act of 6 & 7 Wm. IV., c. 85.	Description of District.
St. Barbara . . .	Aston Underhill . .		Parish of Aston Underhill.
St. Mary Magdalen .	Addlestrop. . . .		„ Addlestrop.
	Abson		„ Wick and Abson.
St. James	Alvington		„ Alvington.
St. Mary	Boddington . . .		„ Boddington.
Christ Church. . .	South Hamlet . . .	Not Licensed under the Act of 6 and 7 Wm. IV., c. 85	South Hamlet, Gloucester.
	Hayles.		Hamlet of Hayles.
	Hardwick		Parish of Hardwick.
Holy Trinity . . .	Kingswood		Hamlet of Kingswood Bitton.
St. John Evangelist .	Kingscote		Parish of Kingscote.
St. James	Lower Slaughter . .		„ Lower Slaughter.
St. John Baptist . .	Lea		Hamlet of Lea.
t.David	Moreton-in-Marsh. .		Parish of Moreton-in-Marsh

C 2

DIOCESE OF GLOUCESTER—(*continued*).

Name of Chapel.	Name or Description of Parish, Chapelry, or other recognized Ecclesiastical Division thereunto annexed.	Whether Licensed under the Act of 6 & 7 Wm. IV., c. 85.	Description of District.
St. James	Marston Meysey . . .		Parish of Marston Meysey.
St. Arild	Oldbury-on-the-Hill . .		,, Oldbury-on-the-Hill
	Owlpen		,, Owlpen.
Holy Trinity . . .	Rodborough		,, Rodborough.
St. John Baptist . .	Ruardean	Not Licensed under the Act of 6 & 7 Wm. IV., c. 85.	,, Ruardean.
St. Paul	Shurdington		,, Shurdington.
All Saints	Stone		Hamlet of Stone, Berkeley.
St. Briavell's . . .	St. Briavell's		Parish of St. Briavell.
	Winson		,, Winson
St. James	Westerleigh		,, Westerleigh.
St. Michael . . .	Yanworth		,, Yanworth.
St. Matthew's . . .	Ebley	Licensed under 6 & 7 Wm. IV., c. 85.	Ebley, in parish of Stonehouse.
St. John's	Beachley		Beachley, in parish of Tidenham.
In the Deaneries of Cricklade and Malmesbury.			
	Leigh		Leigh.
St. Nicholas . . .	Slaughterford		Slaughterford.
St. Nicholas . . .	Tytherton	Not Licensed under 6 & 7 Wm. IV., c. 85.	Tytherton.
St. Giles	Lea		Lea.
St. John Baptist . .	Charlton and Brokenbrow.		Charlton and Brokenbrow.
St. Leonard . . .	Broad Blunsdon and South Marston.		Broad Blunsdon and South Marston.
St. Giles	Alderton		Alderton.

Registry, Gloucester,   (Signed)   THOMAS HOLT, N.P.,
   January 10, 1840.   *Registrar.*

Name of Chapel.	Name or Description of Parish, Chapelry, or other recognized Ecclesiastical Division thereunto annexed.	Whether licensed under the Act of 6 and 7 Wm. IV., c. 85.	Description of District for which it is so Licensed.
Alveston . . .	Chapelry of Alveston	Not licensed.	
Aust	Chapelry of Aust	Not licensed.	
Northwick . .	Chapelry of Northwick and Redwick	Not licensed.	

(Signed)   WILLIAM CLARKE.   }
                        CHARLES S. CLARKE, } *Deputy Registrars.*

Registrar's Office, Bristol,
                                         17th June, 1840.

SIR,

     Annexed we beg to transmit a List of Chapels belonging to the Church of England within that part of the Diocese of Gloucester and Bristol to which our Registry relates.

We have the honour to remain,

Sir,

Your obedient Servants,

(Signed)   WILLIAM CLARKE,   }
                       CHARLES S. CLARKE,} *Deputy Registrars.*

To the Registrar-General of
  Births, Deaths, and Marriages,
    General Register Office, London.

DIOCESE OF HEREFORD.

Name of Chapel.	Name or Description of Parish, Chapelry, or other recognized Ecclesiastical Division thereunto annexed.	Whether licensed under the Act of 6 and 7 Wm. IV., c. 85.	Description of District for which it is so Licensed.
Hightington . . .	Annexed to the Vicarage of the parish of Rock, in the county of Worcester.	No.	
Hentland	Annexed to the Vicarage of the parish of Lugwardine, in the county of Hereford.	No.	
Kinsham	A parochial Chapel in the county of Hereford	No.	
Knighton-upon-Team.	Annexed to the Vicarage of the parish of Lindridge, in the county of Worcester.	No.	
King's Caple . . .	Annexed to the Vicarage of Sellach, in the county of Hereford.	No.	
Langarron . . .	Annexed to the Vicarage of the parish of Lugwardine, in the county of Hereford.	No.	
Little Dewchurch . .	Annexed to the Vicarage of the parish of Lugwardine, in the county of Hereford.	No.	
Madeley, St. Luke's Chapel, consecrated 26th October, 1837, with power to solemnize Matrimony and all other services according to the Rites and Ceremonies of the Church of England.	Annexed to the Vicarage of the parish of Madeley, in the county of Salop.	No.	
Michael Church . .	Annexed to the Vicarage of the parish of Kington, in the county of Hereford.	No.	
Milson	Annexed to the Rectory of the parish of Neen Sollars, in the county of Salop.	No.	
Nash	Annexed to the Rectory of the parish of Burford, in the county of Salop.	No.	
Norbury	Annexed to the Vicarage of the parish of Lydbury, North, in the county of Salop.	No.	
Orcop	A parochial Chapelry in the county of Hereford.	No.	
Orlton	Annexed to the Rectory of the parish of Eastham, in the county of Worcester.	No.	
Pensax	Annexed to the Vicarage of the parish of Lindridge, in the county of Worcester.	No.	
Preston Wynne . .	Annexed to the Vicarage of the parish of Withington, in the county of Hereford.	No.	
Rocheford	Annexed to the Vicarage of the parish of Tenbury, in the county of Worcester.	No.	
Shipton	A parochial Chapelry in the county of Salop.	No.	
St. Weonard's . . .	Annexed to the Vicarage of the parish of Lugwardine, in the county of Hereford.	No.	
Tiberton	Annexed to the Vicarage of the parish of Madley, in the county of Hereford.	No.	
Westhide	Annexed to the Rectory of the parish of Stoke Edith, in the county of Hereford.	No.	
Wormbridge . . .	A parochial Chapelry Donative in the county of Hereford.	No.	
Woolstonmind . .	Annexed to the Rectory of the parish of Worthen, in the county of Salop.	No.	•
Yatton	Annexed to the Vicarage of the parish of Much Marcle, in the county of Hereford.	No.	
Knowbury, St. Paul's, on the Clee-hill, a Church consecrated 29th January, 1840, with power to solemnize Matrimony and all other services according to the Rites and Ceremonies of the Church of England.			

(Signed)   THEO. LANE,

Deputy Registrar of the Diocese of Hereford.

Sir,

     Herewith I forward to you the List of Chapels belonging to the Established Church in the Diocese of Hereford, wherein Marriages may lawfully be solemnized according to the Rites of the Church of England, made up to the 1st of January, 1840.

I am, Sir,

Your very obedient Servant,

Thomas Mann, Esq.,	(Signed)	THEO. LANE,
Chief Clerk,		*Deputy Registrar of the Diocese of Hereford,*
General Register Office, London.		19th June, 1840.

DIOCESE OF LICHFIELD.

A List made by the Registrars of the Diocese of Lichfield, in pursuance of the Provisions of the Acts of 6 and 7 Wm. IV., c. 85, and 7 Wm. IV., c. 1, being a List of all Chapels belonging to the Church of England within that Diocese, wherein Marriages may lawfully be solemnized according to the Rites and Ceremonies of the Church of England—distinguishing which have a Parish, Chapelry, or other recognized Ecclesiastical Division annexed to them, and which are Chapels licensed by the Bishop under the Act of 6 and 7 Wm. IV., c. 85, and stating the District for which each of such Chapels is licensed, according to the Description thereof in the License.

County.	Name of Parish in which the Chapel is situated.	Name of Chapel having a Chapelry or other acknowledged Ecclesiastical Division.
Stafford	Alstonefield	Butterton.
	Aldridge	Barr Magna.
	Tatenhill	Barton-under-Needwood.
	Eccleshall	Chorlton.
	Stone	Fulford.
	Colwich	Trodswell.
	Stoke-upon-Trent	Hanley.
	Lichfield, St. Michael	Hammerwick.
	Hanbury	Marchington.
	Hanbury	Newborough.
	Leek	Rushton.
	Penkridge	Stretton.
	Penkridge	Shareshill.
	West Bromwich	West Bromwich, Christchurch, has a District assigned to it under the Church Building Acts.
Derby	Mackworth	Allestree.
	Bakewell	Ashford.
	Chesterfield	Brampton, St. Thomas.
	Bradborne	Brassington.
	Bakewell	Beighley.
	Bakewell	Baslow.
	Bakewell	Buxton.
	A Donative	Beauchief.
	A Donative	Bretby.
	Chesterfield	Brimington has a District assigned to it and licensed for Marriages under the Act of 4 Geo. 1V., c. 76.
	Spoondon	Chaddesden.
	Bakewell	Chelmorton.
	A Donative	Dale Abbey.
	Youlgreave	Elton.
	Castleton	Edale.
	Hartington	Earlsterndale.
	Bakewell	Fairfield.
	Mickleover	Findern.
	Ashborne	Hognaston.
	Mickleover	Littleover.
	Bakewell	Moniash.
	A Donative	Newton Solney.
	Derby, St. Peter	Normanton.
	Brailsford	Osmaston by Ashborne.
	A Donative	Park Forest.
	Duffield	Quarndon.
	Walton-on-Trent	Rosliston.
	Norbury	Snelstone.
	A Donative	Scropton.
	Spoondon	Stanley.
	Morley	Smalley.
	Bakewell	Sneldon.
	Duffield	Turnditch.
	Bakewell	Taddington.
	Cubley	Marston Montgomery.
	Bakewell	Longston.
	Youlgreave	Winster.
	Bakewell	Wormhill.
	Sawley	Wilne.
Salop	Bridgnorth	Alveley.
	Edgemond	Aston.
	Shrewsbury, St. Mary.	Astley.
	Stockton	Bonninghall.
	A Donative	Buildwas.
	Bridgnorth	Bobbington.
	Bridgnorth	Bridgnorth, St. Leonard's.
	Bridgnorth	Claverley.
	Longnor	Leebotwood.
	Hodnet	Morton Sea.
	Bridgnorth	Quatford.
	Ellesmere	Welch Hampton.
	Hodnet	Weston.

DIOCESE OF LICHFIELD—*(continued)*.

Name of Chapel.	Name or Description of Parish, Chapelry, or other recognized Ecclesiastical Division thereunto annexed.	Whether licensed under the Act of 6 and 7 Wm. IV., c. 85.	Description of District for which it is so Licensed.
Longton, St. James, in the parish of Stoke-upon-Trent, Staffordshire.	The township of Longton.	Licensed under the Act 28th June, 1837.	The township of Longton.
Lower Gornall, St. James, in the parish of Sedgley, Staffordshire.	Lower Gornall .	4th July, 1837	The boundary to coincide throughout with the boundary of the village of Lower Gornall and Gornall Wood, which is known by that name as one of the nine villages into which the parish of Sedgley is divided.
Coseley, Christchurch, in the parish of Sedgley, Staffordshire.	Coseley Township	4th July, 1837	The boundary of the district commences at the point where the common boundary of Coseley and Woodsetton villages meets the boundary of Hipton parish, and comprises the whole of Coseley and Brierley villages, and also two portions of Ettingshall village, one of which lies on the south-east side of the road running through Sodom, past the bottom of Can-lane, and so on towards the Deepfield; and, secondly, all that portion of Ettingshall which lies on the east side of the canal running from Deepfield to Wolverhampton.
New Mills, or Beard, St. George, in the parish of Glossop, Derbyshire.	Township of Beard.	4th July, 1837	The hamlets of Beard, Ollerset, Whittle, and Thornset, in the parish of Glossop.
Hayfield, in the parish of Glossop, Derbyshire.	Chapelry of Hayfield.	4th July, 1837	The chapelry of Hayfield, which consists of the hamlets of Great Hamlet, Phoside, Kinder, Chinley, Bugsworth, and Brownside, in the parish of Glossop.
Newcastle-under-Lyme, Christchurch, Staffordshire.	Newcastle-under-Lyme.	28th July, 1837	Within a line passing through Bath-street, Fog-street, and Market-street, including both sides of those streets, and that portion of the town in which St. George's Chapel is situate, and also the whole of the town of Newcastle lying beyond the Pool Dam towards the west, called the Higher Land.
Long Eaton, in the parish of Sawley, Derbyshire.	Chapelry of Long Eaton.	18th Aug., 1837.	The township or liberty of Long Eaton, in the parish of Sawley, in the county of Derby.
Kingswinford, St. Mary, Staffordshire.	Kingswinford .	23rd Sept., 1837	The district commences on the north side of the Pensnett Pools to the Stourbridge canal, along the canal by Brockmoor bridge, to Haywood's bridge, thence by the road leading from Brockmoor to Bromley-lane; along Bromley-lane to the gate on the Stourbridge and Wolverhampton turnpike-road; thence, in a straight line across Barnett-lane, and through the Rudge plantations to the point where the road leading from Wordesley to Green's Forge intersects the Kidderminster and Wolverhampton turnpike-road; thence to Green's Forge, to the boundary of the parish there; thence, along the boundary of the parish, with the parishes of Womborne, Himley, Sedgley, and Dudley, to the point where the measurement commenced on Pensnett Chase.
Brierley Hill, in the parish of Kingswinford, Staffordshire.	Chapelry of Brierley Hill.	23rd Sept., 1837	The district commences on the north of Brockmoor bridge, and continues by the south side of Pensnett Pools, running eastwardly to the Dudley road, and then to the road leading from Stourbridge to Nethertown, and is bounded on the south by the hamlet of Cradley, on the west by the hamlet of Amblecoate, in the parish of Old Swinford, and continues across Brettle-lane to the Stourbridge canal, by which it is bounded on the north-west, and from thence continues by Haywood's bridge to Brockmoor bridge, the point whence the measurement commenced.
Donnington Wood, St. George, in the parish of Lilleshall, Shropshire.	Chapelry of Donnington Wood.	10th Nov., 1837	The district is bounded on the south by the Watling-street road, commencing at Pain's-lane, and continuing on to the Red-hill gate; on the east, by the parish of Sheriff Hales; on the north, by the Donnington-wood canal; and on the west by Pain's-lane.
Prior's Lee, St. Peter, in the parish of Shiffnal, Shropshire.	Chapelry of Priors Lee.	7th Dec., 1837	The district forming the western part of the parish of Shiffnal, and comprising Snedshill, Oaken-gate, the Nab, south side of Pain's-lane, and Redhill Priors Lee, and the several farms called Lower Woodhouses, Middle Woodhouses, Upper Woodhouses, the Castle Blythbury, the Neard, the Elms, and the Nedge, and is bounded by the townships of Haughton, Wyken, and Shaw, and the parishes of Shickley, Dawley, Wombridge, Wrockwardine, and Lilleshall.

DIOCESE OF LICHFIELD—*(continued)*.

Name of Chapel.	Name or Description of Parish, Chapelry, or other recognised Ecclesiastical Division thereunto annexed.	Whether licensed under the Act of 6 and 7 Wm. IV., c. 85.	Description of District for which it is so Licensed.
Broughton, in the parish of Eccleshall, Staffordshire.	Chapelry of Broughton.	24th Dec.,1837	The district commences at the Hook gate and continues on from thence to the hamlet of Podmore on the north, on the east to the hamlet of Chathill, which it includes, and from thence, across the Chester-road, by Fair Oak, and continues on by Langard-lane, on the south, to some woods, called Bishop's Woods, on the east, and from thence to the Hook-gate, where it commences; which district includes the hamlets of Charnes, Brourly, Wetwood, and Broughton.
Ripley, in the parish of Pentrich, Derbyshire.	The Township of Ripley, in the parish of Pentrich.	6 & 7 Wm. IV., and 1 Vict. 24th May, 1838	The district commences at the Tunnel-road, continuing thence by Butterly Hall to Greenwich, and from thence to the Coppice; and continuing along by the White Lees, to the turnpike-road on the south; and from thence along the boundary of the parish of Pentrich, by the Old Hall, and on to the straight lane through the Hartshay Pit to the Cromford canal, and from thence to the turnpike-road on the north, and so on to the Tunnel road where the district commences.
Tunstall, in the parish of Wolstanton, Staffordshire.	Tunstall, in the parish of Wolstanton.	6 & 7 Wm. IV., and 1 Vict. 24th Sept., 1838	Comprising the townships of Ranscliffe, Oldcott, and Tunstall, in the parish of Wolstanton.
Donisthorpe, in the county of Derbyshire.	Donisthorpe.	4 Geo. IV. 31st Oct., 1838	The district comprises the liberties of Oakthorpe, Donisthorpe, and the village of Moira, bounded on the north-east and east by the parishes of Blackfordby and Willesby, on the south-east and south by the parish of Measham, on the south-west and west by the turnpike-road leading from Measham to Burton-on-Trent, and commonly called Watton-way, and on the north-west and north by Barrett's pool and the brook that flows from it to the River Mease at Acresford
Mellor, in the parish of Glossop, Derbyshire.	Chapelry of Mellor, in the parish of Glossop, Derbyshire.	6 & 7 Wm. IV., 23rd Nov., 1838.	The district comprises the hamlets of Mellor, Ludworth, and New Mills, in the parish of Glossop.
Shelton, St. Mark, in the parish of Stoke-upon-Trent, in the county of Stafford.	Township of Shelton.	6 & 7 Wm. IV., and 1 Vict., c. 22. 21st March,1839.	The district comprises the liberty or township of Shelton, excepting and retaining only such parts and parcels of building land lying in the boundary line, belonging to the ancient glebe of the rectory of Stoke-upon-Trent, and forming as it were the very curtilage of the Mother Church.
Smethwick, Old Chapel, in the parish of Harborne, Staffordshire.	Smethwick . .	6 & 7 Wm. IV., c.85,&1 Vict.,c.22 29th Aug., 1839.	The district is bounded on the north by a lane leading from Langley green to Handsworth, (which lane separates it from the district of North Harborne,) and on the south by the turnpike-road leading from Hales Owen to Birmingham, (which road separates it from the district of Harborne Proper,) and on the south-east by the parish of Birmingham and Handsworth, and on the west by the parish of Hales Owen, in the county of Salop and Diocese of Worcester.
North Harborne, Holy Trinity, Staffordshire.	North Harborne	6 & 7 Wm. IV., c.85,&1 Vict.,c.22 29th Aug., 1839.	The North Harborne district is bounded on the north by the parish of West Bromwich, on the east by the parish of Handsworth, on the south by a lane leading from Langley-green to Handsworth (which lane separates it from the hamlet of Smethwick), and on the west by the parish of Hales Owen and liberty of Oldbury, in the county of Salop.

(Signed)   J. MOTT,   } *Deputy Registrars.*
              J. HAWORTH,

The Close, Lichfield,
     27th June, 1840.

DIOCESE OF LINCOLN.

[No Return.]

DIOCESE OF LLANDAFF.

[No Return.]

DIOCESE OF LONDON.

A List made by the Registrar of the Diocese of London, in pursuance of the provisions of the Act of 6 and 7 Wm. IV. c. 85, and 7 Wm. IV., c. 1, being a List of all Chapels belonging to the Church of England within that Diocese, wherein Marriages may be lawfully solemnized according to the Rites and Ceremonies of the Church of England, distinguishing which have a Parish, Chapelry, or other recognized Ecclesiastical Division annexed to them, and which are Chapels licensed by the Bishop under the Act 6 and 7 Wm. IV. c. 85, and stating the District for which each of such Chapels is licensed, according to the description thereof in the License.

Name of Chapel.	Name or Description of Parish, Chapelry, or other recognized Ecclesiastical Division thereunto annexed.	Whether Licensed under the Act of 6 & 7 Wm. IV. c. 85.	Description of District for which it is so Licensed.
St. John the Baptist, Hoxton.	District of, in the parish of St. Leonard, Shoreditch.	No.	
Holy Trinity . .	Brompton, parish of Kensington.	No.	
St. Mary, Haggerstone.	District of, in the parish of St. Leonard, Shoreditch.	No.	
Stamford Hill Chapel	District, in the parish of Hackney.	No.	
Holy Trinity . .	District of, in the parish of St. Mary, Islington.	No.	
St. Paul , . .	District of, in the parish of St. Mary, Islington.	No.	
St. John the Evangelist, Holloway.	District of, in the parish of St. Mary, Islington.	No.	
South Hackney . .	South Hackney	No.	
Upper Chelsea . .	Upper Chelsea	No.	
St. Michael, Highgate	Consolidated Chapelry of .	No.	
St. John, Paddington.	District of, in the parish of Paddington.	No	
St. John, Hampton Wick.	District, in the parish of Hampton.	No.	
St. George's Chapel, Old Brentford.		Yes;	All that district bounded on the north by a line commencing at and including the house of G. Oliver, Esq., in Boston Road, and passing by Mercury House in Windmill Lane, Mr. Jones's house in Drum Lane, and the Clay Ponds to a point in Bollow Bridge Lane, on the south by the River Thames and the parish of Chiswick, and on the west by the township of New Brentford.
St. Paul	In the parish of Waltham Holy Cross.	Yes;	All that district bounded on the north by the line commencing at the junction of the cross roads leading from Pyner's Green, Honey Lane Green, and the public house known by the name of the King's Oak, and proceeding thence to the extremity of a lane due east, terminated by the boundary which separates the parish of Waltham Holy Cross from the parish of Loughton ; then turning to the right and proceeding along the said boundary to the extreme southern point of the parish of Waltham, on the forest side, where the boundary commences which separates the parish of Waltham from the parish of Chingford ; then following the said boundary in a direction westward to the extreme western part of an assignment laid down as Lady Silvester's assignment ; then turning to the right in a direction north-west along Sewardstone, Bury Lane, and thence proceeding up a green lane which meets the road leading from High Beech to Sewardstone, called "Mott Street;" thence proceeding along the last-mentioned road to certain cottages situated on the right side thereof, and known by the name of the "Barn Houses;" thence proceeding northward along the western boundaries of the property of Captain Charles Sotheby, designated "Hope Hall Farm," and the property of

D

DIOCESE OF LONDON—*(continued.)*

Name of Chapel.	Name or Description of Parish, Chapelry, or other recognised Ecclesiastical Division thereunto annexed.	Whether Licensed under the Act of 6 & 7 Wm. IV., c. 85.	Description of District for which it is so Licensed.
St. Paul—*continued.*	In the parish of Waltham Holy Cross.		John Collingridge to the lane called Avy Lane, thence proceeding along Avy Lane towards the east, then turning to the left up the lane leading to Pyner's Green, then proceeding northward along the lane from Pyner's Green to the junction of the cross roads where the said line commences.
Weld Chapel, Southgate.	Parish of Edmonton . . .	Yes;	All that district bounded on the north by the road leading from Whetstone to Enfield, on the east by a road running at right angles with the above-mentioned road from Pole Farm to Chase Gate, and proceeding from thence to Dog-and-Duck Lane, thence to Beale's Farm, including the house on Palmer's Green, and then by a lane leading to the eastern extremity of Tile-Kiln Lane, on the south and west by the boundaries of the parish of Edmonton.
Holy Trinity, Hounslow.	Consolidated Chapelry . .	No.	
St. Paul, Winchmore Hill.	In the parish of Edmonton .	Yes;	All that district bounded on the north by the parish of Enfield, on the east by the high road leading from Enfield town, towards Edmonton Church, and by the road which runs southward as far Huxley Farm on the south by the road leading from Tanner's End to South Gate, on the west by the road running northward from Chase Gate, and on the north-west by the boundary of the parish of Edmonton.
St. John, Potter's Bar	In the parish of South Mims	Yes;	All that district commencing at the north-east corner of Cooper's Lane opposite premises in the parish of Enfield, now occupied by Mr. Tomlinson, Grocer, proceeding down the south side of Chase Lane, to the north-east boundary or corner where the said parish of South Mims joins the parish of Enfield; then turning to the right it proceeds along the boundary which separates the parish of South Mims from the parish of Enfield, to the south-west corner of the waggon road, and, in its course crossing the road leading to Enfield, and also the road leading to Southgate; it then proceeds from the south-east corner of the waggon road along the south side of the waggon road abutting on the south part of the allotment of the late Enfield Chase to the parish of South Mims, crossing the great London and Hatfield road to Gannick Corner; turning to the left it then proceeds along the lane to the lodge of Wrotham Park, the seat of George Byng, Esq., M.P., then turning to the right through Bentley Heath and Bentley Heath Lane, to the junction of Bentley Heath Lane with Baker Street opposite the lane to Dugdale Hill (all the houses at Bentley Heath and Bentley Heath Lane being included); the western boundary proceeds from the corner of Bentley Heath Lane along Baker Street, including the farms occupied by George Harvey, by Mr. Bossom, and Willcott's Manor Farm, lately occupied by Mr. Wardell, to Dark's Farm, then from Dark's Farm to the north-west corner of the parish of South Mims where it joins the parish of North Mims, then turning to the right along the northern boundary of the parish of South Mims to the stone in the London and Hatfield Road, from thence to the north-east corner of Mr. Hammond's land, then turning to the right into Cooper's Lane by Mr. Hammond's house, it proceeds along the south side of Cooper's Lane to the north-east corner opposite Mr. Tomlinson's, where the boundary commences.
St. Thomas the Martyr	In the parish of Brentwood .	Yes;	All that district bounded on the north by South Weald parish, on the east by Shenfield parish, on the south partly by Shenfield parish and partly by South Weald parish, reserving a small spot in this same district, marked South Weald, lying between the figures 26, 2, 31, 32, in the plan annexed to the license.
St. John, Buckhurst Hill.	In the parish of Chigwell .	Yes;	All that district bounded by a circumference having a radius of one mile, and St. John's Chapel for its centre, and comprising parts of the parishes of Chigwell, Loughton, Woodford, and Chingford.

DIOCESE OF LONDON—(*continued.*)

Name of Chapel.	Name or Description of Parish, Chapelry, or other recognized Ecclesiastical Division thereunto annexed.	Whether Licensed under the Act of 6 & 7 Wm. IV. c. 85.	Description of District for which it is so Licensed.
St. Mary, North-end	In the parish of Fulham . .	No.	
St. John, Walham Green.	In the parish of ·Fulham. .	·No.	
St. Peter, Colney .	In the parish of St. Peter Ridge and St. Stephen.	Yes ;	All that district bounded on the north by Hill End and Smallford, on the south· by Shenley parish, on the east by Colney Heath, and on the west by Mapsbury.
		. .	
St. John, Bethnal Green.	In the parish of St. Mathew, Bethnal Green.	No.	
St. Mark, Clerkenwell	St. Mark's District . . .	No.	
Holy Trinity, Holborn	In the parish of· St. Andrew, Holborn.	No.	

(Signed)   JOHN SHEPHARD, Registrar.

DIOCESE OF NORWICH.

Sir,   *Norwich, 19th June,* 1840.

In reply to your Letter of yesterday's date, I beg to inform you that I am not aware -of there being any Chapels in this Diocese in which marriages may be solemnized according to the Rites of the Church of England.

I am, Sir,

Your obedient, humble Servant,

J. KITSON, Registror.

To the Registrar-General.

DIOCESE OF OXFORD.
[No Return.]

DIOCESE OF PETERBOROUGH.
[No Return.]

DIOCESE OF RIPON.

A List made by the Registrar of the Diocese of Ripon up to the 1st day of January, 1840, in pursuance of the provisions of the Acts of 6 and 7 Wm. IV., being a List of all Chapels belonging to the Church of England within that Diocese, wherein Marriages may be lawfully solemnized according to the Rites and Ceremonies of the Church of England, distinguishing which have a Parish, Chapelry, or other recognized Ecclesiastical Division annexed to them, and which are Chapels licensed by the Bishop under the Act of 6 and 7 Wm. IV., c. 85, and stating the District for which each of such Chapels is licensed, according to the description thereof in the License.

Name of Church or Chapel.	Name or Description of Parish, Chapelry, or other recognized Ecclesiastical Division thereunto annexed.	Whether Licensed under the Act of 6 and 7 Wm. IV. c. 85.	Description of District for which it is so Licensed.
Hunslet Chapel . .	In the parish of Leeds, in the county of York.	4 Geo. IV. c. 76.	Chapelry of Hunslet.
Holbeck Chapel . .	Ditto	Ditto . .	Chapelry of Holbeck.
Beeston Chapel . .	Ditto . ·. . .	Ditto ·. .	Chapelry of Beeston.
Wortley Chapel . .	Ditto	Ditto . .	Chapelry of Wortley.
Farnley Chapel . .	Ditto . ·. . .	Ditto ·. .	Chapelry of Farnley.
Bramley Chapel .	Ditto	Ditto . .	Chapelry of Bramley.
Headingley Chapel .	Ditto· . ·. . .	Ditte . .	Chapelry of Headingley.
Chapelallerton Chapel	Ditto	Ditto . .	Chapelry of Chapelallerton.
St. James's Church, in Halifax.	In the parish of Halifax, in the county of York.	Ditto . .	Township of ·Halifax and Skircoat.

D 2

DIOCESE OF RIPON—(*continued.*)

Name of Church or Chapel.	Name or Description of Parish, Chapelry, or other recognized Ecclesiastical Division thereunto annexed.	Whether Licensed under the Act of 6 and 7 Wm. IV. c. 85.	Description of District for which it is so Licensed.
Trinity Church, in Halifax.	In the parish of Leeds, in the county of York.	4 Geo. IV. c. 76.	Township of Halifax, and the lower division of the township of Skircoat.
Sowerby Bridge Church	Ditto	Ditto . .	Lower division of the township of Warley, the township of Norland, and the upper division of the township of Skircoat.
Sowerby Church . .	Ditto	Ditto . .	Township of Sowerby (except such part thereof as is included within the Turvin quarter.)
Luddenden Church .	Ditto	Ditto . .	Township of Midgley and the upper part of the township of Warley.
Illingworth Chapel .	Ditto	Ditto . .	Township of Ovenden.
Coley Church . . .	Ditto	Ditto . .	Townships of Northowram and Shelf.
Southowram Chapel .	Ditto	Ditto . .	Township of Southowram.
Lightcliffe Chapel .	Ditto	Ditto . .	Township of Hipperholme-cum-Brighouse.
Brighouse Church. .	Ditto	Ditto . .	Township of Hipperholme-cum-Brighouse.
Rastrick Chapel . .	Ditto	Ditto . .	Township of Rastrick.
Ripponden Church .	Ditto	Ditto . .	Townships of Soyland, Barksland, and Rishworth.
Cross Stones Church .	Ditto	Ditto . .	Township of Longfield and the upper and middle thirds of the township of Stansfield.
Mytholme Church. .	Ditto	Ditto . .	Lower third of the township of Stansfield.
St. John's Church in the Wilderness.	Ditto	Ditto . .	Township of Erringden and the Turvin quarter of the township of Sowerby Range.
St. Peter's Church, Earl's Eaton.	In the parish of Dewsbury, in the county of York.	Ditto . .	Township of Soothill Nether.
The Church in the township of Heckmondwicke.	In the parish of Birstall, in the county of York.	Ditto . .	Township of Heckmondwicke.
St. Paul's, Hanging Heaton.	In the parish of Dewsbury, in the county of York.	Ditto . .	Township of Soothill Upper.
St. John's, Dewsbury Moor.	Ditto	Ditto . .	All that part of the parish of Dewsbury that is bounded on the west by the parish of Mirfield, including Dewsbury Moor, Upper and Lower Boothroyd, and so much of the township of Dewsbury on the east as is included between the public roads from Crow West to Dewsbury, and from Dewsbury to Raven's Wharf.
The Church or Chapel of St. Paul's, Birkenshaw.	In the parish of Birstall, in the county of York.	Ditto . .	Hamlets of Birkenshaw, Latham Lane, Fieldhead, Hunsworth Village, Hunsworth Lodge, Toft Shaw, East Bierley, part of Tong Street, Westgate Hill, Hodgson Lane, Wasp Nest, Moor Lane, and Drub Lane.
St. John's, Cleckheaton	Ditto	Ditto . .	Hamlet of Cleckheaton.
Whitechapel, Cleckheaton.	Ditto	Ditto . .	Hamlets of Scholes and Oakenshaw, and the township of Wyke.
Christ Church . . .	In the parish of Bradford, in the county of York.	Ditto . .	The district assigned to the said Church.
Thornton Chapel . .	Ditto	Ditto . .	The district assigned to the said Chapel.
Bierley Chapel . .	Ditto	Ditto . .	The district assigned to the said Chapel.
Wibsey Low Moor Chapel	Ditto	Ditto . .	The district assigned to the said Chapel.
Horton Chapel . .	Ditto	Ditto . .	The district assigned to the said Chapel.

DIOCESE OF RIPON—(*continued.*)

Name of Church or Chapelry.	Name or Description of Parish, Chapelry, or other recognized Ecclesiastical Division thereunto annexed.	Whether Licensed under the Act of 6 and 7 Wm. 1V. c. 85.	Description of District for which it is so Licensed.
Thorn-'s Church or Chapel.	In the parish of Wakefield, in the county of York.	4 Geo. IV. c.76.	The persons residing in the Chapelry.
Wetherby Chapel . .	In the parish of Spofforth, in the county York.	6 and 7 Wm.IV. c. 85.	The township of Wetherby.
Pudsey Chapel . .	In the parish of Calverley, in the county of York.	Ditto . .	The township of Pudsey.
Christ Church New Mills	In the parish of Kirkburton, in the county of York.	Ditto . .	The district belonging to the Church.

27, *Parliament Street,*
27th June, 1840.

(Signed)   JOHN BURDER,
Registrar of the Diocese of Ripon.

DIOCESE OF ROCHESTER.

A List made by the Registrar of the Diocese of Rochester, in pursuance of the provisions of the Acts 6 and 7 Wm. IV., c. 85, and 7 Wm. IV., c. 1, being a List of all Chapels belonging to the Church of England within that Diocese, wherein Marriages may lawfully be solemnized according to the Rites and Ceremonies of the Church of England, distinguishing which have a Parish, Chapelry, or other recognized Ecclesiastical Division annexed to them, and which are Chapels licensed by the Bishop under the Act of 6 and 7 Wm. IV., c. 85, and stating the District for which each of such Chapels is licensed according to the description thereof in the License.

Name of Chapel.	Name or Description of Parish, Chapelry, or other recognized Ecclesiastical Division thereunto annexed.	Whether Licensed under the Act of 6 & 7 Wm.IV., c. 85.	Description of District for which it is so Licensed.

There is no Chapel in this Diocese in which Marriages can be solemnized according to the Rites and Ceremonies of the Church of England.

There is a District Church of Tunbridge Wells.	District Parish of Tunbridge Wells.		Not Licensed under the Act 6 and 7 Wm. IV., c. 85, but deriving its authority under the Church Building Acts.

Rochester, 2nd January, 1840.   (Signed)   GEORGE ESSELL, *Registrar.*

DIOCESE OF SALISBURY.

A Return made by the Registrar of the Diocese of Salisbury, within fifteen days after the 1st day of January, 1840, in pursuance of the provisions of the Acts of 6 and 7 Wm. IV., c. 85, and 7 Wm. IV., c. 1, of all Chapels belonging to the Church of England in that part of the county of Wilts which is within the said Diocese, wherein Marriages may be lawfully solemnized according to the Rites and Ceremonies of the Church of England, distinguishing which have a Parish, Chapelry, or other recognized Ecclesiastical Division annexed to them, and which are Chapels licensed by the Diocesan under the Act of 6 and 7 Wm. IV., c. 85, and stating the District for which each of such Chapels is licensed according to the Description thereof in the License.

Name of Chapel.	Name or Description of Parish, Chapelry, or other recognized Ecclesiastical Division thereunto annexed.	Whether Licensed under the Act of 6 & 7 Wm.IV., c. 85.	Description of District for which it is so Licensed.
Wilts.			
Sedghill	Berwick St. Leonard.		
Alvedestone . . .	Broad Chalk.		
Atworth			
Holt			
Limplestoke . . .			
South Wraxhall . .	Bradford.		
Westwood			
Winsley			
Martin	Damerham.		
Monkton Deverell .	Deverell, Longbridge.		
Netherhampton . .	Wilton.		
Nunton	Downton.		
Porton	Idmiston.		

DIOCESE OF SALISBURY—(*continued.*)

Name of Chapel.	Name or Description of Parish, Chapelry, or other recognized Ecclesiastical Division thereunto annexed.	Whether Licensed under the Act of 6 & 7 Wm. IV., c. 85.	Description of District for which it is so Licensed.
Earlstoke	} Melksham.		
Seend			
Semington	Steeple Aston.		
Stert	Urchfont.		
Plaitford	West Grinstead.		
Itchilhampton . . .	Allcannings.		
Highway	Bremhill.		
Alton Priors . . .	} Overton.		
Fifield			
Pitton	} Alderbury.		
Farley			
South Broom . . .	Bishop's Cannings.		
Berwick Basset . .	} Calne.		
Cherhill			
Broad Blunsden . .	} Highworth . . .	. .	A Peculiar of the Dean of Sarum, locally situate in the Deanery of Cricklade and Diocese of Gloucester and Bristol.
South Marston . .			
Dilton	} Westbury.		
Bratton			
West Harnham . .	Combe Bissett.		
St. Mary, Redlinch .	Downton	Licensed under 6 & 7 Wm. IV.	
Christchurch . . .	Warminster.	Ditto.	
Trinity Chapel . . .	Trowbridge.	Ditto.	
Dorset.			
Longfleet	} Great Canford . .	Licensed under 6 & 7 Wm. IV.	Tithing of Parkstone.
St. Peter's, Parkstone .			
Peculiars of the Dean of Sarum in the same county of Dorset.			
Winterbourne, Kingston	Beer Regis.		
Holnest	Longburton.		
Peculiar of the Official of Gillingham in the same county.			
Bourton	Gillingham . . .	Licensed under 6 & 7 Wm. IV.	Hamlet of Bourton.

(Signed)   EDWARD DAVIES, *Registrar.*

DIOCESE OF WINCHESTER.

A List made by the Registrar of the Diocese of Winchester within the County of Southampton, within fifteen days after the 1st day of January, 1840, in pursuance of the provisions of the Acts of 6 and 7 Wm. IV., c. 85, and 7 Wm. IV. c. 1, being a List of the Chapels belonging to the Church of England, within the said Diocese, wherein Marriages may be lawfully solemnized according to the Rites and Ceremonies of the Church of England, distinguishing which have a Parish, Chapelry, or other recognised Ecclesiastical Division annexed to them, and which are Chapels licensed by the Bishop under the Act of 6 and 7 Wm. IV., c. 85, and stating the District for which each of such Chapels is licensed according to the description thereof in the License.

Name of Chapel.	Name or Description of Parish, Chapelry, or other recognized Ecclesiastical Division thereunto annexed.	Whether licensed under the Act of 6 and 7 Wm. IV. c. 85.	Description of District for which it is so Licensed.
West Cowes . . .	The parish and chapelry of Northwood in the Isle of Wight.	Yes;	Within the district or limits of the town of Cowes, as defined by an Act of Parliament passed in the 56th year of King George III., intituled " An Act for paving, lighting, cleansing, and otherwise improving the town of West Cowes, in the Isle of Wight, in the County of Southampton, and for establishing a market within the said town."
St. James's, Shirley.	Portion of the parish of Millbrook, as set forth in the division.	Yes;	The present boundaries on the south-east, east, north-east, and north, between the parish of Millbrook, and the parish of All Saints, Southampton Common, and the parishes of North Stoneham and Nursling respectively; then turning south out of the road from Aldermoor to Redbridge, at and by the road from Aldermoor to Millbrook, crossing the main road from Romsey to Southampton at Maybush corner; thence continuing south along the road to Millbrook as far as the road leading from Peckle's Coppice (where the direction post now stands) to Redbridge, to Winchester, to Romsey; thence turning east along the said road usually called the Redbridge-road into the village of Shirley, comprehending (in the said district of Shirley) all the houses adjoining the road on both sides into Shirley village, continuing to the edge over Tanner's brook; thence continuing in the line of the boundary between the manors of Millbrook and Shirley, that is to say, the said brook called Tanner's brook into Mousehole-lane; thence turning east, leaving Mouseholelane Flour-mill, west, and not in Shirley district, along Mousehole-lane, including Shirley House and grounds, now occupied by Colonel Fagon; thence continuing along by the lane or road adjoining Mousehole-lane and Foundry-lane or road, leaving Foundry-lane to the south-west, continuing along the dyke or water-course separating Millbrook and Shirley manors to its falling in with the said high-road leading from Romsey to Southampton, continuing thence along the said road up to the wall running south from the Romsey-road into the Lyndhurstroad, cutting off from the district of Shirley all the houses west of the said wall, and which wall is supposed to be the line of separation of the said manors of Millbrook and Shirley, and including in the said district of Shirley all the houses east of the said wall turning from the east end of the said wall adjoining the Lyndhurst-road eastward to the small water-course on the opposite side of the said Lyndhurst-road, and following the said water-course on the opposite side of the said Lyndhurst-road, also following the said water-course under the houses and on the east side of the wall of the house occupied by Mr. Daintry at Hill, until the same joins the Southampton Water, and thence running eastward along the beach to another water-course which is the present boundary between the said parish of Millbrook and the said parish of All Saints.
St. Catherine's, Ventnor, Isle of Wight.	Portion of the parishes of Newchurch and Godshill, in the Isle of Wight.	Yes;	Such parts of the parishes of Newchurch and Godshill as are contained within the several boundaries following, that is to say, the sea on the south, the parish of St. Lawrence on the west, the parish of Bonchurch on the east, and Row Farm, Span Farm, and Wroxhall Manor, in the said parishes of Newchurch and Godshill, on the north.
The Church or Chapel of the Holy Ghost, at Newtown, Isle of Wight.	The parish of Calborne, Isle of Wight.	Yes;	The whole of the parish of Calborne, in the Isle of Wight, and the manor of Newtown, in the said Isle.
Holy Trinity, Bembridge, Isle of Wight.	Parish of Brading, Isle of Wight.	Yes;	All that part of the parish of Brading called Bembridge quarter, separated from the rest of the said parish of Brading by the parish of Yaverland, and surrounded on the parts by the sea.

DIOCESE OF WINCHESTER—*(continued.)*

Name of Chapel.	Name or Description of Parish, Chapelry, or other recognized Ecclesiastical Division thereunto annexed.	Whether Licensed under the Act of 6 & 7 Wm. IV., c. 85.	Description of District for which it is so Licensed.
Holy Trinity, Hawley, Hants.	Partly in the parish of Yateley, Hants, and partly in the parish of Frimley, Surrey.	Yes;	All that part of the parish of Yateley called Blackwater, and which is upwards of two miles from the parish church of Yateley, and the whole of the village of York-town, extending to the upper lodge of the Royal Military College, which is in the parish of Frimley.
St. Paul's	Portsea	Yes;	To commence at South Sea Castle on the south-east, following a straight line to Marmion-place, and thence continuing in the centre of the road to the canal at Keith Bridge, on the north side the boundary extends westward down the centre of the canal to the London-road, thence crosses to the centre of Union-road, terminating at the Lion Ravelin Gate. The outer line of the fortifications of the towns of Portsea and Portsmouth forms the western boundary; on the south it is bounded by the sea.
All Saints	Portsea	Yes;	The boundary to commence on the south side at Williams' bridge on the canal, extending to the London-road, crossing which it is continued along the centre of Union-road to the north side of the Lion Ravelin Gate, to be bounded on the south-west by the outer line of fortifications of the town of Portsea, and on the west by Portsmouth harbour as far as Byerly's Mill, on the north to commence in the centre of Rudmore-lane leading to the London-road, and comprising the houses on the north side of Kingston-crescent, extending as far as the second milestone on the London-road, the line from thence to continue on the west side of Buckland to Lake-lane, down the centre of which to lead to the London-road, turning there to the south into the centre of Paradise-row, and to terminate at Williams' bridge.
Burghclere, New Church.	Burghclere	Yes;	The whole parish of Burghclere.
St. James, East Cowes.	Whippingham	Yes;	A district confined within a line drawn from the toll-gate on the road between East Cowes and Whippingham, eastward through the grounds of Osborne-park to the sea, and westward to the river Medina.
St. Mark, Pennington	Milford	Yes;	The whole of the manor and tything of Pennington, as the same is separated from the other part of the said parish of Milford, by a brook or stream of water, which takes its course from New Forest to Efford Mill, thence to Keyhaven, where it enters the sea, and which said manor and tything of Pennington is bounded by the said brook or stream of water on the south, by the parish of Hordle on the west, by the parishes of Hordle and Boldre on the north, and by the Solent sea on the east.

(Signed)   CHARLES WOOLDRIDGE.
Deputy Registrar.

DIOCESE OF WORCESTER.

Worcester.   A List of all Chapels belonging to the Church of England within this Diocese, wherein Marriages may be solemnized according to the Rites and Ceremonies of the Church of England.

ARCHDEACONRY OF WORCESTER.

Deanery of Blockley.

None.

Deanery of Droitwich.

In Bromsgrove parish,
     The Chapels of King's Norton, Moseley, and Wythall.
In Dodderhill parish,
     The Chapel of Elmbridge.
In Northfield parish,
     The Chapel of Cofton Hackett.
In Tardebigg parish,
     The Chapel of Redditch.

Deanery of Evesham.

The Chapel of South Lyttleton.
The Chapel of Wickhamford.

Deanery of Kidderminster.

In Clent parish,
     The Chapel of Rowley Regis.
In Dudley parish,
     The Chapel of St. Edmund.
     The Chapel of Netherton.
In Hagley parish,
     The Chapel of Frankley.
In Halesowen parish,
     The Chapel of Oldbury.*
     The Chapel of Cradley.

* The only Chapel in the Diocese which has been licensed for the publication of Banns and solemnization of Marriages, under the Act of 4 Geo. IV., c. 76, sec. 3, is that of Oldbury.

DIOCESE OF WORCESTER—(*continued.*)

In Kidderminster parish,
* The Chapel of St. George.
The Chapel of Lower Mitton.

Deanery of Pershore.

In Bredon parish,
The Chapels of Norton and Cuttesden.
In Fladbury parish,
The Chapels of Stock and Bradley, Throck-
morton, and Wyre Piddle.
The Chapel of Dormeston.
In Overbury parish,
The Chapels of Alstone, Teddington, and
Washbourne.
In St. Andrew's parish, in Pershore,
The Chapels of Holy Cross, Besford,
Bricklehampton, Defford, and Pinwin.
In Ripple parish,
The Chapel of Queenhill.

Deanery of Powick.

In Hanley Castle parish,
The Chapel of St. Peter, Malvern Wells.
In Leigh parish,
The Chapel of Bransford.
In Suckley parish,
The Chapels of Alfrick and Lulsley.

Deanery of Worcester.

In Grimley parish,
The Chapel of Hallow.
In Holt parish,
The Chapel of Little Witley.
In Knightwick parish,
The Chapel of Doddenham.
In St. Peter's parish, in Worcester,
· The Chapel of Whittington.

Deanery of Kington, alias *Kineton.*

In Wolford parish,
The Chapel of Burmington.
In Kineton parish,
The Chapel of Combrooke.
In Shipston-upon-Stour parish,
The Chapel of Tidmington.

Deanery of Warwick.

In Wootton Wawen parish,
The Chapels of Ullenhall and Bearley.
In Claverdon parish,
The Chapel of Norton Lindsey.
In Exhall parish,
The Chapel of Wigglesford.
In Kinwarton parish,
The Chapels of Great Alne and Weethley.

IN THE ARCHDEACONRY OF COVENTRY.

Deanery of Arden.

The Chapel of Ashtead, near Birmingham.
The Chapel of Astley.
The Chapel of Atherstone.
The Chapel of Baddesley.
In Birmingham,
The Chapel of St. Bartholomew.
The Chapel of St. John, Deritend.
The Chapel of St. Mary.
The Chapel of St. Paul.
The Chapel of Christ Church.
The Chapel of the Holy Tinity, in Bordesley.
The Chapel of St. Peter.
In Aston parish,
The Chapel of Castle Bromwich.
The Chapel of Erdington.
In Hampton-in-Arden parish,
The Chapel of Nuthurst.
The Chapel of Lea Marston.
The Chapel of Shuttington.
In Sutton Coldfield parish,
The Chapel of St. James.

In Solihull parish,
The Chapel of St. James.
The Chapel of Stockingford.
The Chapel of Whiteacre Superior.
The Chapel of Whiteacre Inferior.
The Chapel of Water Orton.

Deaneries of Moreton, Stoneleigh, and Coventry.

The Chapel of Bobenhull.
The Chapel of Brownsover in Clifton.
The Chapel of Burton Hastings.
· The Chapel of Binley.
The Chapel of Chesterton.
In Coventry,
The Chapel of Hunningham.
The Chapel of Milverton.
The Chapel of Ryton-super-Dunsmore.
The Chapel of Stivichall.
The Chapel of Shilton.
The Chapel of Wyken.

(Signed)   JOHN HILL CLIFTON,

Deputy Registrar,

SIR,

Registry, Worcester,
25th June, 1840.

     Enclosed, I beg to send you a Return for the last year, of the Chapels in this Diocese, in which Marriages may be solemnized.

I am, Sir,

Your most obedient Servant,

Thomas Mann, Esq.,
General Register Office.

(Signed)   J. H. CLIFTON.

DIOCESE OF YORK.

A List made by the Registrar of the Diocese of York, within fifteen days after the 1st day of January, 1840, in pursuance of the provisions of the Acts of 6 and 7 Wm. IV., c. 85, and 7 Wm. IV., c. 1, being a List of all Chapels belonging to the Church of England within that Diocese, wherein Marriages may lawfully be solemnized according to the Rites and Ceremonies of the Church of England, distinguishing which have a Parish, Chapelry, or other recognized Ecclesiastical Division annexed to them, and which are Chapels licensed by the Archbishop under the Act of 6 and 7 Wm. IV., c. 85, and stating the District for which each of such Chapels is licensed according to the description thereof in the License.

Name of Chapel.	Name or Description of Parish, Chapelry, or other recognized Ecclesiastical Division thereunto annexed.	Whether Licensed under the Act of 6 and 7 Wm. IV., c. 85.	Description of District for which it is so Licensed.
	NORTH RIDING.		
Seamer.	Parish of Seamer.		
Ingleby Greenhow.	Parish of Ingleby Greenhow		
Ingleby Arncliffe .	Parish of Ingleby Arncliffe		
Wilton .	Parish of Wilton		
Kirkleavington	Parish of Kirkleavington		
Egton .	Parish of Egton		
Easton .	Chapelry of Easton		
Acklam	Parish of Acklam		
Skelton	} Parish of Skelton-cum-Brotton		
Brotton			
Whorlton .	Parish of Whorlton .		
Yarm .	Parish of Yarm .		
Over Silton	Chapelry of Over Silton		
Bilsdale	Chapelry of Bilsdale		
Brompton .	Parish of Brompton		
Hovingham	Parish of Hovingham		
Kirkdale	Parish of Kirkdale .		
Rosedale	Chapelry of Rosedale		
Old Malton	Parish of Old Malton		
St. Michael	} Parish of Malton		
St. Leonard			
Sinnington.	Parish of Sinnington		
Wykeham .	Parish of Wykeham		
Huttons Ambo	Parish of Huttons Ambo		
Thorganby.	Parish of Thorganby		
Fylingdales	Chapelry of Fylingdales		
Whitby.	Parish of Whitby .		
Birdforth	Chapelry of Birdforth		
Coxwold .	Parish of Coxwold .		
Farlington .	Parish of Farlington		
Kilburne .	Parish of Kilburne .		
Marton.	Parish of Marton .		
Newton-upon-Ouze .	Parish of Newton-upon-Ouze .		
Raskelf	Chapelry of Raskelf		
Thirsk .	Parish of Thirsk		
Sandhutton	Chapelry of Sandhutton		
Carlton Miniot.	Chapelry of Carlton Miniot		
Sowerby	Chapelry of Sowerby		
Ayton .	Parish of Ayton		
Appleton-upon-Wyske	Chapelry of Appleton-upon-Wyske.		
Danby .	Parish of Danby .		
Glaisdale .	Chapelry of Glaisdale		
Liverton	Chapelry of Liverton		
East Harlsey .	Parish of East Harlsey.		
Guisborough .	Parish of Guisborough .		
Upleatham.	Parish of Upleatham		
Carlton	Parish of Carlton .		
Faceby.	Parish of Faceby.		
Hilton .	Parish of Hilton .		
Carlton Hustwaite	Parish of Carlton Hustwaite		
Newton	Parish of Newton .		
Eskdaleside	} Parish of Whitby .	Licensed under Act 6 and 7 Wm. IV., c. 85.	Its own Chapelry.
Ugglebarnby .	. . . .	. .	Its own Chapelry.
	EAST RIDING.		
Ellerton	Parish of Ellerton .		
Holme-in-the-Wolds .	Parish of Holme-in-the-Wolds.		
Kildwick near Watton.	Parish of Kildwick near Watton		
Leckonfield	Parish of Leckonfield .		
North Dalton .	Parish of Norton Dalton		
Skerne .	Parish of Skerne		

DIOCESE OF YORK—(*continued.*)

Name of Chapel.	Name or Description of Parish, Chapelry, or other recognised Ecclesiastical Division thereunto annexed.	Whether Licensed under the Act of 6 and 7 Wm. IV., c. 85.	Description of District for which it is so Licensed.
Seaton Ross . . .	Parish of Seaton Ross		
Skidby	Chapelry of Skidby.		
St. John, Beverley .	Beverley Minster		
Watton	Parish of Watton		
Wilberfoss	Parish of Wilberfoss		
Nunkeeling . . .	Parish of Nunkeeling		
St. Mary, Hull . .	Parish of St. Mary		
St. James, Hull . .	. . . .	Licensed under the Act 6 and 7 Wm. IV., c. 85.	District of South Myton Ward.
Lowthorpe	Parish of Lowthorpe		
Riston	Parish of Riston		
Drypool	Parish of Drypool		
Easington	Parish of Easington		
Kayingham . . .	Parish of Kayingham		
Mappleton	Parish of Mappleton		
Otteringham . . .	Parish of Otteringham		
Marfleet	Parish of Marfleet		
Sunk Island . . .	Parish of Sunk Island		
Bempton	Parish of Bempton		
Bessenby	Parish of Bessenby.		
Sledmere	Parish of Sledmere		
Birdsall	Parish of Birdsall		
Boynton	Parish of Boynton		
Burton Fleming . .	Parish of Burton Fleming . . .		
Carnaby	Parish of Carnaby		
Filey	Parish of Filey		
Flambrough . . .	Parish of Flambrough		
Galmpton	Parish of Galmpton		
Hackness	Parish of Hackness.		
Harwood Dale. . .	Chapelry of Harwood Dale . . .		
Cayton	Chapelry of Cayton.		
Cloughton	Chapelry of Cloughton.		
Butterwick. . . .	Chapelry of Butterwick		
Wold Newton . . .	Parish or Chapelry of Wold Newton .		

WEST RIDING.

Barmby Dun . . .	Parish of Barmby Dun		
Bolton-upon-Dearne .	Parish of Bolton-upon-Dearne. . .		
Campsall	Parish of Campsall		
Frickley with Clayton .	Parish of Frickley with Clayton . .		
Hickleton	Parish of Hickleton.		
Hatfield	Parish of Hatfield		
Melton-on-the-Hill .	Parish of Melton-on-the-Hill . . .		
Marr	Parish of Marr		
Skelbrooke . . .	Chapelry of Skelbrooke.		
Thorne	Parish of Thorne		
Attercliffe	Chapelry of Attercliffe		
Ardwick-upon-Dearne	Parish of Ardwick-upon-Dearne . .		
Barnsley	Chapelry of Barnsley		
Cawthorne. . . .	Parish of Cawthorne		
Wentworth. . . .	Chapelry of Wentworth.		
Worsbrough . . .	Chapelry of Worsbrough		
Nether Poppleton. .	Parish of Nether Poppleton . . .		
Rufforth	Parish of Rufforth		
Selby	Parish of Selby.		
Fulford	Chapelry of Fulford		
Saxton	Parish of Saxton		
Wetherby	. . . .	Licensed under the Act.	Chapelry of Wetherby.
Baildon	Chapelry of Baildon		
Oulton	District of Oulton		
Roundhay	District of Roundhay		
Liversedge. . . .	District of Liversedge		
Cleckheaton . . .	Chapelry of Cleckheaton		
Crostone	Chapelry of Crostone		
East Ardesley . . .	Parish of East Ardesley		
Elland	Chapelry of Elland.		
Hartishead	Chapelry of Hartishead.		
Horbury	Chapelry of Horbury		
Heptonstall . . .	Chapelry of Heptonstall		
Knottingley . . .	Chapelry of Knottingley		
Wragby	Parish of Wragby		

DIOCESE OF YORK—(*continued.*)

Name of Chapel.	Name or Description of Parish, Chapelry, or other recognized Ecclesiastical Division thereunto annexed.	Whether Licensed under the Act of 6 and 7 Wm. IV., c. 85.	Description of District for which it is so Licensed.
Woodkirk	Parish of Woodkirk		
St. John, in Wakefield	Chapelry of St. John, in Wakefield .		
Woolley	Chapelry of Woolley		
Woodhouse . . .	District of Woodhouse		
Acaster Malbis . .	Parish of Acaster Malbis		
Askham Bryan . .	Parish of Askham Bryan		
Bilbrough	Parish of Bilbrough		
Tong	Chapelry of Tong		
Wibsey	Chapelry of Wibsey		
Wilsden-cum-Allerton.	District of Wilsden-cum-Allerton . .		
Shipley-cum-Heaton .	District of Shipley-cum-Heaton . .		
Bolton in Craven . .	Chapelry of Bolton		
Haworth	Chapelry of Haworth		
Horton in Ribblesdale.	Parish of Horton in Ribblesdale . .		
Hubberholme . . .	Chapelry of Hubberholme		
Waddington . . .	Chapelry of Waddington		
Gill, otherwise Barnolds-wick.	Parish of Gill, otherwise Barnoldswick		
Holy Trinity. Ripon .	District not known		
Pateley Bridge . .	Chapelry of Pateley Bridge . . .		

(Signed)   JOSH. BUCKLE,
Deputy Registrar.

LISTS

OF

PLACES OF PUBLIC WORSHIP

Registered for Solemnization of Marriages, under the Provisions of the Acts of 6 and 7 Wm. IV., c. 85;
and 1 Victoriæ, c. 22.

ALSO, OF ALL

SUPERINTENDENT REGISTRARS, AND DEPUTY SUPERINTENDENT REGISTRARS;

OF

REGISTRARS OF MARRIAGES,

AND OF

REGISTRARS OF BIRTHS AND DEATHS, AND DEPUTY REGISTRARS;

With their Places of Abode, and the Districts for which they respectively serve.

UNION, or SUPERINTENDENT REGISTRAR'S DISTRICT.	County.	Places of Public Worship situated therein, registered for Solemnization of Marriages.		SUPERINTENDENT REGISTRARS, and *Deputy Superintendent Registrars.*	
		Name.	Situation.	Name.	Address.
ABERAYRON	Cardigan . .	Nenaddlwyd	Llacthliw, in the parish of Henfeniw.	Geo. Jas. Wigley	Aberayron . . .
		Peniel	Aberayron.		
ABERGAVENNY . . .	Monmouth . .	Ebenezer	Blaenavon, in the parish of Llanover Upper.	William Powell .	Abergavenny . . .
		Horeb	Blaenavon, in the parish of Llanover Upper.	*J. Reynolds,*	*Ditto.*
		Llanwenarth	Govilon, in the parish of Llanwenarth (*ultra*).		
		Nebo	Pen-y-cae, in the parish of Bedwelty.		
		Sharon	Tredegar, in the parish of Bedwelty.		
		Frogmore Street Baptist Chapel.	Abergavenny.		
		The Independent Chapel .	Abergavenny.		
		Hermon Baptist Chapel .	Nantyglo, in the parish of Aberystruth.		
		The Old Blaina Chapel .	Blaina, in the parish of Aberystruth.		
		Siloh	Tredegar Iron Works, in the parish of Bedwelty.		
		St. Michael's	Abergavenny.		
		Sharon	Ebbw Vale, in the parish of Bedwelty.		
ABERYSTWITH . . .	Cardigan. . .	The Tabernacle. . . .	Talybont, in the parish of Llanfihangel Geneu'rglyn.	Robert Rathill . *Thomas Wells,*	Aberystwith . . . *Ditto.*
ABINGDON	Berks . . .	The Baptist Chapel . .	Ock-street, Abingdon . . .	Richard Ellis . *Dennis E. Malony,*	Abingdon . . . . *Ditto.*
ALBAN'S, ST.	Herts	The Baptist Chapel . .	Dagnall-lane, St. Alban's . .	Richard G. Lowe	St. Alban's . . .
		Mount Zion Chapel . .	Library-lane, Redbourn.		
		The Independent Chapel .	Spicer-street, St. Alban's.		
ALCESTER	Warwick . . .	The Baptist Meeting-house	Alcester	Charles Jones .	Alcester . . . .
		The Caughton Catholic Chapel.	Caughton-court, in the parish of Caughton.	*W. H. Mascall,*	*Ditto.*
ALDERBURY	Wilts	The Primitive Methodist Chapel.	Fisherton-street, Fisherton Anger	Wm. Dyke Whitmarsh, jun.	Salisbury . . . .
ALNWICK	Northumberland.	Glanton Meeting-house .	Glanton, in the parish of Whittingham.	W. Dickson . .	Alnwick . . . .
		United Secession Church .	Alnwick.		
		Sion Meeting-house . .	Alnwick.		
ALRESFORD.	Hants . . .	Alresford Chapel . . .	West-street, New Alresford .	Jasper Wright .	Alresford . . . .
ALSTON and GARRIGILL.	Cumberland . .	. . .	. . .	Wm. Bainbridge.	Alston . .
ALTON	Hants . . .	The Independent Chapel .	Normandy-street, Alton. . .	Matthew H. Moss *Robert Caffall,*	Alton . . . . . *Ditto.*
ALTRINCHAM	Chester . . .	The Presbyterian Chapel .	Nether, Knutsford	Charles Poole .	Altrincham . . .
		The Wesleyan Chapel. .	Altrincham.		
		The Styal Presbyterian Chapel.	Styal, in the parish of Wilmslow		
ALVERSTOKE	Hants . . .	The Independent Chapel .	Gosport	Henry Woodrow.	Gosport . . . .
		The Catholic Chapel . .	Gosport.		
AMERSHAM.	Bucks and Herts	The Lower Baptist Chapel	Amersham, Bucks	Thomas Marshall	Amersham. . . .
		The Independent Chapel .	Chesham, Bucks.	*Henry Heath,*	*Ditto.*
		Bethesda Chapel . . .	Beaconsfield, Bucks.		
		The Old Baptist Chapel .	Chesham, Bucks.		
		The General Baptist Chapel	Chesham, Bucks.		
AMESBURY	Wilts	. . .	. . .	Richard M. Wilson	Salisbury . . . .
AMPTHILL	Bedford . . .	Baptist Chapel	Cranfield.	George Robinson	Ampthill . . . .
		Maulden Meeting . . .	Duck End, Maulden, Ampthill, Beds.	*Edward Hanscomb,*	*Ditto.*

REGISTRARS of MARRIAGES.		Registrars' District.	REGISTRARS of BIRTHS and DEATHS.		Deputy Registrars of Births and Deaths.	
Name.	Address.		Name.	Address.	Name.	Address.
David Davis . .	Aberayron.	*Llansantffraed*	David Davies .	Aberayron . . .	Abel Green . .	Aberayron.
Abel Green . .	Aberayron.	*Llandisilio*	Thomas Walters	Llanarth, Aberayron . .	Walter Walters .	Llanina; Aberayron.
Job Davies . .	Abergavenny . . .	*Abergavenny* . . .	Job Davies . .	Abergavenny.		
Edward Pritchard	Llanwenarth (*ultra*), near Abergavenny.	*Abergstruth* . . .	Daniel James .	Nantyglo; Abergavenny.		
John Lewis . .	Tredegar, near Abergavenny.	*Rock*	Evan Jones . .	Rock, near Newport, Monmouthshire.		
		Tredegar	John Lewis . .	Tredegar; Abergavenny.		
		Llanarth	James Powell .	Bryngwyn; Abergavenny.		
		Blaenavon	Edward Pritchard	Llanwenarth (*ultra*), Abergavenny.		
		Llanvihangel . . .	William Watkins	Llanvetherine; Abergavenny.		
John James . .	Aberystwith . . .	*Aberystwith* . . .	John Cole . .	Aberystwith	William Cox. .	Aberystwith.
		Genev'rglyn . . .	John Griffiths .	Trerddol; Aberystwith.		
		Llanrhystyd . . .	John Parry . .	Llanilar; Aberystwith.		
		Rheidol.	John Davies . .	Llanfihangel-y-Croyddin; Aberystwith.	David Jones . .	Llanfihangel-y-Croyddin; Aberystwith.
James Collier .	Abingdon	*Kingston-Bagpuize*	John Bennett .	Kingston Bagpuize; Abingdon.		
		Abingdon . . .	William Grace .	St. Helen's, Abingdon.	Jas. Beckensall .	Broad-street, Abingdon.
		Nuneham . . .	John Polly . .	Toot-Baldon; Dorchester, Oxon.	James Polly .	Marsh-Baldon; Oxford.
		Sutton-Courtenay .	William Porter .	Culham, Oxon	John Bradbery .	Culham, Oxon.
		Cumnor	William Hutt .	Cumnor, Oxford.		
Jacob Blake . .	St. Alban's . . .	*St. Alban's* . . .	Jacob Blake . .	St. Alban's	J. Wingrave, jun.	St. Alban's.
		Harpenden. . . .	Henry J. Leadham	Harpenden; St. Alban's.		
R. H. Harbridge	Alcester	*Studley*	John Reeve . .	Samborn; Alcester . .	T. Richards . .	Studley; Alcester.
		Feckenham. . . .	Henry Taylor .	Feckenham; Alcester.		
		Bidford	John Cox. . .	Bidford; Alcester.		
		Alcester	James Murrell .	Alcester	H. Overbury. .	Alcester.
Joseph Burford .	Fisherton-Anger, Wilts	*Britford*	Joseph Burford .	Fisherton-Anger; Salisbury.		
		Downton	R. H. Hooper .	Downton; Salisbury.		
		Alderbury	C. Smith . . .	Farley; Salisbury.		
Thos. H. Bell .	Alnwick	*Alnwick*	Thos. H. Bell .	Alnwick.		
William Thornton	Felton, Northumberland	*Warkworth* . . .	Wm. Thornton .	Felton, Northumberland.		
Andrew Thompson	Rock, Alnwick.	*Embleton*	A. Thompson .	Rock; Alnwick.		
Wm. H. Moody .	Broad-st., New Alresford.	*Alresford (New)* . .	Richard Ryder .	West-st., New Alresford.		
		Ropley	J. S. Hathaway .	Bishop's Sutton.		
John White . .	Alston	*Alston and Garrigill*	John White . .	Alston; Penrith.		
Edmund Andrews	Alton	*Binstead*	William Harbor .	Binstead; Alton.		
		Selbourne . . .	J. Debenham, jun.	Selbourne; Alton.		
		Alton	Charles Biddle .	Alton.		
William Badcock	Altrincham, Cheshire	*Knutsford*	James Earle . .	Knutsford, Altrincham.		
		Lymm	Samuel Carter .	Lymm; Warrington.		
		Wilmslow	Thos. Robinson .	Wilmslow, Cheshire.		
		Altrincham . . .	Wm. Badcock .	Altrincham.		
Stephen King .	Gosport	*Alverstoke* . . .	Mathias March .	Gosport	H. Woodrow, jun.	50, High-st., Gosport.
James Dorrell .	Amersham, Bucks	*Amersham*	Richard Sims .	Amersham, Bucks.		
		Missenden	John Coughtrey .	Great Missenden, Bucks.		
		Chalfont	John Crisp . .	Chalfont St. Peter, Gerard's Cross, Bucks.		
		Beaconsfield . . .	John Hutchinson	Beaconsfield, Bucks.		
		Chesham	Wm. Ford, jun. .	Chesham, Bucks.		
Edwin A. B. Farr	Winterborne - Gunner, Salisbury.	*Amesbury*	John May . .	Durrington; Amesbury.		
		Orcheston	E. W. Turner .	Maddington; Salisbury.		
		Winterborne . .	Edwin A. B. Farr	Winterborne Gunner; Salisbury.		
Charles Austin .	Ampthill	*Cranfield*	Daniel Bull . .	Cranfield, Newport Pagnell, Bucks.		
		Shitlington	David Simkins .	Shitlington, Hitchin, Herts	Lewis Flint . .	Shitlington Silsoe.
		Ampthill	John Marshall .	Ampthill, Bedfordshire .	Charles Austin .	Ampthill.

UNION, OR SUPERINTENDENT REGISTRAR'S DISTRICT.	County.	Places of Public Worship situated therein, registered for Solemnization of Marriages.		SUPERINTENDENT REGISTRARS, and *Deputy Superintendent Registrars.*	
		Name.	Situation.	Name.	Address.
ANDOVER	Hants . . .	The Baptist Chapel . .	Andover	Thomas Lamb .	Andover . . . .
ANGLESEY	Anglesey . .	Capel Evan.	Llanerchymedd, in the parish of Rhodogeidio.	Samuel Dew . . Edward Jonathan,	Llangefni . . . . Ditto.
ASAPH, ST.	Denbigh and Flint	Particular Baptist Chapel	Henllan, St., in the parish of Henllan.	Thos. K. Roberts	St. Asaph . . . .
		Swan Lane Chapel. . .	Denbigh.		
ASHBOURNE	Derby. . . .	. . .	. . .	C. Hewitt Welch	Ashbourne . . .
ASHBY-DE-LA-ZOUCH .	Leicester . . .	The Independent Chapel . A Baptist Chapel . . .	Ashby-de-la-Zouch . . . . Hugglescote, in the parish of Ibstock, Market Bosworth.	John Davenport	Ashby-de-la-Zouch .
		A Baptist Chapel . . .	Ashby-de-la-Zouch.		
ASHFORD, EAST . . .	Kent	. . .	. . .	Thomas Southee	Willesborough . .
ASHFORD, WEST . . .	Kent	The Baptist Chapel . . The Countess of Hunting-don's Chapel.	St. John's Lane, Ashford . . Ashford.	Alfred Briggs .	Ashford, Kent . .
ASHTON-UNDER-LYNE, and OLDHAM	Lancaster . .	The Old Chapel . . .	Dukinfield, in the parish of Stockport.	J. Higginbottom Robert Newton,	Ashton-under-Lyne . Ditto.
		Methodist New Connection Chapel.	Ashton-under-Lyne.		
		Independent Chapel . . The Independent Chapel .	Ashton-under-Lyne. Dukinfield, in the parish of Stockport.		
		Bethel Chapel	Staley Bridge; Stockport.		
		St. Mary's Catholic Chapel	Astley Street, Dukinfield; Stockport.		
		The Methodist New Con-nection Chapel.	Mossley, in the parish of Ash-ton-under-Lyne.		
		Tintwistle Chapel . . .	Tintwistle, in the parish of Mottram.		
		Mount Pleasant General Baptist Chapel.	Staley Bridge, in the parish of Ashton-under-Lyne.		
		The Particular Baptist Chapel.	Staley Bridge, in the parish of Stockport.		
		Greenacre's Chapel . .	Oldham.		
		The Israelite's Sanctuary .	Ashton-under-Lyne.		
		Hope Chapel	Denton, in the parish of Man-chester.		
		The School Buildings . .	Dukinfield, in the parish of Stockport.		
		Queen Street Chapel . .	Oldham.		
ASKRIGG	York	The Gunnerside Chapel .	Gunnerside, in the parish of Grinton.	George Winn .	Askrigg, Yorkshire .
ASTON	Warwick. . .	The General Baptist Chapel	Lombard-street, Deritend, in the parish of Aston; Birmingham.	Enoch Pearson .	Aston-road, Birming-ham.
		The Chapel of the Holy Trinity.	High-street, Sutton Coldfield .		
ATCHAM	Salop. . . .	Pontesbury Baptist Chapel St. Peter's Chapel . . . Minsterly Chapel . . .	Pontesbury . . . . . . Acton, Burnell. Minsterley, in the parish of Westbury.	Thomas Everest.	Shrewsbury . . .
ATHERSTONE	Warwick. . .	The Independent Chapel .	Atherstone	Stafford S. Baxter	Atherstone . . .
AUCKLAND	Durham . . .	The Primitive Methodist Chapel.	Tofthill, near Bishop Auckland	William Trotter .	Bishop Auckland .
		The Baptist Chapel . .	Hamsterley, in the parish of St. Andrew, Auckland.		

REGISTRARS of MARRIAGES.		Registrars' Districts.	REGISTRARS of BIRTHS and DEATHS.		Deputy Registrars of Births and Deaths.	
Name.	Address.		Name.	Address.	Name.	Address.
John Holdup	Andover	Andover	Robert Cook	Clanville; Andover.		
		Hurstborne Tarrant	John Purver	Hurstborne Tarrant; Andover.		
		Long-Parish	Henry Wheeler	Wherwell, Andover.		
		Ludgershall	George Postans	Amport Green; Andover.		
John Roberts	Amlwch, Anglesey	Bodedern	Daniel Jones	Bryn-Lyn, Bodedern.		
		Holyhead	Richard Morris	Pontægyrog, Holyhead.		
		Llangefni	John Prytherch	Cefn Cwmmwd, near Llangefni.		
		Llanddausaint	Edward Parry	Pen-y-bont, Llanbadrig, Amlwch.		
		Amlwch	John Roberts	Amlwch, Anglesey.		
		Llandyfrydog	John Williams	House, Llanfairmath, afarneithaf Llangefni.		
John Williams	Townsend, Denbigh	St. Asaph	Rich. Humphreys	St. Asaph	W. J. Humphreys	Bryngroow, St. Asaph.
		Abergele	Thomas Owen	Abergele.		
		Denbigh	P. N. Roberts	Denbigh.		
John Bass	Ashbourne	Ashbourne	John Bass	Ashbourne	Samuel Ackerley.	Ashbourne.
		Brailsford	William Rix	Shirley, Derbyshire.		
		Brassington	Thomas Keeling	Parwich, Derbyshire.		
Jos. Davenport	Ashby-de-la-Zouch.	Ashby-de-la-Zouch	Richard Cheatle	Ashby-de-la-Zouch	Benjamin Cheatle	Ashby-de-la-Zouch.
Thomas Wayte	Ashby-de-la-Zouch.	Hartshorn	David Birkin	Nether Seal; Ashby-de-la-Zouch.	William Blastock	Donisthorpe.
		Measham	Joseph Pickard	Measham; Ashby-de-la-Zouch.	Wm. Pickering	Measham.
		Whitwick	William Hill	Packington; Ashby-de-la-Zouch.		
Daniel Pellatt	Willesborough	Brabourne	Wm. Browning	Mersham; Ashford, Kent.	W. Johnson Finn	Mersham-street, Ashford, Kent.
		Wye	John Wildash	Wye; Ashford, Kent.		
		Aldington	John Lucy	Aldington; Ashford, Kent.	Rob. Scott	Aldington, Kent.
Archibald Miles	Ashford, Kent	Colehill	Wm. Cheeseman	Charing; Ashford, Kent.		
		Ashford	Thomas Hall	Hothfield; Ashford, Kent.		
John Whitehead	Ashton-under-Lyne; Manchester.	Ashton Town	John Whitehead	Stamford-street, Ashton-under-Lyne.		
		Audenshaw and Droylsden.	John Ousey	Audenshaw; Ashton-under-Lyne.		
		Knottlanes	James Elliott	Lees, Austerlands; Manchester.		
		Hartshead	Robert Watson	Staley Bridge; Manchester.		
		Denton and Haughton	Frederick Cooke	Denton; Ashton-under-Lyne.		
		Dukinfield	Robert Ivy	Dukinfield, Ashton-under-Lyne.		
		Newton and Godley	Thomas Bradley	Godley, Hyde; Manchester.		
		Staley	John Hussey	Staley, Manchester.		
		Mottram	Ralph Sidebottom	Mottram, Staley Bridge; Manchester.		
		Oldham-below-Town	John Ascroft	Oldham	John Taylor	Hollinwood, Oldham.
		Oldham-above-Town	Edwin Cocks	Oldham.		
		Middleton	Thomas Hilton	Middleton; Oldham.		
		Royton	William Fitton	Royton; Oldham.		
		Chadderton	E. Butterworth	Busk; Oldham.		
		Crompton	Richard Clegg	Crompton, Oldham.		
William Rudd	Muker Reeth	Hawes	J. Wilson Metcalfe	Hawes, Yorkshire.		
T. M. Parke	Askrigg.	Askrigg	T. Moore Parke	Askrigg, Yorkshire.		
		Muker	William Rudd	Muker; Richmond, York.		
Joseph Rawlings	High-street, Deritend, Birmingham.	Sutton Coldfield	George Brentnall	Sutton Coldfield; Birmingham.		
		Duddeston & Nechells	John Goodall	27, Ashted-row, Birmingham.		
		Erdington	John K. Oram	Erdington; Birmingham.		
		Deritend and Bordesley	Jos. Rawlings	High-street, Deritend, Birmingham.		
Richard Croft	Pontesbury; Shrewsbury.	Alderbury	John Dyas	Alderbury; Shrewsbury	John Dyas, sen.	Paddock; Alderbury.
		Westbury	George Jackson	Westbury; Shrewsbury.	John Harris	Westbury; Shrewsbury.
		Pontesbury	Richard Croft	Pontesbury; Shrewsbury.	Pryce Benbow	Pontesbury; Shrewsbury.
		Montford	John Edwards	Montford; Shrewsbury	George Edwards	Montford; Shrewsbury.
		Atcham	Robt. Weatherby	Atcham; Shrewsbury.	And. Weatherby	Wroxeter; Shrewsbury.
		Battlefield	James Hampton	Upton Magna; Shrewsbury	James Rogers	Upton Magna; Shrewsbury.
		Condover	Forester Cross	Condover; Shrewsbury	Joshua Cumpston	Condover; Shrewsbury
Leonard Gisborne	Atherstone	Atherstone	John Baker	Atherstone.	Edward Baker	Atherstone.
William Dean	Bishop Auckland	Hamsterley	John Kirkup	Lynesack and Softly, Bishop Auckland.	Thomas Graham, jun.	Bishop Auckland.
		Bishop Auckland	Ralph Joplin	Bishop Auckland.		

F

UNION, or SUPERINTENDENT REGISTRAR'S DISTRICT.	County.	Places of Public Worship situated therein, registered for Solemnization of Marriages.		SUPERINTENDENT REGISTRARS, and *Deputy Superintendent Registrars.*	
		Name.	Situation.	Name.	Address.
AUSTELL, ST.	Cornwall . . .	Wesleyan Methodist Meeting-house.	St. Austell	J. M. Boyle . . *William Jago,*	St. Austell . . . *Ditto.*
AXBRIDGE	Somerset . . .	Baptist Chapel . . . . The Old Independent Meeting-house.	Cheddar . . . . . . Wrington.	Richard Trew .	Axbridge . . . .
AXMINSTER.	Devon . . .	The Old, or George's Meeting. Combe Street Chapel . . The Baptist Chapel . . Charmouth Chapel . .	Colyton . . . . . . Lyme Regis. Lyme Regis. Charmouth.	Charles Bond .	Axminster. . . .
AYLESBURY	Bucks . . .	The Baptist Meeting-house Hale Ley's Independent Chapel. Wingrave Chapel . . .	Haddenham . . . . . . The New Road leading to London, Aylesbury. Wingrave.	T. S. Chapman . *William Godfree,*	Market-place, Aylesbury *Ditto.*
AYLSHAM	Norfolk . . .	The Baptist Meeting-house Oulton Independent Chapel	Foulsham . . . . . . Oulton.	William Hill .	Marsham ; Norwich .
BAKEWELL	Derby. . . .	The Independent Chapel . The Roman Catholic Chapel	Matlock, Bath ; Derbyshire . Hassop, Bath ; Derbyshire.	John Barker . .	Burre-house, Bakewell
BALA	Merioneth .	Capel Newydd . . . . Calvinistic Methodist Chapel	Bala, in the parish of Llanyeil Bala.	J. Gilbertson .	Bala . . . . .
BANBURY	Oxon	The Aston Catholic Chapel The Independent Chapel . The Baptist Chapel . .	Aston-le-Walls, Northampton . Church lane, Banbury. Upper Middleton, in the parish of Middleton Cheney, Northamptonshire.	George Moore .	Banbury . . . .
BANGOR and BEAUMARIS	Carnarvon and Anglesea.	Ebenezer . . . . . Pennel Baptist Chapel .	High-street, Bangor . . . Well-street, Bangor.	H. Williams . .	Bangor . . . .
BARNET	Middlesex and Herts.	Wood-street Chapel . .	Chipping Barnet, Herts . .	W. N. Franklyn	Chipping Barnet . .
BARNSTAPLE	Devon . . .	The Methodist Chapel . The Independent Chapel . The Independent Chapel . Eastscombe Chapel . .	Boutport-street, Barnstaple . Cross-street, Barnstaple. Ilfracombe. Tawstock.	J. Sherard Clay . *Stephen Bencraft,*	Barnstaple . . . *Pilton ; Barnstaple.*
BARROW-ON-SOAR . .	Leicester . . .	The General Baptist Chapel The General Baptist Chapel	Quorndon . . . . . . Rothley.	Thomas Fewkes.	Barrow-on-Soar . .
BARTON, &c..	Lancaster . .	The Independent Chapel . All Saints Catholic Chapel The Unitarian Chapel. .	Patricroft, Eccles . . . . Barton-upon-Irwell. Monton Green, Eccles.	G. F. Mandley .	Salford, Manchester .
BASFORD	Nottingham . .	The Independent Chapel . Mount Sion Chapel . . The General Baptist Chapel	Ilkeston . . . . . . Marlpool, in Heanor. Nether-street, Beeston.	William Ashton. *Thomas Sleath,*	Bulwell, Nottingham. *Ditto.*
BASINGSTOKE	Hants . . .	The Independent Meeting-house.	London-street, Basingstoke.	George Lamb . *William Challis,*	Basingstoke, Hants . *Ditto.*
BATH . . . ᵇ	Somerset . . .	Argyle Chapel . . . . The late Countess of Huntingdon's Chapel. Pierrepont Place Chapel . New King Street Chapel . Walcot Chapel. . . . Trim Street Chapel . . Saint Austin's or Portland Chapel. York Street Chapel . .	Bath . . . . Bath. Pierrepont-place, Bath. New King-street, Bath. Nelson-place, Bath. Trim-street, Bath. Cottles-lane, Bath. York-street, Bath.	Christian Brown *Edward Brook,*	Abbey-street, Bath 13, *Northgate-street, Bath.*

REGISTRARS of MARRIAGES.		Registrars' Districts.	REGISTRARS of BIRTHS and DEATHS.		Deputy Registrars of Births and Deaths.	
Name.	Address.		Name.	Address.	Name.	Address.
Thomas Drew	St. Austell	*Mevagissey*	Geo. John Dunn	Mevagissey, Cornwall.	Benoni Tim. Ball	Mevagissey, Cornwall.
		Grampound	William Andrew	Cuyte, St. Austell.		
		Fowey	Geo. Beer	Tywardreath; Fowey, Cornwall.		
		St. Austell.	Thomas Drew	St. Austell	John Higman	St. Austell.
William Crease	Axbridge, Somersetshire.	*Wedmore and Mark*	Richard Jones	Weare; Cross, Somersetshire.	John Burdge	Alston Sutton, Weare; Cross, Somerset.
		Banwell and Weston-super-Mare.	Samuel Norman	Worle; Axbridge	Nathan Fry	Worle; Cross, Somerset.
		Axbridge & Winscombe	John Lawrence	Cheddar; Axbridge.		
		Blagdon and Congresbury.	Charles Pope	Langford; Axbridge	William Hall	Blagdon; Cross, Somerset.
		Burnham and Bleadon	George Gane	South Brent, Cross	William Huckman	Lympsham; Cross, Somerset.
Joseph Edwards.	Colyton	*Axminster*	Charles Hayman	Axminster	John Bond	Axminster.
		Colyton.	Thomas Cann	Seaton; Axminster	Joseph Edwards.	Colyton.
		Lyme	George Frederick Codrington.	Lyme Regis.		
		Chardstock	Edw. F. Haskell	Chardstock; Axminster.		
Henry Bird	Aylesbury	*Aston Clinton*	Humphrey Bull	Aston Clinton, Tring, Herts.		
		Haddenham	Dan. Thos. Forster	Upper Winchendon; Aylesbury.		
		Waddesdon	Thomas Horton	Quainton; Aylesbury.		
		Aylesbury	Thomas Fell.	Aylesbury.		
Geo. Morris Bane	Aylsham, Norfolk	*Eynsford*	A. Sands	Reepham; Norwich	Robert Keeler	Reepham; Norwich.
		Buxton	George Legg	Tuttington; Aylsham, Norfolk.	G. M. Bane	Aylsham; Norfolk.
Wm. Stafford	Matlock, Bath	*Bakewell*	James Chapman	Bakewell; Derbyshire.		
James Chapman.	Bakewell.	*Matlock*	William Stafford	Matlock, Bath; Matlock.		
		Tideswell	John Gardom	Tideswell.		
		Bala	William Jones	Lion Hotel, Bala.		
J. G. Walford	Banbury, Oxon	*Banbury*	Wm. Galsworthy	Banbury	Wm. Rusher.	Market-place, Banbury.
William Walford	Banbury, Oxon.	*Swalcliffe*	Edward Charlton	Swalcliffe; Banbury.		
		Cropredy	Thomas Pearce	Williamscott; Banbury.		
		Bloxham	John Bonner	Bodicote; Banbury.	Thomas Bonner.	Bodicote.
Griffith W. Prees	Camgymro; Bangor.	*Bangor.*	John Macintosh	Bangor, Carnarvonshire.		
Rt. Prichard	High-street, Bangor.	*Llanllechid*	Griffith W. Prees	Camgymro; Bangor, Carnarvonshire.		
		Beaumaris	Hugh R. Hughes	Ffordd Deg; Beaumaris, Anglesey.		
Edward Taplin	Chipping Barnet	*Barnet.*	Edward Taplin	Chipping Barnet, Herts.		
		Finchley	John Tattam	Finchley, Middlesex.		
		South Mims	William Acason.	Barnet, Middlesex.		
John Barry	Barnstaple	*Barnstaple.*	John Parry	Barnstaple	William Curtis	High-street, Barnstaple.
George Coats	Ilfracombe.	*Bishop's Tawton*	John Tinson	Bishop's Tawton, Barnstaple.	William Howell.	Newport; Barnstaple.
		Braunton	Wm. Carpenter	Pilton; Barnstaple	G. G. Carpenter	Barnstaple.
		Ilfracombe.	George Coats	Ilfracombe	Edward Hearson.	Ilfracombe.
		Combmartin	John Watts	Combmartin; Ilfracombe.	William Willis	Combmartin; Ilfracombe.
		Paracombe	Thomas Baker	Linton; Devon	William Bale	Linton.
Thomas Raven	Quorndon	*Barrow*	Rob. Shuttlewood	Sileby; Mountsorrel	D. Shuttlewood, jun.	Sileby.
Thomas H. Barsby	Rothley, Mountsorrel.	*Quorndon*	Samuel Wright	Mountsorrel.		
		Rothley	John Buttery	Thurcaston; Mountsorrel.		
		Syston	William C. Dally	Syston; Leicester.		
William Lewis	Patricroft, Eccles	*Barton-upon-Irwell*	J. Cheadle	Broad-street, Eccles, Barton-upon-Irwell.	E. F. Cheadle	Eccles.
		Worsley	J. Berry	Old Clough Lane, Worsley.		
		Flixton.	Rev. W. A. Cave	Parsonage, Flixton.		
Moses Mason	Ilkeston; Derby.	*Wilford*	G. Wingfield	Ruddington; Nottingham.		
John Perrons	Basford; Nottingham.	*Carlton.*	John Deabill.	Gedling; Nottingham.		
		Arnold	William Thomas	Arnold; Nottingham.		
		Bulwell	F. Ward	Hucknall Torkard; Nottingham.		
		Ilkestone	George Norman	Ilkestone; Derby	Dan. G. Thackeray	Ilkestone; Derby.
		Greasley	William Smith	Eastwood; Nottingham	Henry Draper	Eastwood; Nottingham.
		Basford	John Butler	Basford; Nottingham.		
Charles Doman	Basingstoke	*Basingstoke*	George Willis	Oat-street, Basingstoke.		
		Bromley	William Dennis.	Sherfield, Hants.		
		Dummer	Charles Hill	Church Oakley; Basingstoke	Robert Barrett	Church Oakley; Basingstoke.
John Jackson	12, Henrietta-street, Bath.	*Lansdown*	Frederick Field	Northumberland-buildings, Bath.	Geo. Field	5, Chapel-row, Queen-street; Bath.
F. Cottle	22, Charles-street, Bath	*Walcot*	Job Lockyer Seale	Axford-buildings, Bath	Edm. Lansdown	7, Walcot-terrace, Bath.
		Abbey	Willis S. Ritchie.	7, Bridge-street, Bath.		
		Lyncombe & Widcombe	John A. Lloyd	Claverton-street, Bath.		
		Bathwick	John Kilvert	Darlington-street, Bath	Thomas Weston	Willow-cottage, Bathwick, Bath.
		Batheaston	Wm. Mannings	Batheaston, near Bath.		
		Twerton	Thomas Hitchins	Twerton; Bath.		

UNION, or SUPERINTENDENT REGISTRAR'S DISTRICT.	County.	Places of Public Worship situated therein, registered for Solemnization of Marriages.		SUPERINTENDENT REGISTRARS, and *Deputy Superintendent Registrars.*	
		Name.	Situation.	Name.	Address.
BATTLE	Sussex . . .	. . .	. . .	Thomas Ticehurst *Fras. W. Ticehurst,*	Battle . . . . . *Ditto.*
BEAMINSTER	Dorset . . .	Independent Chapel . . Weytown Independent Chapel. The Independent Chapel .	East-street, Beaminster. Weytown, in the parish of Netherbury. Broadwinsor.	George Cox . .	Beaminster . . .
BEDALE	York	. . .	. . .	Thomas Dennis Peacock.	Bedale . . . .
BEDFORD	Bedford . . .	The Old Meeting . . . Howard Chapel . . . The Baptist Meeting-house Roxton Chapel . . . . Cotton End Meeting . . Brook End Meeting . . The Independent Chapel . Christ's Church . . The Harrold Chapel . . The Baptist Meeting-house	Mill-street, Bedford. . . . Mill-street, Bedford. Carlton. Roxton. Cotton End, in the parish of Cardington. Brook End, in the parish of Keysoe. Turvey. Conduit-street, Bedford. Harrold. West End, in the parish of Steventon.	Samuel Wing .	Potter-street, Bedford.
BEDMINSTER	Bristol & Somerset	The Baptist Meeting-house Langton-street Chapel . Ashton Chapel . . . . Wesleyan Chapel . . .	Pill, in the parish of Easton, in Gordano. Bedminster. Long Ashton. Yatton.	E. Peters . . .	Long Ashton, Bristol.
BELFORD	Northumberland	The United Secession Chapel The Scotch Church . .	Belford . . . . Warrenford, in the parish of Bamburgh.	Gerrard Selby .	Alnwick . . . .
BELLINGHAM	Northumberland	The United Secession Chapel Otterburn Chapel . . Bridhope Craig Chapel . Falstone Scotch Church .	Bellingham . . . . . . Otterburn, in the parish of Elsdon. Bridhope Craig, in the parish of Elsdon. Falstone.	Joseph Crawford	Hexham . . . .
BELPER	Derby . . .	The Independent Chapel . Baptist Chapel . . . The General Baptist Chapel The General Baptist Chapel	Belper, in the parish of Duffield Swanwick, in the parish of Alfreton. Wirksworth. Alfreton.	Joseph Pym . .	Belper . . . . .
BERKHAMPSTEAD . .	Herts. . . .	. . .	. . .	Geo. L. Faithfull	Tring . . . . .
BERMONDSEY	Surrey . . .	The Roman Catholic Church of the Most Holy Trinity. Jamaica-row Chapel . .	Parker's-row, Dock-head, Bermondsey. Jamaica-row, Bermondsey.	Beriah Drew . . *George Drew,*	185, Bermondsey-street *Ditto.*
BERWICK	Northumberland.	The Catholic Chapel . . The Second Relief Meeting-house. The Second United Secession Church. The Relief Meeting-house. Golden Square Chapel. . Low Meeting, or Hide Hill Chapel. Haggerston Chapel . . Norham Dissenting Meeting-house. The Scotch Church . .	Ravensdowne-street, Berwick-upon-Tweed. Bankhill, Berwick-upon-Tweed. Church-street, Berwick-upon-Tweed. Chapel-street, Berwick-upon-Tweed. Berwick-upon-Tweed. Berwick-upon-Tweed. Haggerston, in the parish of Ancroft. Norham. Tweedmouth, in the Borough of Berwick-upon-Tweed.	Donald Sinclair . *Edward Willoby,*	Berwick-upon-Tweed. *Ditto.*
BETHNAL GREEN. . .	Middlesex . .	Bethnal Green Meeting .	Cambridge-road, Bethnal Green.	Robert Brutton .	18, Bethnal Green

REGISTRARS of MARRIAGES.		Registrars' Districts.	REGISTRARS of BIRTHS and DEATHS.		Deputy Registrars of Births and Deaths.	
Name.	Address.		Name.	Address.	Name.	Address.
William Burden.	Battle, Sussex. . .	Ewhurst	T. Barham . .	Sedlescomb; Battle . .	James Byner .	Sedlescomb; Battle.
		Battle	William Burden.	Battle	Thomas Foord .	Battle, Sussex.
		Bexhill. . . .	Stephen Thomas	Sidley-green; Battle . .	John Sinden .	Bexhill, Sussex.
Isaac Oliver . .	Beaminster . . .	Beaminster.	Charles Frampton	Beaminster	Anthony Toleman	Beaminster.
		Netherbury . .	John Day . .	Broadwinsor; Beaminster	John Symonds .	Broadwinsor; Beaminster.
		Evershot . . .	Wm. Martyr . .	Evershot; Dorchester .	Thomas Cox .	Evershot; Dorchester.
		Misterton . . .	Jub Gibbs . .	Mosterton; Beaminster .	Mark Storke .	South Perrott; Beaminster.
. . .	. . .	Bedale	John Spencer .	Bedale, Yorkshire.		
		Masham . . .	Christopher Raper	Masham, Yorkshire.		
J. Mackenzie, M.A.	Tavistock-street, Bedford.	Bedford and Cardington.	William Bailey .	Bedford	Thos. Lovelidge.	Bedford.
Nathaniel Godfrey	Turvey, near Olney, Bucks.	Bedford and Kempston	William Blower.	Bedford	William White .	High-street, Bedford.
		Risley	Joseph Gregory .	Risley, Kimbolton, Hunts.	George Langley .	Risley, Kimbolton.
		Barford . . .	Joseph Humbley	Great Barford, St. Neot's, Hunts.	William Wagstaff	Great Barford; Bedford.
		Sharnbrook . .	John Williamson	Sharnbrook, Bedford . .	James Coombs .	Sharnbrook, Bedford.
		Turvey	Nathaniel Godfrey	Turvey, Olney, Bucks . .	John Abrahams .	Turvey; Olney, Bucks.
		Harrold . . .	William Wootton	Harrold; Bedford . .	Hugh Saunders .	Harrold; Bedford.
George Allen .	Pill, Easton in Gordano; Bristol.	Bedminster . .	Benj. John Room	Bedminster	William Ward .	East-street, Bedminster.
Jos. Derham .	Yatton, Bristol.	Lang Ashton . .	Henry J. Macy .	Westown; Bristol . .	J. Sperrin, jun.	Backwell; Bristol.
Charles Castle .	Langton-street, Bedminster.	St. George . .	George Allen .	Pill; Bristol.		
George Scott .	Belford	Yatton . . .	Martin N. Shipton	Clevedon; Bristol . .	Samuel Sprod .	Yatton, Bristol.
		Belford	George Scott .	Belford.		
Robert Hall . .	Thorneyburn; Hexham	Bellingham . .	Robert Hall . .	Thorneyburn; Hexham.		
		Kirkwhelpington	Edward Coulson.	Bridgeford, Lee Mailing; Hexham.		
Jesse Radford .	Belper, Derbyshire .	Alfreton . . .	Francis Mather .	Greenhill-lane, Alfreton	James Higton .	Greenhill-lane; Alfreton.
F. Mather .	Greenhill-lane, Alfreton.	Belper	Jesse Radford .	Belper	William Radford	Belper.
J. Macbeth .	Wirksworth.	Wirksworth . .	Marcellus Peal .	Wirksworth; Belper .	Peter Peal . .	Coldwell-street, Wirksworth.
		Duffield . . .	Joseph Bower .	Duffield; Derby . .	William Parker .	Duffield.
		Horsley . . .	James Eley . .	Horsley Woodhouse; Derby	John Eley . .	Horsley Woodhouse; Derby.
		Ripley	Joseph Mather .	Bull-bridge, Crich, Alfreton	Samuel Henstock	Crich; Alfreton.
John M. Mills .	Great Berkhampstead.	Berkhampstead .	Edward Fentiman	Berkhampstead.		
		Tring	Mark Young . .	Tring	Tho. Fleet, jun. .	Tring.
Richard Hellier .	1, George-terrace, Crimscott-street, Bermondsey.	Leather Market .	William Cross .	Long-lane, Bermondsey .	Thomas Drew .	140, Long-lane, Bermondsey.
Wm. C. Ewbank	5, George-terrace, Crimscott-street, Bermondsey.	St. Mary Magdalen	Richard Hellier .	1, George-terrace, Crimscott-street, Bermondsey.	W. C. Ewbank .	5, George-terrace, Crimscott-street, Bermondsey.
		St. James . . .	James Paul . .	20, Prospect-place, Dockhead, Bermondsey.	W. Groombridge, jun.	New Church Lodge, St. James's-place, Bermondsey.
J. B. Atkinson .	Wool-market, Berwick-upon-Tweed.	Islandshire . .	John Anderson .	Scremerston, Berwick-upon-Tweed.		
William Dods .	Norham, near Berwick.	Norhamshire . .	William Dods .	Norham, Berwick-upon-Tweed.		
		Berwick . . .	J. B. Atkinson .	Berwick-upon-Tweed . .	Mat. Patterson .	Church-street, Berwick
Edward Moore .	43, Ward's-row, Bethnal Green-road.	The Green . . .	Thomas Howard .	1, Barrosa-terrace, Cambridge-heath Gate, Hackney-road.	G. J. Knight . .	2, Queen's-row, Cambridge-road.
		Church	George Reynolds	9, Bethnal Green-road, near the New Church.	Thos. H. Hudson	93, Church-street, near Thorold-square, Bethnal Green-road.
		Town	Henry Gregory .	7, White-street, Bethnal Green-road.	Samuel Ebbut .	1, White-street, Bethnal Green-road.
		Hackney-road . .	James Murray .	8, Suffolk-place, Cambridge Heath Gate, Hackney-road.	Joseph Tennison.	9, Broughton-place; Ann's-place, Hackney-road.

UNION, or SUPERINTENDENT REGISTRAR'S DISTRICT.	County.	Places of Public Worship situated therein, registered for Solemnization of Marriages.		SUPERINTENDENT REGISTRARS, and *Deputy Superintendent Registrars.*	
		Name.	Situation.	Name.	Address.
BEVERLEY	York	The Scotch Baptist Chapel The Baptist Chapel . . The Independent Chapel . The Wesleyan Chapel. .	In Walkergate, Beverley . . Well Lane, Beverley. Lairgate, Beverley. Walkergate, Beverley.	James Boyes. .	Beverley . . . .
BICESTER	Oxford . . .	Trinity Chapel . . . . The Independent Chapel .	Hethe Water-lane, Bicester.	Edward W. Jones *F. H. Lindsey,*	Bicester . . . . Ditto.
BIDEFORD	Devon . . .	The Independent Chapel . The Great Meeting-house . The Wesleyan Chapel	Meeting-street, in Appledore, in the parish of Northam. In Bridgeland-street, Bideford. Chapel-street, Bideford.	H. A. Harvie .	Bideford . . . .
BIGGLESWADE . . .	Bedford . . .	The Baptist Meeting . . The Wesleyan Chapel. . The Baptist Meeting-house The Catholic Chapel . . Union Meeting-house . The Wesleyan Chapel	Biggleswade. . . . . . Biggleswade. Blunham. Shefford, in the Parish of Campton-cum-Shefford. Little Hardwick. Tempsford.	Edward Argles .	Biggleswade . . .
BILLERICAY	Essex . . .	The Independent Chapel . Thorndon Hall Chapel . St. Helen's, Brentwood, Catholic Chapel.	Warley-lane, Brentwood . . Thorndon Hall, in the parish of Ingrave. Brentwood Hamlet, in the parish of South Weald.	James V. Penfold	Billericay . . : .
BILLESDON	Leicester . .	. . .	. . .	T. Ingram, jun. . *Thomas Ingram,*	Leicester . . . . Ditto.
BINGHAM	Nottingham .	Wesleyan Chapel . . .	Bingham	W. Huckerby, jun.	Bingham . . . .
BIRMINGHAM . . .	Warwick. .	The New Meeting-house . The Old Meeting-house . Carr's-lane Chapel . . St. Chad's Chapel . . St. Peter's Chapel . . Cannon Street Meeting-house Bond Street Chapel . . The Scotch Church . . The New Jerusalem Church	Moor-street, Birmingham . . Old Meeting-street, Birmingham Carr's-lane, Birmingham. Shadwell-street, Birmingham. St. Peter's-place, Birmingham. Cannon-street, Birmingham. Bond-street, Birmingham. Islington, in the parish of Birmingham. Birmingham.	Henry Knight . *John Whitehouse Showell.*	Birmingham . . . 48, *New-street, Birmingham.*
BISHOP'S STORTFORD .	Herts	The Old Independent Chapel. Independent Chapel . .	Stansted, Mountfichet . . . Sawbridgeworth	Geo. Welch . . *J. D. Taylor . .*	Stansted, near Bishop's Stortford. *Bishop's Stortford.*
BLABY : :	Leicester . .	The Independent Meeting-house. Independent Chapel . .	Narborough . . . . . . Wigston Magna.	William Gregory	Leicester . . . .
BLACKBURN	Lancaster . .	The Independent Chapel. Ebenezer Chapel . . . St. Mary's Chapel . . . Mount Street Chapel . St. Alban's Catholic Chapel St. Mary's Chapel . . . The Particular Baptist Chapel.	Chapel-street, Blackburn . . Over Darwen, Blackburn. Enfield, Clayton-le-Moors, Blackburn. Blackburn. St. Alban's, Blackburn. Rileys, near Lango, in Billington, Blackburn. Islington, in the township of Blackburn.	Peter Ellingthorpe	Blackburn . . . .
BLANDFORD	Dorset . . .	The Independent Chapel .	Blandford Forum	Thomas Oakley . *William Wiseman,*	Blandford . . . . Ditto.
BLEAN	Kent	. . .	. . .	George Eastes .	Staplegate, Canterbury
BLOFIELD	Norfolk . . .	. . .	. . .	Wm. H. Codling	Blofield ; Norwich .
BLYTHING . : : . .	Suffolk . . .	Cratfield Chapel . . . Walpole Meeting-house . The Independent Chapel .	Cratfield . . . . Walpole. Quay-street, Halesworth.	Dan. Forman, jun. *Dennis Heladon,*	Bulcamp, near Halesworth. *Union Workhouse, Blything.*
BODMIN . : : : . .	Cornwall . .	. . .	. . .	W. R. Hicks. . *S. Hiscutt Liddell,*	Castle-hill, Bodmin . Bodmin.

REGISTRARS of MARRIAGES.		Registrars' Districts.	REGISTRARS of BIRTHS and DEATHS.		Deputy Registrars of Births and Deaths.	
Name.	Address.		Name.	Address.	Name.	Address.
Anthony Atkinson	Beverley, Yorkshire	Beverley	Anthony Atkinson	Beverley	Joseph Hind.	Beverley.
		Leven	George Dunn	Routh; Beverley	Wm. Simpson	Routh; Beverley.
		Cave	John Hill	South Cave; Beverley		
		Lockington	Samuel Wyna	Lockington; Beverley.		
Jno. Williams	Bicester	Bicester	Joseph Reynolds.	Bicester.		
		Blechingdon	James Hore	Somerton, Deddington, Oxon.		
Christmas Smith	Bideford	Hartland	Chas. H. Rowe	Hartland; Devon	Richard South	Hartland, Devon.
		Bradworthy	J. Walter	Redmansford, near Bradworthy; Bideford.		
		Bideford	Thos. L. Pridham	New Buildings; Bideford.	Richard Buss	Mill-street, Bideford.
		Northam	Dr.C.E.Pratt.M.D.	Appledore; Bideford	Benj. Herman	Northam; Bideford.
		Parkham	Lewis S. Hole	Alwington; Bideford	John Chalk	Fairy Cross; Bideford.
Frank Snitch	Southill; Biggleswade	Potton	Robert Barker	Sandy; Biggleswade.		
		Biggleswade	Frank Snitch	Southill; Biggleswade		
George Rolph	Billericay	Great Burstead	William Carter	Billericay.		
		Brentwood	Cornelius Butler	Brentwood.		
		Wickford	C. Thackthwaite	Wickford; Essex.		
Wm. Holyoak	Billesdon	Billesdon	Wm. Holyoak	Billesdon; Leicester.		
B. W. Wright	East Bridgford, Bingham; Nottingham	Ratcliffe-on-Trent	John Marriott	Colston Bassett, Bingham, Notts.	Wm. Allison	Colston, Bassett.
		Bingham	B. W. Wright	East Bridgford, Bingham; Nottingham.	Edward Clough	East Bridgford; Bingham.
John Ryland.	37, Cherry street	All Saints	John White	41, Hall-street, Birmingham	G. White	74, Upper Tower-street.
Mich. Maher.	5, Congreve-street, Birmingham.	St. George's	Thomas Sansom	146, Great Hampton-row, Birmingham.		
		St. Mary's	Wm. Williams	12, Whitehall-street, Birmingham.		
		St. Paul's	Joseph Smith	72, New Hall-street, Birmingham.		
		St. Philip's	Joseph Gell	28, Cannon-street, Birmingham.		
		St. Peter's	George Bynner	16, Bartholomew-row. Birmingham.		
		St. Martin's	Paul Gardner	167, Bristol-street, Birmingham.		
		St. Thomas	Edward Penn	20, Bristol-street, Birmingham.		
		Lady Wood	G. Mills Ryder	19, Parade, Birmingham.		
John Slater, jun.	Bishop's Stortford	Bishop's Stortford.	John S. Alger	Bishop's Stortford.		
		Sawbridgeworth.	Edward Leech	Sawbridgeworth.		
		Stansted	John Seamer.	Stansted, Essex.		
		Braughin	William Walker.	Braughin; Puckeridge.		
John Newby.	Wigston Magna; Leicester.	Wigston	William Sedgley	Wigston Magna; Leicester.		
		Enderby	Michael Pratt	Narborough; Leicester.		
Edward Swarsbrick	Billington; Blackburn	Blackburn	Joseph Fairbrother	Snig Brook, Blackburn.		
Mat. Brockleburst	Branch-road, Blackburn	Mellor	Thomas Counsel.	Mellor; Blackburn.		
Seth. Harwood	Over Darwen, Blackburn	Darwen	Seth Harwood	Over Darwen; Blackburn.		
		Billington	William Axtley	Billington; Blackburn.		
		Great Harwood	Rev. Rob. Dobson	Great Harwood; Blackburn.		
		Oswaldtwistle	Clayton Bradley.	Oswaldtwistle; Blackburn.		
		Witton	John Green	Livesey; Blackburn.		
James Hobbs	Blandford	Blandford	H. F. Lane	The Square, Blandford Forum.		
		Milton Abbas	Stephen Burt	Spettisbury, Blandford Forum.		
William Dunbar.	Herne; Canterbury	Herne	William Dunbar.	Herne; Canterbury	Wm. Eates	Herne Bay.
		Sturry	H. Hills	Villa of St. Gregory; Canterbury.	John Pilcher	St. Dunstan's, Canterbury.
Peter Eade	Blofield; Norwich	Blofield	Peter Eade	Blofield; Norwich.		
		Walsham	W. H. Cufaude	Acle, Norfolk	T. E. Clarke	Acle, Norfolk.
Wm. Fisher, sen.	Cratfield; Halesworth	Halesworth	Wm. Fisher, sen.	Cratfield; Halesworth.	Wm. Fisher, jun.	Cratfield; Halesworth
		Wenhaston	Chas. White, jun.	Wenhaston; Halesworth.	Chas. White, sen.	Wenhaston, Halesworth
		Westleton	Thomas Rous	Westleton; Yoxford.	James Rous	Westleton; Yoxford.
William Ward	Fore-street, Bodmin	Bodmin	Jacob Thomas	Stephen Gelley, Lanivet Bodmin.		
		Lanlivery	John Parkin, jun.	Lostwithiel, Cornwall.		
		Egloshayle	John Mabley	Tredrissick, St. Micvet, Wadebridge, Cornwall.		
		St. Mabyn	Oliver Sleeman	Pool-park, St, Tudy; Bodmin		

UNION, or SUPERINTENDENT REGISTRAR'S DISTRICT.	County.	Places of Public Worship situated therein, registered for Solemnization of Marriages.		SUPERINTENDENT REGISTRARS, and Deputy Superintendent Registrars.	
		Name.	Situation.	Name.	Address.
BOLTON	Lancaster . .	Catholic Chapel . . .	Pilkington-street, Great Bolton	John Woodhouse	Bolton . . . . .
		Independent Chapel . .	Halshaw Moor, Farnworth.	Thomas Holden .	Newport-terrace, Bolton.
		The Independent Meeting-house.	Mawdsley-street, Great Bolton.		
		Duke's Alley Chapel . .	Duke's-alley, Great Bolton.		
		The Presbyterran Chapel of the Unitarian Denomination.	Bank-street, Great Bolton.		
		Unitarian Meeting-house .	Moor-lane, Great Bolton.		
		Independent Methodist Chapel.	Fold's-road, Little Bolton.		
		The New Jerusalem Church	Halsham Moor, in the Township of Kearsley.		
BOOTLE	Cumberland . .	. . .	. . .	Thomas Falcon .	Esk Meals, near Ravenglass.
BOSMERE and CLAYDON	Suffolk . . .	. . .	. . .	Fred. Hayward .	Needham Market .
BOSTON	Lincoln . . .	Grove Street Chapel . .	Grove-street, Boston . . .	J. G. Calthorp .	Boston. . . . .
		The Unitarian Chapel . .	Spain-lane, Boston.	Charles H. Denston	Ditto.
		Zion Chapel	West-street, Boston.		
		The Roman Catholic Chapel	Boston.		
		The General Baptist Chapel	High-street, Boston.		
BOUGHTON, GREAT . .	Chester . . .	The Presbyterian Chapel .	Crook's-lane, Chester . . .	Thomas Parry .	Chester . . . .
		Catholic Chapel . . .	Chester.		
		Queen-street Chapel . .	St. John's, Chester.		
BOURN	Lincoln . . .	The Roman Catholic Chapel	Irnham	Wm. David Bell .	Bourn . . . .
		The General Baptist Chapel.	Bourn.		
BRACKLEY	Northampton .	. . .	. . .	R. Weston . .	Brackley . . . .
BRADFIELD.	Berks. . . .	. . .	. . .	Thomas Beall .	Bradfield; Reading .
BRADFORD	Wilts. . . .	The Independent Chapel .	Morgan's Hill, Bradford, Wilts	William Timbrell	Bradford, Wilts . .
		The Baptists' Chapel . .	At or near St. Margaret-street, Bradford, Wilts.		
		The Wesleyan Chapel. .	Coppice Lane, Bradford.		
BRADFORD	York	Kipping Chapel . . .	Thornton, in Bradford, Yorkshire	J. Reid Wagstaff	Bradford, Yorkshire.
		Horton-lane Chapel . .	Bradford, Yorkshire.	Jas. Alfred Cooper	Manningham, Bradford, Yorkshire.
		Salem Chapel	Bradford, Yorkshire.		
		Rehoboth Chapel . . .	Calverley-with-Farsley.		
		Zion Chapel	Bridge-street, Bradford, Yorkshire.		
		Upper Chapel	Idle, in the parish of Calverley.		
		The Roman Catholic Chapel	Stott Hill, Bradford, Yorkshire.		
		The Baptist Chapel . .	Idle.		
		Westgate Chapel . . .	Bradford, Yorkshire.		
		Bethel Chapel	Shipley, in the parish of Bradford.		
		Red Chapel	Cleckheaton, in the parish of Bristol.		
		The Independent Chapel .	Eccleshill, in the parish of Bradford.		
		The Independent Chapel .	Wilsden, in the parish of Bradford.		
BRAINTREE	Essex. . . .	The Independent Meeting-house.	Bocking End, Bocking . .	John Cunnington	Braintree . . . .
				Augustus Charles Veley,	Ditto.
BRAMPTON	Cumberland . .	. . .	. . .	G. Ramshay . .	Brampton . . . .
BRECKNOCK	Brecknock . .	Maesyberllan	Maesyberllan, in the parish of Talachddu.	J. Davies . . .	Usk-terrace, Brecknock
		Watergate Chapel . . .	Brecknock.		

REGISTRARS of MARRIAGES.		Registrars' Districts.	REGISTRARS of BIRTHS and DEATHS.		Deputy Registrars of Births and Deaths.	
Name.	Address.		Name.	Address.	Name.	Address.
John Prestwich .	Farnworth; Bolton .	Bolton Eastern ..	John S. Scowcroft	Newport-street, Bolton.		
Thomas Turner .	Fletcher-street, Great Bolton.	Bolton Western ..	Thomas Balshaw	Derby-street, Bolton Moor	Wm. Balshaw	Noble street, Great Bolton.
David Nimmo .	Greenhill, Little Bolton	Little Bolton ..	Thomas Dawson.	Kay-street, Little Bolton .	James Wardle .	Bark-street, Little Bolton.
Thomas Kenyon .	Green-street, Great Bolton.	Sharples ..	Robert Knowles .	Sharples; Bolton.		
		Halliwell ..	Robert Makant .	New-road, Halliwell; Bolton	Samuel Makant .	Halliwell.
Samuel Roberts .	Bradshaw-gate, Great Bolton.	Horwich ..	Thomas Hunt .	Lostock; Bolton.		
		Little Hulton ..	John Eckersley .	Rumworth; Bolton.		
		Edgeworth. ..	James Barnes .	Holyland, Edgeworth; Bolton.		
		Turton . ..	Peter Haslan .	Birtenshaw, Turton; Bolton		
		Westhoughton ..	Rev. C. Bateson .	Parsonage, Westhoughton; Bolton.	James Partington	Westhoughton; Bolton.
		Farnworth . ..	Samuel Tonge .	Farnworth; Bolton .	James Longworth	Greenfold, Farnworth.
		Lever . ..	Andrew Nelson .	Darcy Lever; Bolton.		
		Tong-with-Haulgh.	Robert Horrabin.	Lever Bridge, Tong-with-Haulgh, Bolton.		
. . .	. . .	Bootle	John Hunter. .	Woodhouse, Whitbeck.		
		Muncaster . ..	William Mossop.	Ravenglass, Muncaster.	Rev. Jos. Taylor, B.A.	Ravenglass.
Crisp Howard .	Coddenham ..	Coddenham .	Crisp Howard .	Coddenham; Ipswich.		
		Debenham ..	Thomas Edwards	Stonham-parva; Ipswich.		
		Bramford ..	Geo. Kerridge .	Bramford; Ipswich.		
Edw. Coupland .	Boston.	Boston	Edw. Coupland .	Boston	Wm. G. Atkin .	Boston.
		Swineshead ..	R. Odlin Milson .	Swineshead; Boston .	Robert Shaw, jun.	Swineshead; Boston.
		Kirton . ..	Thomas Hampton	Kirton; Boston .	Joseph Knowles .	Kirton; Boston.
		Benington . ..	James Plant . .	Leake; Boston .	Adam Plant .	Leake; Boston.
		Sibsey . ..	James Brummitt .	Sibsey; Boston .	Thos. Brummitt.	Sibsey; Boston.
Robert Roberts .	Chester	Hawarden. .	Thomas Moffatt .	Hawarden, Flint .	Rev. James M. Fitzmaurice.	Hawarden, Flint.
		Tattenhall .	Thos. J. Proudlove	Tattenhall; Handley, Cheshire.		
		Great Boughton Castle	Robert Roberts .	Chester.		
		Great Boughton Cathedral.	Wm. F. J. Bage.	Chester.		
Josh. Robinson .	Bourn	Aslackby ..	John Mansfield .	Billingborough; Falkingham.	Aug. G. Allenson	Billingborough; Falkingham.
G. Stringfellow .	Iraham, Colsterworth.	Bourn	Geo. O. Munton .	Bourn	Wm. Mullett. .	Bourn.
		Deeping . ..	William Page .	Market Deeping . .	Wm. Holland, jun.	Market Deeping.
		Corby . ..	J.Collingwood,jun.	Corby; Colsterworth .	Wm. Collingwood	Corby.
. . .	. . .	Brackley	William Gillett .	Brackley.		
		Sulgrave ..	Daniel Curtis .	Farthinghoe; Brackley.		
John Laws .	Tilehurst, Reading .	Bucklebury ..	William Saunders	Bradfield; Reading.		
		Mortimer . ..	Josh. Lovegrove.	Sulhampstead; Reading.		
		Tilehurst ..	Samuel Lucas .	Tilehurst; Reading.		
Arthur Adye .	Woolley-street, Bradford, Wilts.	Bradford, South-eastern	Arthur Adye .	Woolley-street, Bradford, Wilts.		
		Bradford, North-western	William Adye .	Woolly-street, Bradford, Wilts.		
George Wright .	Horton, Bradford, Yorkshire.	Bradford, East-end	Richard Spencer .	Bradford, Yorkshire . .	John Spencer, jun.	Bradford.
		Bradford, West-end	Thos. Liversedge	Bradford, Yorkshire. .		
		Cleckheaton ..	Robert Broughton	Cleckheaton; Leeds.		
		Idle ..	Samuel Hutton .	Idle; Bradford . .	John Vint. . .	Idle.
		Manningham ..	Edward Firth .	Manningham; Bradford.		
		Thornton ..	Edward Kay. .	Thornton; Bradford.		
		Calverley ..	Rev. Jones Foster	Calverley-with-Farsley; Leeds.		
		Wilsden ..	David Briggs .	Wilsden; Bradford.		
		Drighlington ..	John Barraclough	Drighlington; Leeds.		
		Pudsey ..	Rev. Wm. Colefax	Pudsey; Leeds. . .	James Nayler .	Pudsey; Leeds.
		Horton . ..	George Wright .	Horton; Bradford.		
		North Bierly ..	George Wooller .	North Bierly; Bradford.		
		Bowling ..	Henry Sutcliffe .	Bowling; Bradford.		
Eli Tyler. . .	Bocking . . .	Braintree . .	Robert C. Tomlinson.	Braintree . .	Samuel Figgin	Braintree.
		Bocking ..	Eli Tyler. .	Bocking; Braintree .	J. Tyler, sen. .	Bocking.
		Finchingfield ..	Charles Crawley.	Weathersfield; Braintree.	John Westwood .	Weathersfield; Braintree.
John Routledge .	Brampton	Brampton . ..	John Routledge.	Brampton.		
		Hayton..	Ralph Watson .	Garthfoot; Brampton.		
		Walton ..	William Steele .	Walton; Brampton.		
W. Davies .	Trehendryfawr .	Brecknock. .	John Williams .	Brecknock.		
D. Thomas .	Trecastle.	Merthyr Cynog .	John Prosser. .	Belch-y-ddwy-allt Merthyr Cynog; Brecknock.		
		Devynnock . ..	Daniel Thomas .	Trecastle, Brecknockshire.		
		Llangorse ..	John Williams .	Llanfillo, Brecknock.		
		Penkelly ..	Joshua Jones. .	Penkelly, Llanfigan, Brecknock.		

UNION, or SUPERINTENDENT REGISTRAR'S DISTRICT.	County.	Places of Public Worship situated therein, registered for Solemnization of Marriages.		SUPERINTENDENT REGISTRARS, and *Deputy Superintendent Registrars.*	
		Name.	Situation.	Name.	Address.
BRENTFORD	Middlesex . .	The Independent Chapel . Albany Chapel . . . . Shrewsbury Place . . .	Hanworth Road, Hounslow . Old Brentford. Isleworth.	George Clark . *John James Clark,*	New Brentford . . *Sion Place, Isleworth.*
BRIDGE	Kent. . . .	. . .	. . .	Herbert Collard .	Nackington, Canterbury
BRIDGEND and COW-BRIDGE.	Glamorgan . .	Ruhamah Baptist Chapel Saron . . . . . Carmel	Newcastle, Bridgend . . . Treoes, in the parish of Langan Maestag Iron Works, in the parish of Langonoyd.	Wm. Edmondes .	Cowbridge . . .
BRIDGNORTH	Salop. . . .	Stoneway Chapel . . The Baptist Chapel . .	Bridgnorth . . . . . . Bridgnorth.	John Trevor . .	Bridgnorth . . .
BRIDGWATER	Somerset . .	Christ Church Chapel . Sion Chapel . . . . The Wesleyan Methodist Chapel. The Independent Chapel . The Baptist Chapel . . Sion Chapel	Dampiet-street, Bridgwater . Bridgwater. Ball's-lane, Bridgwater. North Petherton. Bridgwater. Othery.	Robert Underdown *Edwin Down,*	Bridgwater . . . *Ditto.*
BRIDLINGTON	York	The Baptist Chapel . . The Independent Chapel .	Bridlington . . . . . Skipsea.	Sidney Taylor .	Bridlington . . .
BRIDPORT	Dorset . . .	The Unitarian Chapel . The Independent Meeting-house. The Catholic Chapel . .	East-street, Bridport . . . Stake Lane, otherwise Barrack-street. Chideock.	John Pitfield .	Allington, near Bridport.
BRIGHTON	Sussex . . .	Union Street Chapel . . The late Countess of Huntingdon's Chapel. New-road Chapel . . . Hanover Chapel . . . Salem Chapel . . . . St. John the Baptist Chapel The Tabernacle . . .	Union-street, Ship-st., Brighton North-street, Brighton. New-road, Brighton. Church-street, Brighton. Bond-street, Brighton. Upper St. James-street, Brighton. West-street, Brighton.	Robert Becher .	Town Hall, Brighton
BRISTOL	City and County of Bristol.	Lewin's Mead Meeting-house. The Moravian Chapel . . Brunswick Chapel . . . Gideon Chapel . . . . Counterslip Meeting . . Bridge-street Chapel . . The Roman Catholic Chapel The Tabernacle . . . Castle-green Chapel . . Broadmead Meeting-house Zion Chapel . . . . Lady Huntingdon's Chapel Pithay Chapel	Lewin's Mead, Bristol . . . Maudlin-lane, Bristol. Brunswick-square, Bristol. Newfoundland-street, Bristol. Counterslip, Bristol. Bridge-street, Bristol. Trenchard-street, in the parish of St. Michael, Bristol. Penn-street, Bristol. Castle-green, Bristol. Broadmead, Bristol. Coronation-road, Bristol. Lodge-street, Bristol. In the Pithay, Bristol.	Wm. P. Hartley . *Joseph B. Grindon,*	Bristol . . . . . *Bishop-street, Bristol.*
BRIXWORTH	Northampton .	The Baptist Meeting-house The Baptist Chapel . .	Guilsborough . . . . . Moulton.	Robert Hewitt .	Northampton .
BROMLEY	Kent	Bromley Chapel . . .	Widmore-lane, Bromley . .	Robert B. Latter	Bromley, Kent . .
BROMSGROVE	Worcester, Warwick, Stafford, and Salop.	The Independent Chapel .	Bromsgrove	Thomas Day . .	Bromsgrove . . .
BROMYARD	Hereford . .	. . .	. . .	T. Griffiths . .	Bromyard . . . .
BUCKINGHAM	Bucks . . .	The Old Meeting . . . The New Meeting, or Church-street Chapel.	Well-street, Buckingham . . Buckingham.	Thomas Hearn . *George Nelson,*	Buckingham . . . *Ditto.*
BUILTH	Brecknock . .	Panty Celyn . . . . Troedrhewdalar . . .	Panty Celyn, in the parish of Llanfihangel, Abergwessin. Troedrhewdalar, in the parish of Llansvan-Vawr.	Evan Vaughan .	Builth . . . . .

REGISTRARS of MARRIAGES.		Registrars' Districts.	REGISTRARS of BIRTHS and DEATHS.		Deputy Registrars of Births and Deaths.	
Name.	Address.		Name.	Address.	Name.	Address.
John F. Bontems	Brentford	Brentford	John Francis Bontems.	Old Brentford	Benjamin Crabb	Bridge Terrace, Kew Bridge, Brentford.
		Acton	John Williamson	Acton, Middlesex . . .	J. Williamson, jun.	Acton.
		Chiswick	James Foster .	Chiswick, Middlesex . .	G. J. Baynes. .	Turnham-green.
		Isleworth . . .	Llewelyn Lewis .	Worton-lane, Isleworth .	Wm. Winkworth	Isleworth.
		Twickenham . .	James Gooch .	Twickenham	John Lamb . .	Church-st., Hounslow.
C. Holman . .	Littlebourne, Canterbury.	Barham	Charles Holman	Littlebourne ; Canterbury.	W. Smith . .	Littlebourne, Canterbury.
W. Davey . .	Westgate, Canterbury	Chartham	William Davey .	Westgate ; Canterbury	F. Saunders . .	Westgate, Canterbury.
David Jenkins .	Lantwit Major, Glamorganshire.	Cowbridge	David Jenkins .	Lantwit Major, Cowbridge, Glamorganshire.		
		Bridgend	David W. Davies	Bridgend, Glamorganshire.		
		Maesteg	William Prees .	Coity ; Bridgend, Glamorganshire.		
William Grierson	Bridgnorth . . .	Bridgnorth. . . .	John Pinckstone	Bridgnorth.		
		Worfield	William Weaver	Claverley ; Bridgnorth.		
		Chetton. . . .	Edward Edwards	Eardington ; Bridgnorth.		
Edwin Down. .	Bridgwater . . .	Bridgwater . . .	Abraham King .	Bridgwater	James Newman .	Bridgwater.
John Chinn . .	Westonzoyland, Bridgwater.	Huntspill . . .	John Burnett .	Huntspill ; Bridgwater.		
		Polden Hill . .	John Stagg . .	Moorlinch ; Bridgwater.		
		Middlezoy . . .	John Chinn . .	Westonzoyland ; Bridgwater		
		North Petherton .	Thomas Rich .	North Petherton ; Bridgwater.		
		Stowey.	R. B. Ruddock .	Nether Stowey ; Bridgwater	J. Franklin Waites	Nether Stowey ; Bridgwater.
Robert T. Brown	Bridlington . . .	Hunmanby . . .	Thomas Hagyard	Hunmanby ; Bridlington .		
		Skipsea . . .	Robert Lowson .	Burton Agnes ; Bridlington.		
		Bridlington . . .	R. T. Brown . .	Bridlington.		
John Coppock .	Bridport	Bridport	William Tucker .	Allington, Bridport . .	John Coppock .	East-street, Bridport.
John Monteith .	Bridport.	Burton Bradstock .	John Knight .	Burton Bradstock ; Bridport	Richard Hawkins	Burton Bradstock, Bridport.
William Tucker.	Allington, Bridport.	Whitchurch Canonicorum.	Henry Jerrard .	Chideock ; Bridport . .	James Garrard .	Whitchurch Canonicorum.
George Sawyer .	Brighton	Palace	George Sawyer .	Middle-street, Brighton .	G. A. Stonham .	Ship-street, Brighton.
		St. Peter's . . .	T. R Simmonds.	2, Gloucester-place, Brighton		
		Kemp Town . . .	Charles Dumbrell	91, St. James's-street, Brighton.	R. R. Sparrow .	95, St. James's-street, Brighton.
John Ayre . .	Cathay.	Castle Precincts . .	Charles Attwood	Charlotte-street, Queen-square, Bristol.	J. T. Gwyer . .	King-street, Queen-square, Bristol.
		St. Augustine . .	A. N. Ruddock .	Unity-street, Bristol.		
		St. James's . . .	James Prowse .	8, St. James's, Barton, Bristol.		
		St. Mary Redcliffe	T. Field Gilbert .	32, Redcliffe-hill, Bristol.		
		St. Paul's	John Brady . .	3, Gloucester-street, St. Paul's, Bristol.	T. B. Jackson .	4, Wilson-place, Bristol
Robert R. Morris	Brixworth	Moulton	John Flecknoe .	Boughton ; Northampton.	Thomas Parker .	Boughton, Northampton.
William Williams	Guilsborough.	Brixworth	Robert R. Morris	Brixworth ; Northampton.		
John Flecknoe .	Boughton.	Spratton	Wm. Williams .	Guilsborough ; Northampton	Thomas Carter .	Guilsborough.
Charles Freeman	Bromley, Kent . .	Bromley	Charles Bourne .	Bromley, Kent.		
		Chislehurst . . .	T. H. Smith . .	St. Mary Cray, Footscray, Kent.		
W. Ward, jun. .	Bromsgrove . . .	Bromsgrove . . .	Wm. Johnson .	Bromsgrove	W. Johnson, jun.	Bromsgrove.
		Tardebigg . . .	John Osborne .	Redditch ; Bromsgrove	B. Colewick .	Redditch ; Bromsgrove
		Belbroughton and Hagley.	William Gardner	Clent ; Stourbridge . .	Daniel Osborne .	Belbroughton, Stourbridge.
W. Wilkes . .	Bromyard	Bromyard	Wm. Vernalls .	Bromyard.		
		Brockhampton . .	R. Perkins . .	Norton ; Bromyard.		
		Bishop's Frome .	John Rann . .	Bishop's Frome ; Bromyard.		
Samuel King .	Buckingham . . .	Buckingham . . .	Samuel King .	Buckingham.		
		Tingewick . . .	J. Phillips . .	Tingewick ; Buckingham.	William Everett	Tingewick ; Buckingham.
		Leckhamstead . .	Robert Roper .	Maidsmorton ; Buckingham.		
Peter Jones . .	Llwyncus, Llanleonville, Builth.	Builth	Thomas Powell .	Builth	John Price . .	Builth.
David Williams .	Builth.	Colwyn.	Thomas Lloyd .	Hundred House, Builth.		
		Abergwesin . . .	Peter Jones . .	Llywncus ; Builth.		

UNION, or SUPERINTENDENT REGISTRAR'S DISTRICT.	County.	Places of Public Worship situated therein, registered for Solemnization of Marriages.		SUPERINTENDENT REGISTRARS, and *Deputy Superintendent Registrars.*	
		Name.	Situation.	Name.	Address.
BURNLEY	Lancaster . .	The Catholic Chapel . .	Burnley Wood, Burnley . .	Richard Shaw .	Burnley . . . .
		Bethesda Chapel . . .	Burnley.	*Robert Artindale,*	*Ditto.*
		Sion Chapel.	Burnley.		
		Independent Chapel . .	Colne, in the parish of Whalley.		
		Unitarian Chapel . . .	Spring Gardens, in Padiham, in the parish of Whalley.		
BURTON-ON-TRENT . .	Stafford . . .	The Independent Chapel .	Tutbury	William Coxon .	Burton-on-Trent . .
		The Independent Chapel .	High-street, Burton-on-Trent.		
		The General Baptist Chapel	Burton Extra, in the parish of Burton-on-Trent.		
BURY	Lancaster . .	The Independent Chapel .	New-road, Bury	William Harper	Bury, Lancashire . .
		The Catholic Chapel . .	Bury.	*William H. Norris,*	*Ditto.*
		Bamford Chapel . . .	Bamford, in the parish of Middleton.		
		The Presbyterian Chapel .	Stand, in Pilkington, in the parish of Prestwich.		
		The Presbyterian Chapel .	Bury.		
		The Independent Chapel .	Chapelfield, in Pilkington, in the parish of Prestwich.		
		The Brunswick Wesleyan Association Chapel.	North-street, Bury.		
BURY ST. EDMUNDS . .	Suffolk . . .	The Independent Meeting	Whiting-st., Bury St. Edmunds	Frederick Wing .	Bury St. Edmunds .
		Northgate-street Chapel .	Bury St. Edmunds.		
		The Churchgate-street Chapel.	Bury St. Edmunds.		
CAISTOR	Lincoln . . .	. . .	. . .	George Marris .	Caistor . . . .
CALNE	Wilts	The Baptist Meeting . .	Castle-street, Calne	John Broxholm .	Calne, Wilts . . .
CAMBERWELL	Surrey . . .	Hanover Chapel	High-street, Peckham . . .	Thomas Plum .	21, Addington-square, Camberwell.
		Mansion House Chapel .	Camberwell Road.		
		Marlboro' Chapel . . .	Old Kent Road, Camberwell.		
CAMBRIDGE	Cambridge . .	The Baptist Chapel . .	St. Andrew's-street, Cambridge.	Jos. Deacon Fetch	Sidney-street, Cambridge.
		Eden Chapel	Burleigh-street, Cambridge.		
		Zion Chapel	East-road, Cambridge.		
CAMELFORD	Cornwall . . .	A Bible Christian Chapel.	St. Teath, Church Town . .	Claud. C. Hawker	Boscastle, Camelford .
		The Wesleyan Methodist Association Chapel.	Boscastle.		
CANTERBURY	Kent	Guildhall-street Chapel .	Canterbury	John Nutt . .	Canterbury . . .
		King-street Chapel . .	King-street, Canterbury.	*Wm. Hobday,*	*Ditto.*
		St. Peter's-street Chapel .	Canterbury.		
		Union Chapel	Watling-street, Canterbury.		
CARDIFF	Glamorgan . .	Bethany.	St. Mary's-street, Cardiff . .	Thomas Watkins	Cardiff. . . . .
		Tabernacle	Cardiff, in the parish of St. Mary.		
		Tonyfelin	Caerphilly, in the parish of Eglwysilian.		
		Ainon	Tongwynlais, in the parish of Eglwysilian.		
		White Cross	Eglwysilian.		
		Ebenezer	Union-street, Cardiff.		
		Ararat	Waentrodau, in the parish of Whitchurch.		
CARDIGAN	Cardigan & Pembroke.	Blaenywaun Chapel . .	Blaenywaun, in the parish of St. Dogmells.	Caleb Lewis .	Cardigan . . . .
		Bethany Chapel . . .	Cardigan.	*David Jenkins,*	*Ditto.*
		Pen-y-Bryn.	Pen-y-Bryn, in the parish of Bridell.		
		Bethlehem Chapel. . .	Newport, Pembrokeshire.		
		Siloam Chapel	Verwick.		
CARLISLE	Cumberland . .	The Old Presbyterian Chapel	Fisher-street, Carlisle . . .	James Mouncy .	Carlisle . . . .
		Catholic Chapel . . .	Lowther-street, in the parish of St. Mary.		
		Scotch Presbyterian Chapel	Lowther-street, Carlisle.		

REGISTRARS of MARRIAGES.		Registrars' Districts.	REGISTRARS of BIRTHS and DEATHS.		Deputy Registrars of Births and Deaths.	
Name.	Address.		Name.	Address.	Name.	Address.
Thomas Sutcliffe John Conyers William West	Burnley Colne, Lancashire. Padiham, Lancashire.	*Pendle* *Colne* *Burnley* *Padiham*	James Dixon John Conyers Thomas Sutcliffe William West	Newchurch, in Pendle; Burnley. Colne. Burnley Padiham; Burnley.	Chas. Sutcliffe	34, St. James's-street, Burnley.
John Whitehurst	High-street, Burton-on-Trent.	*Tutbury* *Burton-on-Trent* *Repton* *Greeley*	Henry Edwards John Killingly Gervase Smedley William Wright	Tutbury, Burton-on-Trent. New-st., Burton-on-Trent. Repton; Burton-on-Trent. Newhall, Burton-on-Trent.	E. R. Palmer Rupt. Baldwin Wm. Thorp John Heap	High-street, Tutbury. Burton Extra. Newton Solvey, Repton; Burton-on-Trent. Newhall; Burton-on-Trent.
Joseph Whittam	Bury	*Bury, North* *Bury, South* *Walmersley* *Birtle* *Heywood* *Pilkington* *Radcliffe* *Elton* *Holcombe* *Tottington, lower end*	Joseph Whittam Thomas Barker Robt. Thompson James Jackson S. Wolstenholme John Lancashire George Barlow G. Hargreaves R. Wolstenholme Thomas Coop	Stanley-street, Bury, Lancashire. Bury, Lancashire. Walmersley; Bury Birtle, Bury Heywood, Bury Pilkington, Manchester Radcliffe, Manchester. Elton, Bury Dickfield, Holcombe; Bury Tottington, Bury	Joseph Johnson Dennis Barker John Mawdsley Thomas Jackson John Hardman G. Wolstenholme William Hague Richard Olive T. Wolstenholme Samuel Coop	Barlow-street, Bury. Bury, Lancashire. Walmersley; Bury. Bamford; Bury. Heywood; Bury. Sheep Hey, in Pilkington; Manchester. Radcliffe, Manchester. Elton, Bury, Lancashire. Dickfield, Holcombe; Bury. Tottington, Bury.
T. C. Newby. W. J. Chilton	Angel Hill, Bury St. Edmunds. Bury St. Edmunds.	*Bury St. Edmunds*	John Priest	Bury St. Edmunds.		
Robert Lamming	Caistor, Lincoln	*Caistor* *Market Rasen* *Great Grimsby*	John Thompson Zephauiah Barton H. M. Leppington	Caistor, Lincoln Market Rasen Great Grimsby.	John Monday M. S. Barton Thomas Lamming	Caistor. Market Rasen. Laceby; Great Grimsby
Thomas Broxholm	Calne, Wilts	*Calne*	John Ladd	Calne, Wilts	J. N. Ladd	Calne, Wilts.
Edward Clark	Hanover-street, Rye-lane, Peckham.	*Camberwell* *Peckham* *St. George's* *Dulwich*	Thomas Prebble Edward Clark William Wilson Thomas Bartlett	6, Union-row, High-street, Camberwell. Hanover-street, Rye-lane, Peckham. 2, Prospect-place, Old Kent-road. Charity School, Dulwich	John Wm. Prebble E. P. Clark Thomas Cooper J. Maddison	6, Union-row, High-street, Camberwell. 2, Hanover-street, Rye-lane, Peckham. Cottage Green, Camberwell. Near the School-house, Dulwich.
Peter Bays	St. Edward's-passage, Cambridge.	*Great St. Mary's* *St. Andrew the Less* *Great St. Andrew's* *St. Giles's*	Peter Bays Thomas Denny Samuel Knowles Robert Peters	St. Edward's-passage, Cambridge. Downing-terrace, St. Andrew the Less, Cambridge. King-street, Holy Trinity, Cambridge. Magdalen-street, Cambridge		
William Burt	Camelford.	*Camelford* *Boscastle*	William Burt William Symons	Camelford. Hendra, Camelford, Cornwall.		
Thomas Hobday	8, St. George's-terrace, Canterbury.	*Canterbury*	John Aris	3, Bridge-street, Canterbury.	Samuel White	6, Blackfriars, St. Alphage, Canterbury.
Thomas Hopkins Evan Edwards	Cardiff. Caerphilly.	*Cardiff.* *St. Nicholas* *Llantrissent* *Caerphilly*	James Lewis D. W. Davis Evan Davis Evan Edwards	Cardiff Cardiff. Newbridge. Caerphilly.	Thomas Hopkins	Cardiff.
Joshua M. Thomas	Cardigan	*Cardigan* *Llandygwidd* *Newport*	Thomas Langdon Rev. Isaac Hughes Edward Rees	Cardigan Kirw Castle, Cardigan. Newport.	Isaac Thomas	Cardigan.
A. Birrell John Donald	Abbey-street, Carlisle Botchergate, Carlisle.	*St. Mary's* *St. Cuthbert* *Stanwix* *Burgh* *Dalston* *Wetheral*	A. Birrell John Donald Jabez Duxbury Joseph Borrodaile James Finlinson. David Modlin	Abbey-street, Carlisle. Botchergate, Carlisle. Kingstown, Carlisle. Burgh-by-Sands, Carlisle. Dalston, Carlisle. Wetheral, Carlisle.		

UNION, or SUPERINTENDENT REGISTRAR'S DISTRICT.	County.	Places of Public Worship situated therein, registered for Solemnization of Marriages.		SUPERINTENDENT REGISTRARS, *and Deputy Superintendent Registrars.*	
		Name.	Situation.	Name.	Address.
CARMARTHEN	Carmarthen . .	Moriah	Castellmawr, in the parish of Llanwinio.	David Griffiths .	King-street, Carmarthen.
		Tabernacle	Waterloo-terrace ; Carmarthen.		
		Car Salem	Pontyberem, in the parish of Llangendeirne.		
		Penygraig	Penygraig, in the parish of Llandefeylog.		
		Rock Chapel	Rhydwenog, in the parish of Treleach, ar Bettws.		
		Peniel	On Rhydshaw Farm, in the parish of Abergwilly.		
		Bwlchnewydd Chapel . .	Bwlchnewydd, in the parish of Abernant.		
		Hermon.	Pencraigfach, in the parish of Conwyl Elvet.		
		Lammas-st. Meeting-house	Carmarthen.		
		Bethlehem	Pwlltrap, in the parish of St. Clear's.		
		Capel Newydd Meeting-house.	Llanbri, in the parish of Llanstephan.		
		Pantteg.	Llygadcatty, in the parish of Abergwilly.		
		Rhydyceisiaid	Llangunin.		
		Philadelphia	Llangunnor.		
CARNARVON	Carnarvon . .	Ebenezer Independent Chapel.	Ebenezer, in the parish of Llanddeniolet.	John Thomas .	Carnarvon . . . .
		The Pendre Independent Chapel.	Carnarvon.		
CASTLE WARD. . . .	Northumberland	Cheeseburne Grange Chapel	CheeseburneGrange, in the parish of Stamfordham.	Rob. R. Dees .	Newcastle-on-Tyne .
CATHERINGTON . . .	Hants . . .	Providence Chapel. . .	Rowland's Castle, in the parish of Idsworth.	Henry Glasse .	Horndean, Hants. .
CAXTON & ARRINGTON.	Cambridge . .	The Old Baptist Meeting.	Gamlingay	Henry Mortlock .	Caxton. . . . .
CHAPEL-EN-LE-FRITH .	Derby . . .	Chinley Chapel . . .	Chinley, in the parish of Glossop.	William Bennett	Chapel-en-le-Frith, Derby.
CHARD	Somerset, Dorset, and Devon.	The Old Meeting . . .	Ilminster.	William Fowler .	Chard . . . . .
		North-street Chapel . .	Crewkerne.		
		Presbyterian Meeting-house	Hermitage-street, Crewkerne.		
		Zion Chapel	Langport-street, Ilminster.		
		The Independent Chapel .	Fore-street, Chard.		
CHEADLE	Stafford . . .	St. Peter's Chapel . .	Alton Towers, in the parish of Alton.	Thomas Walters.	Cheadle, Staffordshire
		St. Mary's Chapel, Creswell	Creswell, in the parish of Draycott-in-the-Moors.		
CHELMSFORD	Essex . . .	Ingatestone-hall Chapel	Ingatestone	Robert Bartlett .	Chelmsford . . .
		The Independent Chapel .	Baddow-lane, Chelmsford.		
		Old Meeting-house . .	Baddow-lane, Chelmsford.		
CHELTENHAM. . . .	Gloucester . .	Salem Chapel	Regent-street, Cheltenham.	Wm. H. Gyde .	Cheltenham . . .
		The Roman Catholic Chapel	Somerset-place, Cheltenham.	*James Boodle,*	*Ditto.*
		Highbury Chapel . . .	Grosvenor-street, Cheltenham.		
		The Unitarian Chapel .	Manchester-place, Cheltenham.		
CHEPSTOW	Monmouth and Gloucester.	Lydney Baptist Meeting-house.	Lydney, Gloucestershire . .	William E. Toye	Chepstow . . . .
		The Baptist Chapel . .	Chepstow.		
CHERTSEY	Surrey . . .	. . .	. . .	Hy. G. Grazebrook	Chertsey . . . .
				Durley Grazebrook,	*Ditto.*
CHESTERFIELD . . .	Derby . . .	The Independent Chapel	Soresby-street, Chesterfield .	John Marsh . .	Chesterfield . . .
		The Dissenting Protestant Meeting-house.	Elder-yard, Chesterfield.		
		The Independent Chapel .	Dronfield.		
CHESTER-LE-STREET. .	Durham . . .	. . .	. . .	James Gray . .	Chester-le-Street. .
CHESTERTON	Cambridge . .	Ebenezer Meeting-house .	Cottenham	Fred. Barlow .	Cambridge . . .

REGISTRARS of MARRIAGES.		Registrars' Districts.	REGISTRARS of BIRTHS and DEATHS.		Deputy Registrars of Births and Deaths.	
Name.	Address.		Name.	Address.	Name.	Address.
J. White White.	Carmarthen	Carmarthen	G. White White.	Carmarthen	J. White White .	Carmarthen.
William Howell.	Pilmawr, Llanwinio-Carmarthen.	Llangendeirne	Thomas Lewis	Llangendeirne; Carmarthen.		
John White .	Llettycary, Llandefeilog.	Conwyl	Joseph Lewis	Conwyl; Carmarthen.		
		St. Clear's	David Lloyd .	Llanstephen, St. Clear's; Carmarthenshire.		
Robert Williams.	Carnarvon	Carnarvon.	Robert Williams.	Carnarvon.		
		Llanidan	Thomas Smith .	Llangeinwen; Anglesey.		
		Llandwrog .	Thomas Hughes.	Groeslon, Llandwrog; Carnarvon.		
		Llanrug	William Williams	Tyddynbiale; Carnarvon.		
. . .		Stamfordham	George Crow .	Hawkwell; Stamfordham, Newcastle-on-Tyne.		
		Ponteland	Proctor Shotton .	Ponteland, Newcastle-on-Tyne.		
Richard Gale .	Horndean, Hants. .	Horndean	Richard Gale .	Horndean, Hants.		
William Holder .	Caxton	Caxton and Arrington	William Holder.	Longstow, near Caxton.		
James Bennett .	Chinley, Chapel-en-le-Frith.	Chapel-en-le-Frith.	Robert Bardsley.	Chapel-en-le-Frith.		
		Buxton.	Joseph Vernon .	Buxton.		
Henry Burnard .	Ilminster	Chard	Wm. Pitt Ware .	Chard Borough.		
J. L. Burnard .	Crewkerne.	Combe St. Nicholas	Joseph Winter .	Combe St. Nicholas, Chard.		
Wm. Pitt Ware .	Chard.	Crewkerne	J. L. Burnard .	Crewkerne.		
		Ilminster	Henry Burnard .	Ilminster.		
Anthony Hordern	Cheadle	Cheadle	Geo. Fallows .	Cross-street, Cheadle.		
		Alton	Joseph Waterall	Alton; Cheadle . . .	Charles Smith .	Alton; Cheadle.
		Dilhorn	Jonathan Whalley	Dilhorn; Cheadle.		
		Ipstones	Anson Green .	Ipstones; Cheadle.		
William Wicks .	Chelmsford	Chelmsford	William Wicks .	Chelmsford.		
		Writtle.	William Burr .	Writtle, Essex.		
		Ingatestone.	Richard Lewis .	Ingatestone, Essex.		
		Great Baddow	Jeremiah Suckling	Sandon, near Danbury, Chelmsford.		
		Great Waltham	John Dannat, jun.	GreatWaltham; Chelmsford		
Samuel Charles Harper.	318, High-street, Cheltenham.	Cheltenham	Samuel Charles Harper.	318, High-street, Cheltenham.	A. Harper .	318, High-st., Cheltenham.
		Charlton Kings	Robert Pearman.	Leckhampton; Cheltenham.		
Benjamin Tayler	Chepstow	Chepstow	B. M. Bradford, sen.	Chepstow	James Clark .	Chepstow.
		Lidney	Wm. Packer, jun.	Brook-end, Woolastone.		
		Shire Newton	George Howell .	Caerwent, Chepstow	Isaac Spencer .	Caldicott; Caerwent.
W. J. Lovett .	Chertsey	Chertsey	W. J. Lovett .	Chertsey	Alfred Grave.	Chertsey.
		Walton.	J. Higgins .	Hersham; Esher, Surrey.		
		Chobham	Thos. Hudson, jun.	Chobham; Bagshot, Surrey	Charles Howard .	Chobham, Bagshot, Surrey.
Sam. Hollingworth	Chesterfield	Chesterfield	Samuel Hollingworth.	Chesterfield.	George Black .	Brampton.
		Bolsover	O. Stevenson .	Bolsover; Chesterfield.		
		Eckington	Charles Taylor .	Eckington; Chesterfield	J. J. Hayes . .	Mosbro', Eckington.
		Ashover	George Allen .	Ashover; Chesterfield	Thos. Gratton .	Rose Cottage, Ashover.
		Dronfield	Joseph Biggin .	Coalaston; Chesterfield.		
Chas. John Scott.	Chester-le-Street . .	Chester-de-Street	Chas. John Scott	Chester-le-Street.		
		Harraton	Mattw. Henderson	Low Pelaw, Chester-le-Street.		
		Lamesley	Ralph Coulthard	Birtley, Chester-le-Street.		
John R. Lyon .	Cherry-Hinton; Cambridge.	Willingham	Robert Ellis . .	Willingham; Cambridge.		
		Fulbourn	F. R. Hitch .	Fulbourn; Cambridge.		
		Shelford, Great	J. Allen Ramsey	Great Shelford; Cambridge.		

UNION, or SUPERINTENDENT REGISTRAR'S DISTRICT.	County.	Places of Public Worship situated therein, registered for Solemnization of Marriages.		SUPERINTENDENT REGISTRARS, and *Deputy Superintendent Registrars*.	
		Name.	Situation.	Name.	Address.
CHICHESTER	Sussex . . .	The Unitarian Chapel. .	Baffin's-lane, Chichester . .	James Powell .	Chichester . . . .
		Ebenezer Chapel . . .	St. Martin's-square, Chichester		
		The Independent Chapel .	Chapel-street, Chichester.		
		The Roman Catholic Chapel	Slindon House, in the parish of Slindon.		
CHIPPENHAM	Wilts	Tabernacle	Emery Lane, Chippenham. .	West Awdry .	Chippenham . . .
		The Independent Chapel .	Corsham.		
		The Baptist Chapel . .	Chippenham.		
CHIPPING-NORTON .	Oxford . . .	The Church of the Blessed Virgin Mary.	Heythrop	A. L. Rawlinson. *John Biggerstaff,*	Chipping-Norton . . *Ditto.*
		The Baptist Meeting-house	Chipping-Norton.		
		The Wesleyan Chapel. .	Chipping-Norton.		
CHIPPING SODBURY .	Gloucester . .	. . .	. . .	Ethelbert Holborow.	Chipping Sodbury . .
CHORLEY	Lancaster. . .	South Hill	Whittle-le-Woods, in the parish of Leyland.	Peter Stringfellow *Edward Bibby,*	Chorley . . . . *Ditto.*
		St. Joseph	Brindle.		
		St. Gregory	Weldbank, in the parish of Chorley.		
		Hollinshead Street Chapel	Chorley.		
		St. Bede's Chapel . . .	Clayton Green, in the parish of Leyland.		
		The Presbyterian Chapel .	Rivington, in the parish of Bolton-le-Moors.		
		Ebenezer Chapel . . .	Bretherton, in the parish of Croston.		
		The Presbyterian Chapel .	Park-street, Chorley.		
CHORLTON	Lancaster . .	A Chapel	Jackson's-lane, Hulme, Manchester.	John Latham, jun. *John Latham, sen.*	Chorlton-upon-Medlock, Manchester, *5, Egerton Terrace, Hulme.*
		The Dissenting Chapel .	Gorton, Manchester.		
		The Independent Chapel .	Rusholme-road, Chorlton-upon-Medlock, Manchester.		
		Tipping Street Chapel .	Tipping-street, in the township of Ardwick, in the parish of Manchester.		
		The Independent Chapel .	Stretford, in the parish of Manchester.		
		Evangelical Friends' Chapel	Grosvenor-street, Chorlton-upon-Medlock.		
		The Upper Brook-street Chapel.	Chorlton-upon-Medlock.		
CHRISTCHURCH . . .	Hants . . .	The Independent Meeting-house.	Meeting - house - lane, Christchurch.	Henry Pain . .	Bridge-street, Christchurch, Hants.
CHURCH STRETTON. .	Salop	. . .	. . .	John Belton . .	Church Stretton . .
CIRENCESTER	Gloucester and Wilts.	The Baptist Chapel . .	Cirencester	John Bevir . .	Cirencester . . . .
		The Baptist Meeting-house	Milton-end, Fairford.		
CLEOBURY MORTIMER.	Salop	. . .	. . .	Wm. Cooke, jun.	Cleobury Mortimer .
CLERKENWELL . . .	Middlesex . .	Spencer Place Meeting-house.	Goswell-road, in the parish of Clerkenwell.	George A. M'Phail *Edmund Boulter,*	17, Wilmington-square, Clerkenwell. *5, Northampton-square, Clerkenwell.*
		Claremont Chapel . . .	Pentonville.		
		Northampton Tabernacle .	Upper Rosoman-street, Clerkenwell.		
		The Freethinking Christians' Meeting-house.	St. John's-square, Clerkenwell.		
CLIFTON	Gloucester and Bristol.	Anvill Street Chapel . .	Anvill-street, Bristol . . .	C. A. Latcham .	Stoke's Croft, Bristol.
		Kingsland Chapel . . .	Kingsland-road, Bristol.		
CLITHEROE	Lancaster . .	St. Peter's Church. . .	Stonyhurst, Aighton Bailey and Chaigley; Lancashire.	Jno. Wilkinson .	Clitheroe . . . .
		The Catholic Chapel in Lower-gate.	Lower-gate, within Clitheroe.		
		St. William's	Thornley, in the parish of Chipping.		
		St. Mary's	Chipping.		
		Well-gate Chapel . . .	Clitheroe.		
		The Baptist Chapel . .	Sabden, near Pendle Hill; Pendleton.		

REGISTRARS of MARRIAGES.		Registrars' Districts.	REGISTRARS of BIRTHS and DEATHS.		Deputy Registrars of Births and Deaths.	
Name.	Address.		Name.	Address.	Name.	Address.
H. W. Duddan .	North-street, Chichester.	*Chichester*	James Cheesman	Chichester.		
		Sutton	Henry Foard	Sutton, near Petworth.		
		South Bersted . . .	George Peskett .	Bognor, South Bersted.		
Edward Bradbury	Chippenham . . .	*Chippenham*	Henry Spencer .	Chippenham	Charles Bayliffe.	Chippenham.
		Corsham	Aaron Little. .	Corsham.		
		Christian Malford. .	Geo. S. Stiles .	Sutton-Benger; Chippenham.		
		Castle Combe . .	Edward Spencer .	Castle Combe; Chippenham		
John Liddiard .	Chipping-Norton. .	*Chipping-Norton* .	Samuel Vokins .	Chipping-Norton.		
William Hood .	Chipping-Norton.	*Charlbury*	John Godfery .	Charlbury; Enstone, Oxon.		
S. B. Dutfield .	Chipping Sodbury .	*Chipping Sodbury.*	Henry Morton .	Chipping Sodbury.		
		Iron Acton. . . .	John Roberts .	Wickwar, Wotton-under-Edge.	Wm. Minett . .	Wickwar.
		Hawkesbury . . .	Ebenezer Bletchley	Hawkesbury; Dunkirk.		
		Marshfield. . . .	Thomas Boulton	Wick and Abson; Lansdowne, Bath.		
George Houghton	Chorley	*Chorley*	Rev. T. Todhunter	Chorley	Richard Tootell .	St. George's-street, Chorley.
J. Riley . . .	Brindle, Preston.	*Leyland*	F. S. Pilkington .	Leyland; Chorley.		
H. Harrison . .	Bretherton, Chorley.	*Brindle*	Joseph Parker .	Brindle; Chorley.		
		Rivington	Rev. J. Jackson .	Rivington; Chorley . .	Charles Holt. .	Rivington; Chorley.
		Croston	Rev. R. W. King	Croston; Chorley . . .	W. R. Wright .	Croston, Chorley.
John Pownall .	Hulme, near Chorlton-upon-Medlock.	*Chorlton-upon-Medlock*	P. H. Holland .	108, Grosvenor-street, Chorlton-upon-Medlock.	F. W. Holland .	108, Grosvenor-street, Chorlton-upon-Medlock.
John Appleby .	York-street, Chorlton-upon-Medlock.	*Hulme*	John Pownall .	York-street, Hulme; Manchester.	John Pownall, jun.	57, York-street, Hulme. Manchester.
		Ardwick	John Watkinson	Ardwick; Manchester.		
		Stretford	H. T. Bagshaw .	Stretford; Manchester.		
		Didsbury	Samuel Gaskell .	Didsbury; Manchester.		
Richard Sharp .	Christchurch . . .	*Christchurch* . . .	Joseph Scott .	Church-lane, Christchurch, Hants.	John Gould . .	Christchurch.
Thomas Lloyd .	Church Stretton . .	*Church Stretton* . .	Richard Home .	Church Stretton . .	John Lucas . .	Church Stretton.
		Wall	Thomas Dodd .	Cardington, Wall; Church Stretton.		
J. H. White. . .	Cirencester . . .	*Cirencester.* . . .	Henry Light .	Cirencester.		
Edward Thomson	Fairford.	*Fairford*	R. Adams . .	Poulton, Fairford.		
		Cotswold	S. H. Eeles . .	Duntisbourne Abbotts; Cirencester.		
Edmund B. Whitcombe.	Cleobury Mortimer .	*Cleobury Mortimer* .	E. B. Whitcombe	Cleobury Mortimer.		
		Stottesden	W. Bradnee . .	Wheathill; Bridgnorth .	John Bradnee .	Wheathill.
Henry Aldwinckle	18, Exmouth-street, St. James, Clerkenwell.	*Pentonville.* . . .	George Pyne .	43, Henry-street, Pentonville	Joseph Taylor .	55, Southampton-street Pentonville.
		Amwell.	William Foster .	8, Lloyd-square, Clerkenwell.	Henry Aldwinckle	18, Exmouth-street, Clerkenwell.
		Goswell street . . .	Robert C. Fair .	3, Charles-street, St. John-street-road.	Walter Burrows .	5, Lower Charles-street Northampton-square.
		St. James	A. Western . .	5, Clerkenwell-close . .	Samuel Pike. .	72, St. John's-street, Clerkenwell.
Henry Read. .	45, Picton-st., Bristol	*Clifton.*	Jno. Colthurst .	Mall, Clifton; Bristol . .	Jno. Princep. .	Beaufort Cottage; Clifton, Bristol.
		St. Philip and Jacob .	E. S. Mayor . .	Stapleton-place, St. Philip and Jacob; Bristol.	W. P. Haythorne	Stapleton-place, Bristol.
		Ashley	George Coles .	Picton-street; Bristol . .	G. E. Coles . .	26, Picton-street; Bristol
		Westbury and Henbury	C. Rendall . .	Westbury-on-Trym; Bristol	Peter Pope . .	Westbury-on-Trym; Bristol.
		Stapleton	Edwin Day . .	Hambrook; Bristol . .	Geo. Good . .	Hambrook; Bristol.
		St. George. . . .	James Parsons .	St. George; Bristol . .	Joseph Baker .	Upper Easton; Bristol.
Henry Whalley .	Clitheroe	*Clitheroe*	Henry Whalley .	Clitheroe.		
		Whalley	Archb. Wm. Dewhurst.	Whalley; Blackburn.		
		Chipping	Rev. E. Wilkinson	Chipping; Preston . .	Henry Wood. .	Chipping.
		Gisburn	Lambert Crabtree	Gisburn, Yorkshire.		
		Slaidburn	T. D. Jackson .	Slaidburn; Clitheroe.		

H

UNION, or SUPERINTENDENT REGISTRAR'S DISTRICT.	County.	Places of Public Worship situated therein, registered for Solemnization of Marriages.		SUPERINTENDENT REGISTRARS, and *Deputy Superintendent Registrars*.	
		Name.	Situation.	Name.	Address.
CLUN	Salop	The Catholic Chapel . .	Plowden Hall, in the parish of Lydbury, North.	Chas. Rhodes .	Bishop's Castle, Salop.
CLUTTON	Somerset . . .	St. Michael's Chapel . . The Independent Chapel . The Wesleyan Methodist Chapel.	Shortwood, in the parish of Hinton Blewett. Clutton. Midsomer Norton.	J. R. Mogg . . *Wm. Rees Mogg,*	Cholwell House, Bath. *Cholwell.*
COCKERMOUTH . . .	Cumberland .	Presbyterian Chapel . . Crosby Street Chapel . . The Independent Chapel . The Catholic Chapel . .	Workington . . . . . . Maryport, Cross Canonby. Cockermouth. Workington.	Robert Benson . *E. B. Steel,*	Cockermouth . . . *Ditto.*
COLCHESTER	Essex . . .	The Independent Chapel . The Baptist Chapel . . East Stockwell Chapel . St. John's Green Meeting-house. St. James's Catholic Church	Lion Walk, Colchester . . . Eld-lane, Colchester. East Stockwell-street, Colchester. St. John's Green, Colchester. Colchester.	F. G. Abell . . *Edgar Church,*	20, Crouch-street, Colchester. *Colchester.*
COLUMB, ST., MAJOR	Cornwall . . .	The Wesleyan Chapel .	Tregona, in the parish of St. Eval.	T. Collins . . *Thomas Whitford,*	St Columb, Cornwall *St. Columb.*
CONGLETON	Chester . . .	The Catholic Chapel . . Hope Chapel	West-road, Congleton . . . Sandbach.	William Latham	Congleton . . . .
CONWAY.	Carnarvon and Denbigh.	. . .	. . .	Wm. Hughes .	Conway . . . .
COOKHAM	Berks.	Independent Meeting-house	Maidenhead	William J. Ward	Maidenhead . . .
CORWEN	Merioneth . .	. . .	. . .	David Pugh . .	Corwen . . . .
COSFORD.	Suffolk . . .	The Great Meeting . .	Market-place, Hadleigh . .	Isaac Last . .	Hadleigh, Suffolk
COVENTRY	Warwick . . .	Vicar-lane Chapel . . . West Orchard Chapel . . The Baptist Chapel . . St. Mary's Chapel . . . The Great Meeting-house .	Coventry . . . . . . Coventry. Cow-lane, Coventry. Hill-street, Coventry. Smithford-street, Coventry.	Henry Merridew *Thomas Daffern,*	Coventry . . . . *Ditto.*
CRANBROOK	Kent	. . .	. . .	J. E. Wilson. .	Cranbrook . . .
CREDITON	Devon . . .	The Presbyterian Chapel .	Bowden-hill, Crediton . . .	Thomas Pring .	Crediton . . .
CRICKHOWELL . . .	Brecknock . .	Carmel . . . . . . Siloam . . . . . . Bethesda	Rhyd-y-Blew, in the parish of Llangunnides. Clydach Iron Works, in the parish of Llanelly. Llangattock.	Thomas Williams	Crickhowell . . .
CRICKLADE and WOOTTON-BASSETT.	Wilts	The Primitive Methodist Chapel. Bethesda Chapel . . .	Wootton-Bassett . . . . Ashton Keynes.	James Pratt . .	Wootton-Bassett . .
CROYDON	Surrey . . .	George Street Chapel . . St. Mary's Chapel. . .	Croydon . . . . Southbridge, Croydon.	James Andrews .	Duppas-hill, Croydon.
CUCKFIELD	Sussex . . .	Independent Chapel . .	Lindfield.	Samuel Waller .	Cuckfield . . . .
DARLINGTON	Durham . . .	St. Augustine's Chapel . Bethel Chapel	Paradise-row, Darlington . . Union-street, Darlington .	Jervis Robinson .	Darlington . . . .
DARTFORD	Kent	The Baptist Chapel . . The Independent Chapel .	Eynsford . . . . . . Lowfield-street, Dartford.	Thomas B. Fooks	Dartford . . . .
DAVENTRY	Northampton .	The Independent Chapel . The Baptist Chapel . . The Independent Chapel .	Long Buckby . . . . . Braunston Daventry.	George Norman .	Daventry . . . .

REGISTRARS of MARRIAGES.		Registrars' Districts.	REGISTRARS of BIRTHS and DEATHS.		Deputy Registrars of Births and Deaths.	
Name.	Address.		Name.	Address.	Name.	Address.
Geo. Rhodes .	Bishop's Castle, Shropshire.	Bishop's Castle . .	George Rhodes .	Bishop's Castle.		
		Chun	Jno. Davies . .	Clun; Ludlow.		
		Lydbury	John Williams .	Lydbury, near Bishop's Castle.		
		Norbury	John Medlicott .	Walk Mill, Wentnor; Bishop's Castle.		
John Hunt . .	Hinton Blewett; Bath	Clutton.	James Crang .	Timsbury, Bath.		
John Parfitt . .	Clutton.	Midsomer Norton .	Thomas Baynton	Radstock, Bath.		
John Smith . .	Midsomer Norton, near Bath.	Chew Magna . .	Robert Collins .	Chew Magna, Pensford, Somerset.		
		Harptree	Charles Pope .	Temple Cloud, Bath.		
Rob. Richardson .	Cockermouth . . .	Cockermouth . .	Nich. Williamson	Cockermouth.		
Pearson Taylor .	Cockermouth.	Keswick	Fletcher Greenup	Keswick.		
Joseph Thompson	Curwen-street, Workington.	Workington . . .	John Thompson .	Workington	John Askew . .	Workington.
		Maryport	Foster Peurice .	Maryport.		
		North Derwent .	John Fawcett .	Great Broughton.		
H. S. Goody . .	Colchester	Colchester, First Ward	Charles Pretty .	Priory-street, Colchester .	Henry Turner .	Wire-street, Colchester.
G. F. Fenton .	51, High-street, Colchester.	Colchester, Second Ward.	W. F. Brill .	High-street, Colchester .	Edward Clarry .	147, High-street, Colchester.
		Colchester, Third Ward	John Bland . .	George-street, Colchester .	W. H. Bland .	15, George-street, Colchester.
William Jane Geach.	St. Columb, Major, Cornwall.	St. Columb, Major	James Whitefield	St. Columb, Cornwall . .	Nicholas Kent .	St. Columb.
J. W. Phillips .	Padstow, Cornwall.	Padstow	John Phillips .	Padstow, Cornwall . .	J. W. Phillips .	Padstow.
		Newlyn	William Olver .	Newlyn, near Truro .	Robert Stephens.	Newlyn; Truro.
T. Brightmore .	Congleton	Congleton . . .	Joseph Bullock .	Congleton, Cheshire.		
Thomas Burgess	Sandbach, Cheshire.	Sandbach	William Sutton .	Sandbach, Cheshire.		
		Church Hulme . .	W. Worthington Barlow.	Church Hulme, Cheshire.		
		Conway	Robert H. Jones.	Conway.		
		Llechweddisa . .	Bartw. Williams	Llanbelr; Conway.		
		Creuddyn	Robert Williams	Llansaintfraid, Glan Conway, Mochdre; near Conway.		
F. T. Ward . .	Maidenhead . . .	Bray	John Bowyer .	Bray; Maidenhead.		
		Cookham	Richard Poulton	Cookham; Maidenhead.		
T. Jones . . .	Corwen	Corwen	Robert Davies .	Corwen.		
		Gwyddelwern . .	Hugh Edwards .	Stamp, Curwen.		
J. G. Stow . .	Hadleigh Hamlet, Suffolk.	Hadleigh	J. G. Stow .	Hadleigh Hamlet, Suffolk.		
George Scott. .	Cockfield.	Lavenham	George Scott. .	Cockfield.		
John Weston .	Coventry	Holy Trinity . .	Charles Holt. .	Well-street, Coventry.		
W. H. Hill . .	Fleet-street, Coventry.	St. John's and St. Michael's.	James Clarke .	Much Park-street, Coventry	Joseph Cooper .	Much Park-street, Coventry.
Thomas Perigoe.	Hawkhurst . . .	Cranbrook . . .	George Landsell.	Benenden, Kent.		
		Hawkhurst. . . .	Thomas Perigoe.	Hawkhurst; Lamberhurst.		
Wm. Amery, jun.	Crediton	Crediton	Edward Yard .	Crediton.		
		Morchard Bishop .	Henry Brutton .	Morchard Bishop.		
		Bow	William Bibbings	Zeal Monachorum, Crediton	John Bibbings .	Bow, Crediton.
		Cheriton Fitzpaine	William Morgan	Sandford, Crediton . .	William Shopland	Sandford.
David Edwards .	Brynmawr, Abergavenny.	Crickhowell . . .	Henry Morgan .	Crickhowell.		
		Llanelly	John Thomas .	Llanelly; Abergavenny.		
		Llangattock . .	Wm. Rumsey .	Penallt; Crickhowell.		
		Cwmdu	George Morgan .	Cwmdu; Crickhowell.		
		Langwnder . . .	Benj. Williams .	Langunder, Crickhowell.		
Robert Little. .	Cricklade, Wilts .	Cricklade . . .	Robert Little .	Cricklade.		
B. Horsell, jun. .	Wootton-Bassett.	Wootton Bassett .	B. Horsell, jun. .	Wootton Bassett.		
William Smith .	George-street, Croydon.	Mitcham . . .	Geo. Chas. Searle.	Merton, Surrey.		
		Croydon	William Smith .	George-street, Croydon, Surrey.		
William Cooper .	Cuckfield	Lindfield . . .	William Chillcott	Lindfield; Cuckfield.		
		Cuckfield	William Cooper .	Cuckfield.		
		Hurstperpoint . .	Billy Heaver. .	Hurstperpoint; Brighton .	Henry Muzzell .	Hurstperpoint; Brighton.
Wm. Thompson .	High-row, Darlington	Darlington. . . .	John Tweddle .	Bridge-street; Darlington.		
		Aycliffe	Wm. Wilkinson .	Heighington; Darlington.		
W. C. Fooks . .	Dartford, Kent.	Farningham . .	Joseph Beckley .	Farningham; Dartford .	Thos. Sharwood .	Farningham; Dartford.
		Bexley	S. Levens . .	Crayford, Dartford; Kent.		
		Dartford	W. C. Fooks. .	Dartford, Kent. . .	J. K. Shepherd .	Dartford.
William Bird . .	Daventry	Daventry . . .	William Bird .	Daventry	William Bird, jun.	Daventry.
Wm. Bird, jun. .	Daventry.	Werdon	James Bliss . .	Weedon Beck; Daventry.	N. C. Billing .	Weedon Beck; Daventry.
		Long Buckby . .	William Judkins .	Long Buckby, Daventry .	Thomas March .	Long Buckby, Daventry.

H 2

UNION, or SUPERINTENDENT REGISTRAR'S DISTRICT.	County.	Places of Public Worship situated therein, registered for Solemnization of Marriages.		SUPERINTENDENT REGISTRARS, and *Deputy Superintendent Registrars*.	
		Name.	Situation.	Name.	Address.
DEPWADE	Norfolk . . .	The Unitarian Chapel . . The Independent Meeting-house. Wortwell Independent Meeting-house. The Baptist Chapel . .	Diss . . . . Denton. Wortwell. Diss.	John Hotson. .	Long Stratton, Norfolk
DERBY	Derby . . .	Brookside Chapel . . . The Baptist Meeting-house The General Baptist Chapel Friar-gate Chapel . . .	Derby . . . . . . Brook-street, Derby. Sacheverel-street, Derby. Derby.	John Moody . .	Wardwick, Derby. .
DEVIZES	Wilts . . .	St. Mary's Chapel . . . The Presbyterian Chapel .	Northgate-street, Devizes . . Sheep-street, Devizes.	W. E. Tugwell .	Devizes . . . .
DEWSBURY	York	Ebenezer Chapel . . . Rehoboth . . . . . The Lower Chapel. . . Salem Chapel . . . . Grove Chapel	Dewsbury . . . . . . Morley, in the parish of Battley. Liversedge, in the parish of Birstal. Dewsbury. Gomersal, in the parish of Birstal.	William Carr *Charles Carr,*	Gomersall ; Leeds . *Ditto.*
DOCKING	Norfolk . . .	. . .	. . .	Francis Oakes .	Burnham Westgate, Norfolk.
DOLGELLY	Merioneth . .	Hên Gapel, otherwise Capel-yr-Annibynwyr. Capel Rehoboth, otherwise Capel Corris. Capel Sardis . . . . Capel Horeb . . . . Capel Ebenezer. . . . Capel Ebenezer. . . . Capel Salem	Meyrick-square, Dolgelly . . Corris, in the parish of Talyllyn. Llanfihangel-y-Pennant. Parish of Llanenddwyn. Llanegryn. Dinas Mowddwyn, in the parish of Mallwyd. Dolgelly.	Richard Jones .	Dolgelly . . . .
DONCASTER	York and Nottingham.	The Independent Chapel .	Hall-gate, Doncaster . . .	J. Falconar . . *Thomas White,*	Doncaster . . . . *New-street, Doncaster.*
DORCHESTER and CERNE	Dorset . . .	Durngate Street Chapel . The Old Presbyterian Meeting-house. Dorford Chapel. . . . The Independent Chapel .	Durngate-street, Dorchester . Pease-lane, Dorchester. Dorchester. Cerne Abbas.	Thomas Abbott . *Henry Lock,*	Dorchester ; Dorset . *Ditto.*
DORKING	Surrey . . .	West Street Chapel . .	West-street, Dorking . . .	George Hills. . *J. R. Cousins,*	Dorking . . . . *Ditto.*
DOVER	Kent . . .	Zion Chapel . . . . General Baptist Chapel . Wesleyan Chapel . . . The Catholic Chapel . . Pentside, Baptist . . .	Last-lane, Dover . . . . Adrian-street, Dover. Snargate-street, Dover. Dover. Commercial-quay, in the parish of St. Mary, Dover.	William Cross .	Charlton ; Dover . .
DOWNHAM	Norfolk . . .	. . .	. . .	Edward Hett . *F. B. Bell,*	Downham Market . *Ditto.*
DRAYTON	Salop	. . .	. . .	W. M. Wilkinson	Market Drayton . .
DRIFFIELD	York	Providence Chapel . . Bethesda Chapel . . .	Great Driffield . . . . . North Frodingham.	E. D. Conyers .	Great Driffield . .
DROITWICH	Worcester . .	Grafton Chapel. . . .	Grafton Manor	T. Richards . .	Hill-end House, Droitwich.
DROXFORD	Hants . . .	. . .	. . .	Henry C. Smith .	Hambledon ; Horndean, Hants.

REGISTRARS of MARRIAGES.		Registrars' Districts.	REGISTRARS of BIRTHS and DEATHS.		Deputy Registrars of Births and Deaths.	
Name.	Address.		Name.	Address.	Name.	Address.
Thomas Cotman.	Diss, Norfolk . . .	*Diss*	Thomas Cotman	Diss	Thomas Barkham	Diss.
Benjamin J. Crisp	Redenhall-with-Harleston, Norfolk.	*Harleston*	Benjamin J. Crisp	Harleston	Richard Priest	Harleston.
		Stratton	James Aldis . .	Long Stratton, Norfolk .	James Perfitt	Long Stratton.
		Forncett	Robert Holmes .	Tacolnestone, Long Stratton, Norfolk.	Elisha Philippo .	Tacolnestone, Long Stratton, Norfolk.
James Jay . .	Vernon-street, Derby .	*St. Peter's.* . . .	James Jay . .	Vernon-street, Derby . .	Samuel Harvey .	George-street, Derby.
J. T. Swanwick .	St. Mary's-gate, Derby	*St. Alkmund's.* . .	J. T. Swanwick .	St. Mary's-gate, Derby. .	E. Collumbell .	1, King-street, Derby.
Thomas Heppell.	Devizes	*Lavington*	John Glass . .	Lavington, Devizes.		
		Bishop's Cannings. . .	Edwin Sloper . .	Bishop's Cannings, Devizes.		
		Bromham and Potterne	James Tayler . .	Rowde, Devizes.		
		Devizes	John Withers . .	Devizes.		
William Pearson	Dewsbury	*Thornhill and Whitley.*	Thomas Beatson	Briesfield, Wakefield . .	William Beatson	Briesfield ; Wakefield.
William Swainson	Morley, Leeds.	*Mirfield*	William Oates . .	Mirfield, Dewsbury.		
		Liversedge and Heckmondwike.	Joseph Croft . .	Heckmondwike ; Leeds.		
		Gomersal	Thomas Clapham	Birstal ; Leeds.		
		Morley.	William Swainson	Morley ; Leeds.	John Harrison .	Havercroft, Batley ; Dewsbury.
		Batley.	Henry Brearely .	Carlinghow, Batley ; Dewsbury.		
		Soothill	Benj. Mortimer .	Hanging Heaton ; Dewsbury		
		Ossett	Benj. Pickersgill	Ossett ; Wakefield.		
		Dewsbury	William Pearson.	Dewsbury	Joshua Firth .	Dewsbury.
F. H. Church .	Burnham Westgate, Norfolk.	*Burnham*	F. H. Church .	Burnham Westgate, Norfolk.		
		Docking	F. Upjohn . .	East Rudham, Rougham, Norfolk.		
		Snettisham	Thomas Davies .	Snettisham, Lynn . .	William Purdy .	Snettisham, Lynn.
John Pugh . .	Barmouth	*Barmouth*	John Pugh . .	Barmouth	William Price .	Barmouth.
Hugh Evans . .	Talyllyn ; Dolgelly.	*Talyllyn*	Hugh Evans. .	Talyllyn ; Dolgelly. . .	Hugh Humphrey	Pentre-'r-Wern ; Mallwyd.
Charles Dunwell.	Doncaster	*Doncaster*	W. H. Scholfield	Fishergate, Doncaster.		
		Campsall	John Parish . .	Askern ; Doncaster.		
		Burnbrough . . .	Richard Bagshaw	Barmbrough ; Doncaster.		
		Tickhill	Jonathan Tyas .	Wadworth ; Doncaster.		
		Bawtry	Joseph Blythman	Bawtry.		
J. P. Aldridge .	Dorchester ; Dorset .	*Dorchester.* . . .	George Cull . .	Dorchester ; Dorset.		
		Piddletown . . .	John Cox . .	Piddletown ; Dorset.		
		Maiden Newton . .	William Burt . .	Maiden Newton ; Dorchester	James Elias Burt	Maiden Newton.
		Cerne	H. W. Norman .	Cerne Abbas ; Dorchester .	Edwin Norman .	Cerne Abbas ; Dorchester.
John Bull . .	Dorking	*Dorking*	John Bull . .	Dorking	John Norman .	Dorking.
David James. .	Capel ; Surrey.	*Capel*	David James. .	Capel ; Dorking.		
Rich. Beal . .	Hawkenbury-street, Pier, Dover.	*St. Mary*	William Bourher	St. Mary ; Dover . . .	Thomas King .	Chapel-street, Dover.
		St. James	S. M. Pain . .	Charlton-road, Dover . .	John Miles . .	Charlton, Dover.
		Hougham	Henry Mutton .	Buckland, Dover . . .	Thomas Curling.	Buckland ; Dover.
Charles Mumford	Downham Market .	*Downham*	Thomas G. Wales	Downham Market ; Norfolk		
		Wiggenhall. . . .	William Johnson	Watlington ; Downham Market, Norfolk.		
		Fincham	Henry C. B. Steele	Stoke Ferry ; Norfolk.		
Isaac Griffith .	Market Drayton . .	*Hodnet*	James Boydon .	Hodnet, Market Drayton .	Andrew Ashley .	Hodnet, Market Drayton
		Market Drayton . .	Robert Grosvenor	Market Drayton . . .	Thos. Mountford	Market Drayton.
		Moreton Say . .	Joseph Betteley .	Knighton, Market Drayton	Wm. Betteley .	Knighton, Market Drayton.
Abel Holtby . .	Great Driffield . .	*Driffield*	Henry Crozier .	Great Driffield.		
		Foston	T. Hebb, jun. .	Frodingham ; Great Driffield		
		Bainton	F. Hardy. . .	Bainton, Great Driffield.		
		Langtoft	John Atkinson .	Weaverthorpe, Great Driffield.	W. Belwood . .	Weaverthorpe, Great Driffield.
James Kitsell .	Droitwich	*Claines.*	James Willis . .	Fearnal Heath, Claines.		
		Omberstey and Hartlebury.	Thomas P. Medwin	Hartlebury, Stourport . .	Richard Lea . .	Hartlebury, Stourport.
		Droitwich	W. R. Jacques .	Droitwich	Thomas Heming	Droitwich.
Louis J. Lovekin	Bishop's Waltham .	*Westmeon*	George V. Rogers	Westmeon, Alton.		
		Bishop's Waltham .	L. J. Lovekin .	Bishop's Waltham.		
		Hambledon . . .	Francis Hoad .	Droxford, Alton.		

UNION, or SUPERINTENDENT REGISTRAR'S DISTRICT.	County.	Places of Public Worship situated therein, registered for Solemnization of Marriages.		SUPERINTENDENT REGISTRARS, and Deputy Superintendent Registrars.	
		Name.	Situation.	Name.	Address.
DUDLEY	Worcester , .	Independent Chapel . .	Ruiton, in the parish of Sedgley.	T. Shorthouse .	Vicar-street, Dudley .
		The Baptist Meeting-house	New-street, Dudley.		
		The Old Meeting-house .	Cosely, in the parish of Sedgley.		
		The Independent Chapel .	King-street, Dudley.		
		Wesley Chapel. . . .	Wolverhampton-street, Dudley.		
		All Saints	Sedgley.		
		The Protestant Dissenters' Chapel.	Wolverhampton-street, Dudley.		
DUNMOW	Essex	The Independent Meeting	New-street, Great Dunmow. .	Wm. Thos. Wade	Dunmow . . . .
		The Dissenting Meeting-house.	Mill Lane, Stebbing.	*Benj. Anderson.*	*Great Dunmow.*
		Old Independent Meeting	Bolford-street, Thaxted.		
DURHAM & LANCHESTER	Durham . . .	The Croxdale Roman Catholic Chapel.	Croxdale	John Wm. Hays	Durham . . . .
		St. Cuthbert's Chapel .	Old Elvet, in the parish of St. Oswald.		
		Esh Laude Chapel. . .	Esh Laude, in the parish of Lanchester.		
		St. Cuthbert's Chapel .	Brooms, in the parish of Lanchester.		
		Framwellgate Chapel .	Framwellgate, in the parish of St. Oswald.		
DURSLEY.	Gloucester . .	Old Town Meeting . .	Wotton-under-Edge . . .	Alfred Jackson .	Dursley . . .
		Bethesda Chapel . . .	Clap Yate-lane, Uley.		
		The Dursley Tabernacle .	Dursley.		
EASINGTON	Durham . . .	. . .	. . .	Robert Richardson	Easington, Sunderland, Durham.
EASINGWOLD	York	. . .	. . .	John Haxby .	Easingwold . . .
EASTBOURNE	Sussex . . .			George Whiteman	Eastbourne . . .
EAST GRINSTEAD. . .	Sussex . . .	Zion Chapel	Chapel-lane, East Grinstead .	John Smith . .	East Grinstead . .
		Copthorn Chapel . . .	Copthorn, in the parish of Worth.		
EASTHAMPSTEAD . .	Berks. . . .	. . .	. . .	Charles Cave .	Bracknell, Berks . .
EAST RETFORD . . .	Nottingham . .	. . .	. . .	Thomas Bigsby .	East Retford . . .
				John Mee,	*Ditto.*
EASTRY	Kent	Wingham Chapel . . .	Wingham	Edward Greey .	Potter's-st., Sandwich
		Independent Chapel . .	Lower-street, Deal.		
		Baptist Chapel. . . .	Eythorne.		
EAST STONEHOUSE . .	Devon . . .	St. Mary's Chapel . . .	St. Mary's-street, EastStonehouse	Richard Rodd .	East Stonehouse, Plymouth.
				Francis Hooff,	*Ditto.*
EAST WARD.	Westmoreland .	The Baptist Chapel . .	Market Brough	M. Hewitson . .	Kirkby Stephen, Market Brough.
ECCLESALL BIERLOW .	York	South-street Chapel . .	Ecclesall Bierlow	Benjamin Slater .	Sharrow Cottage, Sheffield.
		Hall of Science. . . .	Rockingham-street, Sheffield.	*William Firth,*	*Hanover-square, Ecclesall Bierlow, Sheffield.*
ECCLESFIELD	York	Holy Rood Chapel. . .	Barnsley, in the parish of Silkston.	Sam. Warburton.	Howsley Hall, Ecclesfield.
EDMONTON.	Middlesex, Essex, and Herts.	Enfield Highway Chapel .	Enfield	John Sawyer. .	Edmonton . . .
		St. Mary's Chapel. . .	Holly-place, Hampstead.	*W. C. Sawyer,*	*Enfield.*
		The Baptist Chapel . .	Paradise-row, Walsham Abbey.		
		Baptist Chapel . . .	Tottenham.		
		St. Francis-de-Sale's Chapel	Chapel-place, White Hart-lane, Tottenham.		
		St. John's Chapel . . .	Meeting-house-lane, Edmonton.		
		The Independent Chapel .	Chase-side, Enfield.		

REGISTRARS of MARRIAGES.		Registrars' Districts.	REGISTRARS of BIRTHS and DEATHS.		Deputy Registrars of Births and Deaths.	
Name.	Address.		Name.	Address.	Name.	Address.
Thomas Allen .	Abberley-street, Dudley	*Rowley Regis* . . .	John Whitehouse	Tippity-green, Rowley Regis, Dudley.	Richard Parkes .	Rowley Regis, Dudley.
		Tipton	T. Shorthouse .	Horsley-heath, Tipton; Dudley.	T. Shorthouse, jun.	Horsley-heath, Tipton ; Dudley.
		Sedgley	Benjamin Parker	Gornall, Sedgley, Dudley .	Richard Parker .	Gornall, Dudley.
		Dudley.	Thomas Allen .	Abberley-street, Dudley .	Joseph Shaw, jun.	Kates-hill, Dudley.
John Warner .	Great Dunmow . .	*Thaxted*	James Frye . .	Thaxted, Dunmow.		
		Stebbing	Stephen Ralph .	Bardfield Saling, Braintree.		
		Hatfield	Thomas Cocks .	Hatfield Broad Oak, Bishop's Stortford.		
		Dunmow	Joseph Grice. .	Great Dunmow, Essex.		
Thomas Clamp .	South-street, Durham	*St. Nicholas* . .	John Dubson. .	St. Giles's Gate, Durham.		
Anthony Hedley	Tanfield, Chester-le-Street.	*St. Oswald* . . .	Thomas Clamp .	South-street, Durham.		
		Lanchester . . .	Anthony Hedley.	Tanfield, Chester-le-Street		
		Tanfield	Robert Stott . .	Cawsey-hall, Tanfield, Chester-le-Street.		
Abraham Warner	Dursley	*Wotton-under-Edge*	Edward Page . .	Wotton-under-Edge.		
John Rogers . .	Wotton-under-Edge.	*Uley*	R. C. Harding .	Uley, Dursley.		
		Dursley	Abraham Warner .	Dursley.		
John Snaith . .	South Hetton ; Easington, Sunderland.	*Easington* . . .	John Snaith . .	South Hetton ; Easington.	George Snaith .	South Hetton ; Easington, Sunderland.
. . .	. . .	*Easingwold* . . .	R. T. Skaife . .	Easingwold . .	J. Langdale . .	Coxwold, Easingwold.
		Stillington . . .	F. Flower . .	Huby, Easingwold.		
		Coxwold	G. Spenceley .	Coxwold; Easingwold.		
George Wilson .	Seaford	*West Ham.* . . .	Harry Hurst . .	Willingdon, Eastbourne.		
Harry Hurst . .	Willingdon, Eastbourne	*Eastbourne.* . .	George Wilson .	South-street, Eastbourne.		
T. Charlwood .	East Grinstead . .	*Worth*	John Hunter. .	West Hoathley, East Grinstead.		
		Withyham. . . .	William Wallis .	Hartfield, East Grinstead.	Wm. Wallis, sen.	Hartfield, East Grinstead.
		East Grinstead .	Edward Heaver .	Ashurst Wood, East Grinstead.		
Wm. Wilcocks .	Bracknell, Berks .	*Bracknell* . . .	Thomas Croft .	Bracknell, Berks.		
		Sandhurst . . .	Joseph Warton .	Sandhurst, Blackwater, Hants.		
G. K. Holmes .	East Retford . .	*Clareborough* . . .	Jacob Ogle . .	Moorgate, Clareborough; East Retford.	R. Hodgkinson .	Clareborough.
		Retford	George Thornton	East Retford.		
		Gringley	Henry Raynes .	Gringley-on-the-Hill, Bawtry.	William Parkin .	Everton, Bawtry.
		Tuxford	Peter Whitington	Tuxford, Notts	J. T. Sharp .	Tuxford.
T. V. Cavell . .	17, Griffin-street, Deal	*Wingham*	Thomas Chandler	Wingham	Henry Denne .	Wingham.
J. L. Lass . .	Strand-street, Sandwich	*Eythorne* . . .	John Nash . .	Easole, Nonington, Wingham.	John Chandler .	Easole, Nonington, Wingham.
		Sandwich . . .	J. L. Lass . .	Strand-street, Sandwich .	John Friend .	Strand-street, Sandwich.
		Deal	T. V. Cavell . .	17, Griffin-street, Deal .	William Dear .	6, Coppen-street, Deal.
C. Chapple . .	Edgcumbe-street, East Stonehouse, Plymouth.	*East Stonehouse* .	John Capron. .	Clarence-place, East Stonehouse, Plymouth.	J. J. Boulter .	West Emma-place, East Stonehouse, Plymouth.
Thomas Tapp .	Edgcumbe-street, East Stonehouse.					
G. H. Bailey .	Brough	*Appleby*	Wm. Hewitson .	Appleby	Thomas Hewitson	Appleby.
		Kirkby Stephen . .	G. H. Bailey. .	Market Brough.		
		Orton	George Spencer .	Ravenstonedale, Market Brough.		
Rev. W. T. Kidd	Sheffield Cemetery .	*Ecclesall Bierlow* .	Rev. W. T. Kidd	Sheffield General Cemetery, Sheffield.	R. T. Taylor .	30, South-street, Sheffield Moor, Sheffield.
C. Poyner . .	Sharrow Moor, Sheffield	*Norton*	John Wreaks .	Norton, Derbyshire .	Francis Shaw .	Norton, Sheffield.
		Nether Hallam . .	William Birtles .	Bank view, near Crookes Workhouse; Sheffield.	Joseph Skelton .	Crookes, Sheffield.
		Upper Hallam and Dore	Richard Furness.	Dore, Derbyshire.		
Robert Cauwood .	Barnsley	*Barnsley*	John Ostcliffe .	Barnsley.		
		High Hoyland . .	George Wilby .	Denby Dale, Barnsley.		
		Cawthorn . . .	Thomas Shaw .	Cawthorn, Barnsley.		
		Royston . . *. .* .	John Ball . .	Royston, Barnsley .	J. Laverack . .	Royston.
		Darfield	Edward Watson .	Darfield, Barnsley.		
		Worsbrough . . .	Thomas Guest .	Worsbrough, Barnsley.		
H. Sawyer . .	Silver-street, Enfield .	*Edmonton* . . .	Daniel Judd . .	Bury-street, Edmonton.		
F. J. Robotham, jun.	High-street, Hampstead	*Tottenham* . . *. .*	George Ross . .	Church-road, Tottenham.		
		Hornsey and Highgate	Thomas Grimes .	Near the Church, Hornsey.		
		Enfield	George Capes .	Baker-street, Enfield .	G. L. Smartt. .	Baker-street, Enfield.
		Hampstead . . .	F. J. Robotham .	High-street, Hampstead.		
		Waltham Abbey .	John Mayhew .	Town, Waltham Abbey.		
		Cheshunt	Robert Archer .	Church Gate, Cheshunt.		

UNION, or SUPERINTENDENT REGISTRAR'S DISTRICT.	County.	Places of Public Worship situated therein, registered for Solemnization of Marriages.		SUPERINTENDENT REGISTRARS, and Deputy Superintendent Registrars.	
		Name.	Situation.	Name.	Address.
ELHAM	Kent	Ebenezer Chapel . . . The Baptist Meeting-house	Chapel-street, St. Leonard, Hythe Mill Bay, Folkestone.	Robert Thompson N. H. Chubb,	Lympne ; Hythe, Kent Lyminge.
ELLESMERE.	Salop	Independent Chapel . .	Chapel-street, Ellesmere . .	Robert Morrall . George Salter,	Plas Yollen; Elles-mere. Ellesmere.
ELY	Cambridge . .	Baptist Meeting-house . Countess of Huntingdon's Chapel. Baptist Meeting-house .	Haddenham . . . . . Parish of St. Mary, Ely. Sutton.	W. Marshall, jun.	Ely . . . . .
EPPING	Essex. . . .	The Baptist Chapel . The Baptist Chapel . Chigwell-row Chapel . The Baptist Chapel .	Loughton . . . . . Potter's-street, Harlow. Chigwell-row, Chigwell. Harlow Town.	John Windus .	Epping . . . .
EPSOM	Surrey . . .	The Independent Chapel .	Church-street, Epsom . .	William Everest. J. P. Bell,	Epsom . . . . . Ditto.
ERPINGHAM	Norfolk . . .	. . .	. . .	Joseph Covell .	Runton, Cromer, Nor-folk.
ETON	Bucks . . .	The Independent Chapel .	Chalvey, in the parish of Upton-cum-Chalvey.	C. P. Barrett. .	Register Office, High-street, Eton.
EVESHAM	Worcester & Glou-cester.	Baptist Chapel. . . .	Cowl-street, Evesham . .	J. B. Saunders .	Evesham . . . .
EXETER	Devon . . .	George's Meeting . . St. Nicholas' Chapel . Mint-lane Chapel . . Castle-street Chapel . Grosvenor Chapel . .	South-street, Exeter. . . The Mint, Exeter. Exeter. Exeter. St. Sidwell's, Exeter.	James Terrell . Edw. H. Roberts,	Exeter . . . . Ditto.
FAITH, ST.	Norfolk . . .	. . .	. . .	P. L. Carman .	St. Faith's, Norwich .
FALMOUTH	Cornwall . . .	The Baptists' Chapel . . The Wesleyan Methodist Chapel.	Webber's-street, Falmouth . . Falmouth.	W. J. Genn . .	Falmouth . . . .
FAREHAM	Hants . . .	The Independent Chapel .	Titchfield	Benj. P. Rubie .	Union Workhouse, Fareham.
FARINGDON	Berks, Oxon, and Gloucester.	The Baptist Chapel .	Faringdon	John Haines .	Faringdon . . .
FARNHAM	Surrey . . .	The Independent Chapel .	East-street, Farnham . .	Wm. J. Hollest . J. L. Hollest,	Farnham . . . Ditto.
FAVERSHAM	Kent	Partridge-lane Chapel .	Faversham	M. T. Irish . .	Faversham . . .
FESTINIOG	Merioneth . .	. . .	. . .	John Prichard .	Beddgelert, Carnarvon
FLEGG, EAST and WEST.	Norfolk . . .	. . .	. . .	R. B. Norman .	Rollesby, Norfolk. .
FOLESHILL	Warwick . . .	The Independent Chapel . The Independent Chapel .	Bedworth . . . . . Church-lane, Foleshill.	Richard Dewes . John Chattaway,	Foleshill . . . . Ditto.
FORDINGBRIDGE . . .	Hants and Wilts	The Independent Chapel .	Fordingbridge	G. C. Rawlence .	Fordingbridge, Hants
FOREHOE	Norfolk . . .	St. Augustine of England's Chapel. The Independent Chapel .	Cossey Hall, Cossey . . . . The Fairstead, in the parish of Wymondham.	Edward Press .	Hingham, Norfolk .
FREEBRIDGE LYNN . .	Norfolk . . .	. . .	. . .	Boys Aldham .	King's Lynn . . .
FROME	Somerset . . .	Zion Chapel . . . . Badcox-lane Meeting . The Wesleyan Chapel . Rook-lane Meeting . . The Baptist Chapel . Sheppard's Barton Chapel	Frome, Selwood . . . . Frome, Selwood. Frome. Frome. Beckington. South Parade, Frome, Selwood.	Lawrence Hagley John Hagley,	Frome . . . . . Ditto.

REGISTRARS of MARRIAGES.		Registrars' Districts.	REGISTRARS of BIRTHS and DEATHS.		Deputy Registrars of Births and Deaths.	
Name.	Address.		Name.	Address.	Name.	Address.
W. H. Birch.	Hythe	*St. Leonard, Hythe*	W. H. Birch.	Hythe.		
		Folkestone . . .	S. Macdonald .	Sandgate; Folkestone.		
		Elham	William Pittock	Elham.		
Joseph Hignett .	Ellesmere	*Ellesmere*	Joseph Hignett .	Ellesmere.		
		Baschurch . . .	William Parry .	Middle, Wem.		
		Overton . . .	Enoch Williams .	Penley, Ellesmere.		
		Hanmer	John Hunt . .	Hanmer, Ellesmere.		
M. Fisher . .	Ely	*Ely*	George Cole .	Ely	M. Fisher . .	St. Mary, Ely.
Henry Robinson.	Haddenham.	*Littleport* . .	R. Cheeseright .	Littleport, Ely	M. Cheeseright .	Littleport, Ely.
		Sutton . . .	R. Russell .	Witcham, Ely	S. C. Russell. .	Witcham, Ely.
		Haddenham	Henry Robinson.	Haddenham, Ely . . .	William Cuttriss	Haddenham, Ely.
Frederick Payne.	Epping	*Harlow*	John Chew . .	Potter's-street, Harlow, Essex.		
		Epping	George Moore .	Epping.		
		Chigwell . . .	P. Harding . .	Loughton, Essex.		
Charles Hills .	Epsom	*Leatherhead* . .	John Hill . .	Leatherhead.		
		Sutton	Geo. Henry Green	Sutton, Epsom.		
		Epsom	William Dorling	Epsom	Henry Dorling .	High-street, Epsom.
H. T. Murrell .	Cromer, Norfolk .	*Holt*	John Banks .	Holt.		
		Walsham . . .	John Coleby .	North Walsham.		
		Cromer . . .	T. Murrell .	Sustead, Cromer.		
Chas. Fox Barton	Eton	*Eton*	Jas. Wm. Needham	High-street, Eton.		
		Iver	Jas. Stratton .	Iver, Uxbridge.		
		Burnham . . .	John Williams .	Burnham, Maidenhead.		
John Wadams .	Bengeworth, Evesham	*Evesham* . . .	John Wadams .	Bengeworth, Evesham	Thomas Foster .	High-street, Evesham.
		Broadway . . .	John Tustin . .	Broadway, Evesham .	John Tustin, jun.	Broadway, Evesham.
Rob. T. Head .	Exeter . . .	*St. David* . . .	John Daw . .	Bedford Circus, Exeter.		
John Porter . .	The Mint, Exeter.	*St. Sidwell* . .	Fred. G. Farrant	St. Sidwell, Exeter. . .	S. Hooker . .	St. Sidwell, Exeter.
John Scarnett, jun.	St. Faith's, Norwich .	*St. Faith's.* . . .	Robert Richards .	St. Faith's, Norwich .	John Scarnett, jun.	St. Faith's, Norwich.
		Sprowston . . .	William Durrant.	Catton, Norwich.		
N. T. Tresidder .	Church-street, Falmouth.	*Constantine* . . .	Thomas Dunstan	Trecombe; Falmouth.		
		Falmouth . . .	Robert White .	High-street, Falmouth.	W. N. Buckett .	Falmouth.
		Penryn . . .	S. S. Street . .	Penryn	Thomas Pearce .	Lower-street, Penryn.
		Mylor	Henry Symons .	Flushing, Falmouth .	Samuel Steel .	Flushing, Falmouth.
William Case .	Fareham	*Titchfield* . . .	Edward Andrews	Titchfield, Hants.		
R. R. Brock . .	Titchfield.	*Fareham* . . .	William Case .	Fareham, Hants	Jas. Stubington .	High-street, Fareham.
James Fidel, jun.	Faringdon . . .	*Buckland* . . .	William Church.	Stanford, Faringdon, Berks.		
		Shrivenham . .	William Barnes .	Shrivenham, Faringdon .		
		Faringdon . .	John Pottow . .	Langford; Lechlade, Gloucestershire.		
William Mason .	Farnham	*Ash*	Henry Randall .	Frimley, Bagshot.		
		Farnham . . .	D. D. Brooke .	Farnham.		
		Farnborough . .	William Brown .	Cove, Bagshot, Surrey.		
		Headley . . .	Charles Berry .	Liphook, Hants.		
John Smith . .	Faversham . . .	*Teynham* . . .	James Flood . .	Teynham	William Stiles .	Green-st., Sittingbourne.
Henry Pringuer.	Selling, Kent.	*Boughton* . . .	Henry Pringuer .	Selling	Edward Amos .	Selling, Faversham.
James Flood .	Teynham, Kent.	*Faversham* . . .	John Smith . .	Faversham	J. L. Smith . .	Faversham.
Evan Evans .	. . .	*Festiniog* . . .	Evan Evans .	Tanybwlch; Carnarvon.		
Robert Morgan.		*Llanfihangel-y-Traethau*	Robert Morgan .	Harlech; Carnarvon.		
Thos. Roberts.		*Tremadoc* . . .	Thomas Roberts .	Tremadoc; Carnarvon.		
William Cooper .	Martham, Yarmouth .	*East Flegg* . . .	Robert S. Beare .	Ormesby St. Margaret, Norfolk.		
		West Flegg . .	William Cooper .	Martham, Great Yarmouth	James Cooper .	Filby, Great Yarmouth.
E. P. Turner .	Foleshill, Coventry .	*Foleshill* . . .	E. P. Turner .	Foleshill, Coventry.		
		Sowe	C. H. Parsons .	Shilton, Coventry.		
Joseph Langford .	Fordingbridge. . .	*Fordingbridge* . .	Joseph Langford	Fordingbridge	John Atkins . .	Fordingbridge.
J. A. Nash . .	Wymondham . .	*Costessey* . . .	H. Daveney, jun.	Bawburgh, Norfolk.		
Thomas Roulson	Costessey, Norwich.	*Wymondham* . .	Robt. Jas. Tunaley	Wymondham, Norfolk.		
J. G. Etches . .	Gaywood, King's Lynn	*Castle Rising* . .	J. G. Etches .	Gaywood, King's Lynn.		
William Pickrell.	Grimstone, King's Lynn	*Middleton* . . .	W. Pickerill . .	Grimstone, King's Lynn.		
		Hillington . . .	James Fisher .	Gt. Massingham, Rougham.		
		Gayton	John Headley .	Gayton, King's Lynn.		
Edw. Culverhouse .	Frome	*Kilmersdon* . .	John Brice . .	Kilmersdon, Frome.		
		Nunney . . .	James Nuth .	Nunney, Frome.		
		Road	T. W. Langley .	Road Beckington, Frome.		
		Frome	T. H. Payne .	Frome	John Payne . .	Cork-street, Frome.

UNION, or SUPERINTENDENT REGISTRAR'S DISTRICT.	County.	Places of Public Worship situated therein, registered for Solemnization of Marriages.		SUPERINTENDENT REGISTRARS, and Deputy Superintendent Registrars.	
		Name.	Situation.	Name.	Address.
FYLDE	Lancaster . .	St. Mary's Roman Catholic Chapel.	Lytham	R. B. Fisher . .	Kirkham . . . .
		St. Mary's Roman Catholic Chapel.	Westby, in the parish of Kirkham.		
		The Willows' Chapel . .	The Willows, within the township of Kirkham.		
GAINSBOROUGH . . .	Lincoln and Nottingham.	The Independent Chapel .	Gainsborough	Thomas Oldman	Gainsborough . .
GARSTANG	Lancaster . .	St. Thomas's Roman Catholic Chapel.	Claughton, in the parish of Garstang.	J. Gardner . .	Garstang . . . .
		Roman Catholic Chapel .	Great Eccleston.		
		Garstang Catholic Chapel.	Garstang.		
GATESHEAD	Durham . . .	Gateshead Presbyterian Chapel.	Half-Moon-lane, Gateshead .	Robert Lowthin .	Gateshead . . . .
		Bethesda Chapel . . .	Melbourne-street, Gateshead.		
		The Congregational Chapel	Melbourne-street, Gateshead.		
		Stella Catholic Chapel .	Stella, in the parish of Ryton.		
GEORGE, ST., HANOVER-SQUARE.	Middlesex . .	. . .	. . .	T. B. Chappell .	Board Room, Mount-street.
GEORGE, ST., EAST . .	Middlesex . .	. . .	. . .	Thomas Stone .	6, Wellclose-square, Minories.
GEORGE, ST., SOUTHWARK.	Surrey . . .	The Belgian Chapel . .	London-road, Southwark . .	J. Fitch . . .	17, Union-street, Southwark.
		The Independent Chapel .	Union-street, High-street, Southwark.		
		Guildford-street Chapel .	Little Guildford-st., St. George's, Southwark.		
		Great Suffolk-street Chapel	Great Suffolk-street.		
		St. John's Episcopal Chapel	London-road, in the parish of St. George, Southwark.		
GERMAN'S ST.	Cornwall and Devon.	. . .	. . .	E. H. Pedler .	Liskeard . . . .
GILES, ST., & ST. GEORGE	Middlesex . .	Sardinian Chapel . . .	Duke-street, Lincoln's Inn Fields	William Newbury	Chenies-street, Bedford-square.
		Eagle-street Meeting-house	Eagle-street, Holborn.		
		Gate-street Chapel . .	Gate-street, Lincoln's Inn Fields.		
		Eglise Suisse	Moor-street, in the parish of St. Giles-in-the-Fields.		
GLANDFORD BRIGG . .	Lincoln . . .	The General Baptist Chapel	Kirton-in-Lindsey	John Hett . .	Brigg . . . . .
		The Independent Chapel .	Brigg.	Thos. Freer,	Ditto.
GLENDALE	Northumberland.	Relief Chapel	Cheviot-street, Wooler . .	G. W. Howey .	Wooler, Northumberland.
		Branton Meeting-house .	Branton, in the parish of Eglingham.		
		The Presbyterian Meeting-house.	Crookham, in the parish of Ford.		
		Bethel Chapel	Lowick, in the parish of Lowick.		
		West Chapel	Wooler.		
GLOUCESTER	Gloucester . .	Barton-street Chapel .	Gloucester	J. F. Lexingham	Berkeley-street, Westgate-street, Gloucester.
		Southgate Independent Chapel.	Lower Southgate-street, Gloucester.		
		St. Mary's Chapel . . .	St. Mary's-square, Gloucester.		
GODSTONE	Surrey . . .	. . .	. . .	A. G. Davidson .	Bletchingley, Surrey .
GOOLE	York	. . .	. . .	J. Wilson . .	Goole, Yorkshire . .
GRANTHAM.	Lincoln . . .	Independent Chapel . .	Little Gonerby, Grantham . .	R. H. Johnston .	Grantham . . . .
GRAVESEND and MILTON	Kent	Prince's-street Chapel .	Gravesend	F. Southgate. .	King-street, Gravesend.

REGISTRARS of MARRIAGES.		Registrars' Districts	REGISTRARS of BIRTHS and DEATHS.		Deputy Registrars of Births and Deaths.	
Name.	Address.		Name.	Address.	Name.	Address.
M. M'Donnell	Lytham	Kirkham	William Gradwell	Kirkham.		
R. C. Richards	Kirkham.	Lytham	M. M'Donnell	Lytham, Kirkham.		
		Poulton	R. H. Porter.	Poulton.		
John W. Pashley	Gainsborough	Gainsborough	John W. Pashley	Gainsborough	J. C. Borwell	Gainsborough.
		Scotter	William Forman	Laughton, Gainsborough	John Cooling	Laughton, Gainsborough.
		Willingham	Thomas Jackson	Willingham, Gainsborough	Abraham Torn	Willingham, Gainsborough.
		Marton	George Oliver	Newton and Marton, Gainsborough.	W. Watkinson	Torksey, Gainsborough.
		Misterton	William Cross	Beckingham, Gainsborough	John Raynor	Saundby, Gainsborough.
		Owston	Robert Sharp	Owston, Bawtry	Wm. Fletcher	Owston, Bawtry.
Henry Threlfall	Garstang	Garstang	Henry Threlfall	Garstang	Gawen Benson	Garstang.
Hy. Walker	Great Eccleston.	St. Michael's	Henry Fisher	St. Michael's, Garstang.		
		Stalmine	William Birch	Stalmine, Garstang.		
Robert Foreman.	High-street, Gateshead	Gateshead	John Pattison	Darncrook, Gateshead.	Robert Foreman.	Gateshead.
		Heworth	Thomas Sill	Kirton Gate, Gateshead	John Sill	Kirton Gate.
		Whickham	William Oxwald.	Whickham, Gateshead.		
		Winlaton	Thomas Angus	Winlaton, Gateshead.		
Robert Lees	Board Room, Mount-street.	Hanover-square	Edward Jay	63, Davies-street, Berkeley-square.	G. B. Mason.	16, Duke-st., Grosvenor-square.
		May-fair	C. E. Chowne	Hertford-street, May-fair.		
		Belgrave	W. P. Jorden	9, Lower Belgrave-street, Eaton-square.		
Henry Baddeley	27, Colet-place, Commercial-road.	St. Paul's	Henry Baddeley.	27, Colet-place, Commercial-road.	J. B. Talbot.	9, Lower John-street, Commercial-road.
		St. Mary's	William L. Howell	40, Ratcliffe-highway,		
		St. John's	John Verrall	Charles-street, Old Gravel-lane.		
J. H. Fitch	17, Union-street, Southwark.	Kent-road	Richard Bell.	12, White-street, Southwark	Wm. Hammond.	5, White-street.
D. C. Lyon	4, Pitt-street, Old Kent-road.	Borough-road	James Bedwell	146, Blackfriars'-road, Southwark.		
		London-road	Arthur Redford	96, London-road, Southwark	E. A. Redford	96, London-road.
W. S. Porter.	St. Stephen's, Saltash	St. German's	Richard Pollgreen	St. German's.		
		Saltash	W. S. Porter.	St. Stephen's, Saltash.		
		Antony	Charles Chappell	St. John's, Torpoint, Cornwall.		
H. F. Pargues	15, Caroline-street, Bedford-square.	South District	George Lee	50, Great Queen-street, Lincoln's Inn Fields.	John Lee	50, Great Queen-street, Lincoln's Inn Fields.
		North District	James Wood	6, Great Russell - street, Bloomsbury.	John Sherrard	240, Tottenham Court-road.
		St. George	John Yardley	5, Thorney-street, Bloomsbury.	F. Tweeddale	14, Plumptre-street, Bloomsbury.
A. M. Serjeant	Brigg	Brigg	Wm. Bennett	Brigg	Henry Bourn	Brigg.
		Barton.	John Morley	Barton-upon-Humber.		
		Winterton	L. M. Bennett	Winterton ; Brigg.		
Wm. Wightman.	Wooler, Northumberland.	Ford	Ralph Patterson	Crookham ; Coldstream, Berwickshire.		
		Wooler.	Wm. Wightman.	Wooler ; Northumberland.		
Wm. Whitehead	4, College-court, Holy Trinity, Gloucester.	St. Nicholas	Wm. Whitehead	4, College-court, Gloucester	James Whitehead	College-ct., Gloucester.
		St. John Baptist	Samuel Jordan	Alvin-street, Gloucester.		
		South Hamlet	James Tanner	1, St. James's-place, Spa, South Hamlet, Gloucester.	Wm. Howitt.	Spa Pump-room, South Hamlet, Gloucester.
		Kingsholm	James Pilford	Wotton, St. Mary's Hamlet, Gloucester.	James Bloxsome	Wotton ; Gloucester.
		Godstone	L. A. Teather	Limpsfield, Godstone	John Sanderson	Limpsfield ; Godstone.
James Wake.	Goole, Yorkshire	Goole	W. E. Cass	Goole.		
		Snaith	A. J. Hodgson	Snaith.		
		Swinefleet	J. W. Hodgson	Swinefleet, Goole.		
John Newton	Grantham	Grantham	John Marshall	Little Gonerby, Grantham	J. R. Doughty	Grantham.
		Denton	Stephen Brice	Harston ; Grantham	Thos. Travis.	Harston ; Grantham.
		Colsterworth	Benj. Bright.	Colsterworth ; Grantham	Wm. Lamb	Colsterworth ; Grantham.
E. B. Arnold.	High-street, Gravesend	Gravesend and Milton	E. B. Arnold.	Gravesend	T. B. Butcher	Milton ; next Gravesend.

UNION, or SUPERINTENDENT REGISTRAR'S DISTRICT.	County.	Places of Public Worship situated therein, registered for Solemnisation of Marriages.		SUPERINTENDENT REGISTRARS, and *Deputy Superintendent Registrars*.	
		Name.	Situation.	Name.	Address.
GREENWICH	Kent	Maize-hill Chapel . . . Salem Chapel . . . . Greenwich-road Chapel The Catholic Chapel . . St. Mary's Catholic Chapel High-street (formerly Butt-lane) Meeting.	Maize-hill, Greenwich . . . Powis-street, Woolwich. Greenwich-road. Clark's-buildings, East-street, Greenwich. Green's-end, New-road, Wool-wich. High-street, Deptford.	E. W. James. .	Croom's Hill, Green-wich.
GUILDFORD.	Surrey . . .	The Independent Chapel. The Sutton Place Catholic Chapel.	Chapel-street, Guildford . . Woking.	G. S. Smallpiece	Guildford . . . .
GUILTCROSS . . .	Norfolk . . .	. . .	. . .	Thomas Turner .	Kenninghall, East Har-ling, Norfolk.
GUISBOROUGH . . .	York	. . .	. . .	William Walker. *Jas. Bird,*	Guisborough . . . *Ditto.*
HACKNEY	Middlesex . .	New Gravel-pit Meeting-house. Old Gravel-pit Meeting-house. Kingsland Chapel . . . The Baptist Chapel . . St. Thomas's-square Meet-ing-house. Abney Chapel . . . . The New Chapel . . .	Paradise-fields, Hackney . . Morning-lane, Hackney. Robinson's-row, Kingsland. Mare-street, Hackney. St. Thomas's-square, Hackney. Church-street, Stoke Newington. Upper Clapton.	C. H. Pulley . .	Upper Homerton . .
HAILSHAM	Sussex . . .	Independent Chapel . . The Baptist Chapel . .	Lionscross, in the parish of Herstmonceux. Hailsham.	Henry Isted . .	Hellingly, Hailsham .
HALIFAX.	York	Hanover-street Chapel Ebenezer Primitive Metho-dist Chapel. Square Chapel . . . Northgate-end Chapel. Sion Chapel . . . Providence Chapel. . Bridge-end Chapel. . Harrison-road Chapel. Providence Chapel. . Booth Chapel . .	Halifax . . . . . . Pellon-lane, Halifax. Halifax. Halifax. Wade-street, Halifax. Stainland, in the parish of Halifax. Rastrick, in the parish of Halifax. Halifax. Ovenden, in the parish of Halifax. Midgley, in the parish of Halifax.	Charles Barstow. *H. B. Brunett,*	Halifax . . . . *Ditto.*
HALSTEAD	Essex. . . .	The Old Independent Chapel	Parsonage-lane, in the parish of Halstead.	C. D. Hustler .	Halstead . . . .
HALTWHISTLE . . .	Northumberland.	. . .	. . .	John Lee. . . .	Brampton, Cumberland.
HAMBLEDON	Surrey . . .	. . .	. . .	C. J. Woods . .	Godalming . . .
HARDINGSTONE . . .	Northampton .	The Baptist Chapel . . Yardley Chapel . . .	Road . . . . Yardley-Hastings.	C. Markham . .	Northampton . . .
HARTISMERE	Suffolk . . .	The Baptists'	Eye	H. W. Buchanan	Eye, Suffolk . . .
HARTLEY WINTNEY. .	Hants . . .	Odiham Chapel . . . The Baptist Chapel . .	Odiham . . . . Hartley-row.	James Brooks .	Odiham, Hants . .
HASLINGDEN	Lancaster . .	Goodshaw Higher Chapel Baptist Chapel. . . . New Jerusalem . . .	Goodshaw, in the parish of Higher Booths. Accrington. Abbey-street, Accrington.	Henry King . .	Haslingden . . .
HASTINGS	Sussex . . .	The Croft Chapel . . .	The Croft, Hastings . . .	Henry Thatcher . *Richard Harmon,*	Hill-street, Hastings. Union *Workhouse*
HATFIELD and WELWYN	Herts. . . .	Park-street Chapel . .	Hatfield	John H. Binyon.	Northaw, Barnet . .

REGISTRARS of MARRIAGES.		Registrars' Districts.	REGISTRARS of BIRTHS and DEATHS.		Deputy Registrars of Births and Deaths.	
Name.	Address.		Name.	Address.	Name.	Address.
Thos. Marchant .	High-street, Deptford	*St. Paul's, Deptford*	Thos. Marchant .	High-street, St. Paul's, Deptford.	G. R. Scudamore	22, King-street. New-Town, Deptford.
James Black .	Powis-street, Woolwich.	*St. Nicholas, Deptford*	T. Gathercole, jun.	Creek Bridge-road, St. Nicholas, Deptford.		
Arthur Waller .	Norfolk-place, Woolwich-road, Greenwich.	*Woolwich Arsenal.*	Richard Rixon .	Beresford-square, Woolwich.	Wm. Cock . .	Green's-end ; Woolwich.
Robert Suter. .	London-street, Greenwich.	*Woolwich Dock-yard*	William Nokes .	Rectory-place, Woolwich.		
		Greenwich, East .	Arthur Waller .	Norfolk-place, Woolwich-road, Greenwich.	M. P. Stoneham.	Trafalgar-road, Greenwich.
		Greenwich, West .	Robert Suter. .	London-street, Greenwich.	T. Jarman . .	South-street, Greenwich
G. W. Bailey .	Guildford	*Guildford* . .	Richard Eager .	St. Mary, Guildford .	G. W. Bailey .	Guildford.
		Godalming . . .	Richard Balchin .	Godalming	C. A. Parsons .	Godalming.
		Albury . . .	John Higgins .	Shere, Guildford . .	John Clarke .	Godalming.
		Ripley . . .	Henry White .	Ripley, Guildford . .	Robert Gavill .	Ripley, Guildford.
		Woking . . .	John Hooper. .	Woking, Guildford. .	William Hart .	Woking, Guildford.
Thomas Rackham	Kenninghall, Harling	*Eastern or Banham, and Buckenham.*	J. Cunningham .	Winfarthing, Diss. .	J. W. Jarrett .	Winfarthing, Diss.
		Western or Kenninghall, and Harling.	Thomas Rackham	Kenninghall, Harling .	W. Wells . .	Kenninghall.
William Wilson .	Guisborough . . .	*Guisborough* .	H. W. Wilson .	Guisborough . . .	William Wilson .	Guisborough.
		Lofthouse . .	John Yeoman .	Lofthouse, Guisborough.		
		Marske . . .	Thomas Bird .	Marske, Guisborough.		
		Kirkleatham . .	Charles Bailey .	Kirkleatham, Guisborough.		
		Danby . . .	Thomas Appleby	Castleton, Guisborough.		
Thos. Christie .	Upper Homerton .	*Hackney* . . .	Robert Butts. .	Church-street, Hackney.		
		Stamford-hill .	J. W. Montaigne	Upper Clapton, Hackney.		
		South Hackney .	William Drewett.	Grove-street, South Hackney.		
		West Hackney .	W. B. Robinson.	Shacklewell-lane, West Hackney.	W. H. Robinson.	Shacklewell-lane, West Hackney.
		Stoke Newington .	William Yardley	Stoke Newington-road.	Richard Stieb, jun.	Mare-street, South Hackney.
Henry Potter .	Wartling, Battle .	*Hailsham* . . .	Henry Potter .	Cowbeech, Battle . .	Jabez Pureglove.	Herstmonceux, Battle.
		Hellingly . . .	Isaac Wratten .	Hellingly, Hailsham.		
William Corke .	Halifax	*Halifax* . . .	J. Crowther .	Halifax	Abel Wadsworth.	Great Albion-street, Halifax.
Jeremiah Stead .	Ovenden.	*Elland.* . . .	Walter Smith .	Elland, Halifax . .		
Walter Smith .	Elland.	*Southowram* . .	Thomas Mann .	Southowram, Halifax.		
		Brighouse . . .	Thomas Jessop .	Brighouse, Halifax .	Thomas Cawthra	Brighouse, Huddersfield.
		Rastrick . . .	Jos. Wrigley .	Rastrick, Huddersfield.		
		Sowerby . . .	J. Utley . .	Sowerby-bridge, Halifax .	B. Utley . . .	Sowerby Bridge.
		Rippenden . .	J. Shaw . . .	Barkisland, Halifax.		
		Luddenden . .	Joshua Wormald	Luddenden, Halifax .	Joshua Wormald, jun.	Riding Head, Warley, Halifax.
		Northowram . .	William Moore .	Northowram, Halifax .	J. Greenwood .	Schoolcroft, Ovenden.
		Ovenden . . .	Alexander Spencer	Ovenden, Halifax . .		
George Evans .	Halstead	*Halstead* . . .	Benjamin Gilson	Halstead, Essex . .	S. Rodick . .	Halstead, Essex.
James Cardinall .	Halstead.	*Hedingham* . .	Fred. Fitch . .	Sible Hedingham, Essex	F. N. Fitch . .	Sible Hedingham, Halstead.
George Pickering	Stonehall, Haltwhistle, Northumberland.	*Haltwhistle* . . .	George Pickering	Stonehall, Haltwhistle, Northumberland.		
Frederick Yate .	Hambledon, Godalming	*Cranley* . . .	Jacob Ellery .	Cranley, Guildford .	R. R. Sutliffe .	Cranley, Guildford.
		Witley . . .	Fred. Yate . .	Hambledon, Godalming .	James Yate . .	Hambledon, Godalming
Charles Sawbridge	Piddington, Northampton.	*Hardingstone* . .	Charles Sawbridge	Piddington, Northampton.		
F. Longland .	Yardley-Hastings, Northampton.	*Brafield* . . .	F. Longland . .	Yardley-Hastings, Northampton.		
F. T. Jeyes .	Wootton, Northampton	*Milton* . . .	F. T. Jeyes . .	Wootton, Northampton.		
George Mudd, jun.	Eye, Suffolk . . .	*Botesdale* . . .	R. H. Harris. .	Botesdale, Suffolk.		
		Eye	George Edwards.	Eye.		
		Mendlesham . .	William Cuthbert	Mendlesham, Thwaite, Suffolk.		
Geo. Cook, jun. .	Odiham, Hants . .	*Hartley Wintney* . .	C. T. Howard .	Hartley-row, Hartford Bridge, Hants.		
		Odiham and Crondall .	Samuel Andrews.	Odiham.		
Daniel Nuttall .	Accrington, Bury . .	*Accrington* . . .	Daniel Nuttall .	Accrington, Bury, Lancashire.		
Richard Pickup .	Edenfield, Bury, Lancashire.	*Haslingden.* . .	James Wilding .	Haslingden.	T. Wilding . .	Haslingden.
George Ashworth	New Church, Rochdale, Lancashire.	*Edenfield* . . .	Richard Pickup .	Edenfield, Bury, Lancashire.	T. Pickup . .	Edenfield.
William Robinson	Haslingden.	*Rossendale* . . .	James Rawstron.	New Hall, Hey, Rawtenstall ; Manchester.		
		New Church . .	George Ashworth	New Church, Rochdale	John Ogden . .	Booth Fold, Rochdale.
James Swale .	Hastings	*All Saints* . . .	Fred. C. Inskipp	Hastings	B. Breeds . .	Hastings.
		St. Mary's. . .	J. G. Glandfield.	Hastings	W. Longley . .	7, West-street, Hastings.
		Ore	John Cloke . .	Guestling	T. Cloake . .	Guestling.
William Sandon .	Hatfield	*Hatfield*	William Sandon.	Hatfield	J. Bridgens . .	Hatfield.
		Welwyn . . .	John B. Ring .	Welwyn.		

UNION, or SUPERINTENDENT REGISTRAR'S DISTRICT.	County.	Places of Public Worship situated therein, registered for Solemnization of Marriages.		SUPERINTENDENT REGISTRARS, and Deputy Superintendent Registrars.	
		Name.	Situation.	Name.	Address.
HAVANT	Hants . . .	The Havant Meeting-house	The Pallant, Havant . . .	C. B. Longcroft .	Havant . . . . .
HAVERFORDWEST . .	Pembroke . .	Old Meeting-house . .	Upper Solva, in the parish of Whitechurch, in Dewsland.	Richard James .	High-street, Haverfordwest.
		Treffgarne	Treffgarne, in the parish of Brawdy.		
		Tabernacle	St. Martin's, Haverfordwest.		
		Rhosycaeran	Rhosycaeran.		
		Tabernacle	Milford, in the parish of Steynton.		
		Short Lane Chapel .	Milford, in the parish of Steynton.		
		Baptist Chapel. . . .	Fishguard.		
		Saron	Letterston.		
		Ebenezer Chapel . . .	St David's.		
HAY	Brecknock . .	. . .	. . .	Thomas Lewis .	Hay, S. W. . . . .
HAYFIELD and GLOSSOP.	Derby . . .	The Independent Chapel .	Charlesworth, in the parish of Glossop.	E. Adamson . .	Hayfield, Stockport .
		The Marple Bridge Chapel	Marple Bridge, in the parish of Glossop.		
		All Saints' Chapel . . .	Glossop.		
HEADINGTON	Oxon and Bucks	The Roman Catholic Chapel	High-street, St. Clement's, Oxford.	P. Walsh, jun. .	St. Giles's, Oxford .
HELMSLEY	York	Ampleforth College . .	Ampleforth	William Rowland	Helmsley . . . . .
HELSTON	Cornwall . . .	. . .	. . .	Glynn Grylls .	Helston . . . .
HEMEL HEMPSTED . .	Herts . . .	Baptist Meeting-house .	Hemel Hempsted	Rev. T. Hopley .	Hemel Hempsted . .
HENDON	Middlesex . .	Mill-hill Chapel . . .	Mill-hill, in the parish of Hendon	W. S. Tootell .	Edgeware . . . .
HENLEY	Oxon	The Independent Chapel .	Rotherfield Grays, Henley-on-Thames.	C. H. Chapman .	Henley-on-Thames .
		Stonor Chapel . . .	Stonor, in the parish of Pirton.		
		Providence Chapel . .	Rotherfield Peppard.		
HENSTEAD	Norfolk . . .	. . .	. . .	Thomas Faulkner	Swainsthorpe, Norwich
HEREFORD and DORE .	Hereford . . .	Eign Brook Chapel . .	Eign Brook, Hereford . . .	N. Lanwarne .	St. John-st., Hereford
HERTFORD	Herts . . .	Cowbridge Chapel . .	Hertford	Thomas Sworder	Hertford . . . .
HEXHAM.	Northumberland	The Broad-Gate's Chapel	Hexham	John Stokoe . . *William Turner*,	Hexham . . . . Ditto.
HIGHWORTH and SWINDON.	Wilts. . . .	. . .	. . .	A. S. Crowdy .	Swindon, Wilts . .
HINCKLEY	Leicester. . .	The Independent Chapel .	Stockwell Head, Hinckley .	Benjamin Law .	Hinckley . . . .
		The General Baptist Chapel	Stockwell-road, Hinckley.		
		The Catholic Chapel . .	Priory, Hinckley.		
HITCHIN	Herts. . . .	Back-street Meeting . .	Back-street, Hitchin . . .	William Stevens .	Hitchin . . . .
		Tillhouse-street Meeting .	Hitchin.		
HOLBEACH	Lincoln . . .	The General Baptist Chapel	Fleet Hargate, in the parish of Fleet.	Edward Key *F. W. Beeston*,	Holbeach . . . . Ditto.
		The General Baptist Chapel	Sutton St. James.		
		The Independent Chapel .	Sutton St. Mary, in the parish of Long Sutton.		

REGISTRARS of MARRIAGES.		Registrars' Districts.	REGISTRARS of BIRTHS and DEATHS.		Deputy Registrars of Births and Deaths.	
Name.	Address.		Name.	Address.	Name.	Address.
Henry Parker	Havant	Havant.	Henry Parker	Havant.		
Thomas Ellis	Hill-lane, Haverford-west.	Haverfordwest.	Thomas Ellis	Hill-lane, Haverfordwest.		
Thomas James	Solva, St. David's.	Milford	James Saies	Middle-street, Milford.		
D. Bateman	Rhosycaeran, St. Nicholas, Fishguard.	Fishguard	Thomas Williams	Wallis; Haverfordwest.		
		St. David's	Thomas James	Solva, St. David's.		
James Watkins	Hay, S. W.	Hay, S. W.	John Games	Hay, S. W.		
		Clyro	William Morgan	Glasbury, Hay, S. W.		
		Talgarth	John James	Aberlluavy, Hay, S. W.		
Dennis Rangeley	Hayfield, Stockport	Hayfield	George Lomas	Disley; Stockport.		
T. Dickinson	Glossop.	Glossop.	Tobias Dickinson	Glossop, Manchester.		
H. A. Maybury	St. Giles's, Oxford	St. Clement's	Richard Wood	St. Clement's, Oxford.		
		Wheatley	John Smith	Wheatley, Oxon.		
John Ness	Helmsley	Oswaldkirk	John Sootheran	Ampleforth, Helmsley.	Richard Pipes	Ampleforth.
		Kirby Moorside	Thomas M. Cole	Kirby Moorside.		
		Helmsley	John Ness	Helmsley	R. Allcroft	Helmsley.
John Kerby	Meneage-st., Helston	Helston	J. Kerby	Meneage-street, Helston.		
		St. Keverne	Thomas Pearce	Church-town, St. Keverne, Helston.		
		Wendron	John Pascoe	Trussell Wendron, Helston	John Pascoe, jun.	Trussell Wendron.
		Breage	Thomas Mitchell	Rinsey, Breage, Helston.		
		Crowan	William Floyd	Praze, Crowan, Camborne.		
Henry Humphrey	Hemel Hempsted.	Hemel Hempsted	Henry Humphrey	Hemel Hempsted.		
		King's Langley	Joseph Hill	King's Langley.		
		Flamstead	Thomas Hoar	Flamstead Market-street.		
A. R. Greene.	Little Stanmore	Hendon	W. Charsley.	Hendon.		
		Willesden	George Bilney	Kensall-green, Harrow-road.		
		Edgeware	Alfred Greene	Stanmore.		
		Harrow	F. Winkley	Harrow	W. Winkley	Harrow.
Joseph Soundy	Fair-mile, Henley-on-Thames.	Henley	Thomas Hester	Market-place, Henley-on-Thames.	T. Allen	Henley.
		Watlington	Thomas Nightingale.	Watlington, Tetsworth, Oxford.	William Barnes	Watlington.
John Lee	Shottisham, Norwich.	Henstead	Henry Larke	Framingham Pigot, Norwich	J. W. Girling	Framingham Pigot, Norwich.
		Humbleyard	M. B. Petchell	Bracon Ash, Norwich.		
James Fowler	St. John-street, Hereford.	Hereford	George R. Terry	St. Owen-street, Hereford.		
		Fownhope	James Morgan	Nunnington, Hereford.		
		Burghill	William Lewis	Holmer, Hereford.		
		Dewchurch	Daniel West	Much Birch, Hereford.		
		Kentchurch	John Farr	Abbey, Dore, Hereford.		
		Clodock	John Price	Longtown, Hereford.		
		Madley.	C. T. Bigelstone.	Madley, Hereford.		
John Simson.	Hertford	Watton.	James Bowdler	Watton, Hertford.		
		Hertford	John Simson.	Hertford	H. H. Carter	Hertford.
Joseph Fairless	Hexham	Hexham	James Fairlam	Hexham	J. Murton	Hexham.
		Allendale	George Dickenson	Allendale Town, Hexham.	J. Shield	Allendale Town, Hexham.
		Bywell	John Hunter	Prudhoe, Hexham	William Jordan	Ovingham, Hexham.
		Chollerton	William Hemsley	Acomb, Hexham	Robert Storey	West Acomb, Hexham.
J. C. Salmon	Highworth	Highworth.	J. C. Salmon	Highworth.		
		Swindon	W. E. T. Goodenough.	Wroughton, Marlborough.		
Thomas Vann	Hinckley	Hinckley	Thomas Vann	Hinckley.		
		Earl Shilton	W. T. Walker	Earl Shilton, Hinckley.		
		Burbage	Richard Garner	Burbage, Hinckley.		
John Palmer	Bucklersbury, Hitchin	Hitchin.	James Coleman	Hitchin.		
		Baldock	John Smith	Baldock.		
E. B. Vise	Holbeach	Holbeach	E. B. Vise	Holbeach	T. Bingham	Holbeach.
		Long Sutton	James Newman	Long Sutton, Lincolnshire	J. Markillie	Long Sutton, Lincolnshire.
		Gedney-hill	James Perkins	Holbeach Drove, Lincolnshire.		

UNION, or SUPERINTENDENT REGISTRAR'S DISTRICT.	County.	Places of Public Worship situated therein, registered for Solemnization of Marriages.		SUPERINTENDENT REGISTRARS, and Deputy Superintendent Registrars.	
		Name.	Situation.	Name.	Address.
HOLBORN	Middlesex	John-street Chapel The New Jerusalem Church	John-street, Doughty-street Cross-street, Hatton-garden.	W. R. James. E. W. James,	23, Ely-place, Holborn Ditto.
HOLLINGBOURN	Kent	Ebenezer Chapel Ebenezer Chapel	Sutton Valence Harrietsham-lane, in the parish of Lenham.	William James	Maidstone
HOLSWORTHY	Devon	Bethesda Chapel	Corfcott Green, in the parish of Clawton.	Charles Kingdon	Holsworthy
HOLYWELL	Flint	Cyssegr St. Winifred's Chapel. The Independent Chapel. Ebenezer Bethel Chapel	Heol Mostyn, in the parish of Whitford. Holywell. Chapel-street, Holywell. Rhes-y-cae, in the parish of Halkin. Pen-y-ball, St., in the parish of Holywell.	J. Oldfield, jun.	Holywell
HONITON	Devon	The Baptist Bridge Meeting The Independent Meeting The Baptist Meeting Marsh Chapel The Old Dissenting Meeting-house. The Independent Meeting-house.	High-street, Honiton High-street, Honiton. Silver-street, Honiton. Sidmouth. Sidmouth. Ottery St. Mary.	Philip Mules	Honiton
HOO	Kent			H. Wickham	Strood, Kent
HORNCASTLE	Lincoln	The Independent Chapel . The General Baptist Chapel The Wesleyan Methodist Chapel.	Horncastle Coningsby. Horncastle.	Edward Babington	Horncastle
HORSHAM	Sussex	General Baptist Chapel	Chapel-lane, Horsham	William Stedman	Horsham
HOUGHTON-LE-SPRING	Durham	Bethel Chapel	Easington Lane, Houghton-le-Spring.	William Archbold	Houghton-le-Spring
HOWDEN	York	The Independent Chapel	Howden	George England	Howden
HOXNE	Suffolk	Horham Chapel	Horham	George Pearl	Hoxne, Eye
HUDDERSFIELD	York	Highfield Independent Chapel. Salendine Nook Baptist Chapel. St. Patrick's Church Moorbottom Independent Chapel. The Wesleyan Methodist Chapel. Lockwood Baptist Chapel . The Independent Chapel.	Highfield, in the parish of Huddersfield. Salendine Nook, in the parish of Huddersfield. Huddersfield. Honley, in the parish of Almondbury. Holmfirth, in the parish of Almondbury. Buxton-road, Lockwood, in the parish of Almondbury. Lane, Holmfirth, in the parish of Almondbury.	C. S. Floyd . Horatio Haldenby.	Huddersfield Ditto.
HUNGERFORD	Berks.	The Independent Chapel .	High-street, Hungerford	William Rowland C. Culverhouse,	Ramsbury, Wilts Ditto.
HUNTINGDON	Hunts	The Dissenting Chapel . The Baptist Chapel The Baptist Meeting-house Particular Baptist Chapel	Huntingdon In the Great White, in the parish of Ramsey. Spaldwick. Godmanchester.	Charles Margetts Richard Cross,	Huntingdon Ditto.
JAMES, ST., WESTMINSTER.	Middlesex	Craven Chapel The Bavarian Chapel .	Marshall-street, Golden-square Warwick-street, Regent-street.	George Buzzard .	50, Poland-street, Oxford-street.

REGISTRARS of MARRIAGES.		Registrars' Districts.	REGISTRARS of BIRTHS and DEATHS.		Deputy Registrars of Births and Deaths.	
Name.	Address.		Name.	Address.	Name.	Address.
J. W. Wilkes .	7, Little Gray's-inn-lane	St. George the Martyr	Charles Marchant	13, East-street, Lamb's Conduit-street.	G. Stripling . .	21, Eagle-street.
		St. Andrew's (Western)	Richard Bardons	75, Red Lion-st., Holborn	John Bardons .	27, Bedford-street, Bedford-row.
		St. Andrew's (Eastern)	John Lloyd . .	66, Gray's-inn-lane. . .	Lazarus Holmes.	7, Dorrington-street, Leather-lane.
		Saffron-hill . . .	Thomas Truman.	23, Vine-st., Hatton-garden	John Cover . .	12, Charles-street, Hatton-garden.
J. West . . .	Hollingbourn . .	Hollingbourn . .	C. Sedgwick . .	Hollingbourn.		
		Lenham . . .	George Baily .	Lenham.		
		Headcorn . . .	John Leaver .	Chart-next-Sutton, Maidstone.		
Samuel Fry, jun..	Holsworthy . . .	Black Torrington .	James Gilbert .	Black Torrington; Hatherleigh.		
		Broadwoodwidger .	William Bond .	Ashwater; Holsworthy.		
		Clawton . . .	Robert Veale .	Clawton; Holsworthy.		
		Holsworthy . .	Samuel Fry, jun.	Holsworthy.		
		Milton Damerel .	P. Saunders . .	Milton Damerel, Holsworthy		
Wm. Jones . .	Holywell	Mold	Dr. Edward Thos. Hughes.	Mold.		
		Holywell . . .	Peter Williams .	Holywell.		
		Whitford . . .	Thomas Vickers .	Holywell.		
		Flint	John Haywood .	Flint.		
George Turner .	Honiton	Honiton . . .	George Turner .	Honiton.	G. Turner, jun. .	Honiton.
		Ottery St. Mary, and Sidmouth.	Edward Carter .	Ottery St. Mary, Devon.		
. . .	. . .	. . .	. . .	. . .	John Blyther .	Hoo, Rochester.
W. R. King . .	Coningsby. . . .	Horncastle.	William Ward .	Horncastle	Thomas Fawssett	Horncastle.
Thomas Johnson	Horncastle.	Tattershall . . .	Richard Martin .	Coningsby, Horncastle	T. Cuthbert .	Coningsby; Horncastle
		Tetford. . . .	Jarvis Barnes .	Tetford, Horncastle	John Foster .	Tetford; Horncastle.
		Wragby . . .	William Brothwall	Wragby, Lincolnshire. .	Richard Brothwell	Wragby.
Robert Rowland	Horsham	Horsham . . .	Wm. Adamthwaite	Horsham	John Clarke . .	Horsham.
J. Humphrey .	Near Painshaw, Sunderland.	Houghton-le-Spring .	J. Humphrey .	Near Painshaw, Sunderland.		
John Elliott . .	East Rainton, Durham.	Hetton-le-Hole . .	John Elliott . .	East Rainton, Durham.		
Thomas Turton .	Howden	Howden . . .	Thomas Turton .	Howden.		
		Newport . . .	H. J. Raines .	Newport ; Howden.		
		Hulme . . .	Robert Burnham	Holme-upon-Spaldingmoor, Market Weighton.		
		Bubwith . . .	George Newstead	Bubwith ; Howden.		
Benaiah Bryant .	Wilby, Woodbridge .	Stradbroke . . .	John Claxton .	Stradbroke.		
		Dennington . . .	William Bloss .	Brundish ; Framlingham.		
William Bradley	Commercial-square, Huddersfield.	Huddersfield . .	William Bradley	Commercial-square, Huddersfield.	John Bradley .	King-street, Huddersfield.
Richard Harrison	Holmfirth ; Huddersfield.	Almondbury . .	Joseph Dean .	Almondbury, Huddersfield.		
		Kirkheaton . .	George S. Dyson	Kirkheaton ; Huddersfield.		
		Kirkburton. . .	James Binns . .	Kirkburton, Huddersfield.		
		New Mill . . .	John Ibberson .	Butterley, Fulstone, Huddersfield.		
		Holmfirth . . .	Richard Harrison	Holmfirth ; Huddersfield.		
		Honley . . .	Rev. Jas Potter .	Honley ; Huddersfield.		
		Meltham . . .	Joseph Taylor .	Meltham ; Huddersfield.		
		Lockwood . . .	Rev. F. W. Dyer,	Lockwood; Huddersfield.		
		Slaithwaite . .	John Roberts .	Linthwaite ; Huddersfield.		
		Golcar. . . .	John Wilkinson .	Golcar; Huddersfield.		
James Jelfs . .	Hungerford, Berks	Lambourn . . .	David Kennard .	Lambourn	A. Gearing . .	Lambourn.
		Hungerford . .	James Jelfs . .	Hungerford	Thomas Jelfs .	Hungerford.
		Kintbury . . .	John Lidderdale	Kintbury ; Newbury.	J. Philips. . .	Kintbury ; Newbury.
Edward Goodrick	Godmanchester, Huntingdon.	Huntingdon . .	Robert Fox . .	Godmanchester, Hunts.		
Richard Bond .	Ramsey, Huntingdon	Sawtry. . . .	William Burton .	Sawtry ; Stilton.		
		Spaldwick . . .	J. E. Lindeman .	Spaldwick, Huntingdon.		
		Ramsey . . .	G. S. Ravenscroft	Ramsey ; Huntingdon.		
John Buzzard .	50, Poland-street, Oxford-street.	Berwick-street . .	Henry Robinson	4, Cambridge-street, Golden-square.	James Botton .	59, Berwick-street.
		Golden-square. . .	George Lawford .	6, Saville-passage, Saville-row.		
		St. James's-square.	James Roberts .	38, Duke-street.		

UNION, or SUPERINTENDENT REGISTRAR'S DISTRICT.	County.	Places of Public Worship situated therein, registered for Solemnization of Marriages.		SUPERINTENDENT REGISTRARS, and *Deputy Superintendent Registrars.*	
		Name.	Situation.	Name.	Address.
IPSWICH	Suffolk . . .	St. Nicholas Old Meeting-house.	St. Nicholas-street, Ipswich .	Thomas Grimsey	Ipswich . . . .
		Stoke-green Chapel . .	Ipswich.		
		Tacket-st. Meeting-house .	Tacket-street, Ipswich.		
		Salem Chapel	Globe-lane, Ipswich.		
		The Independent Chapel .	St. Nicholas-street, Ipswich.		
		Bethesda Chapel . . .	Dairy-lane, Ipswich.		
ISLINGTON	Middlesex . .	Union Chapel	Compton-terrace, Islington	William May .	1, Devonshire-terrace, Barnsbury-square, Islington.
		The Independent Chapel .	Lower-street, Islington.		
		Islington Chapel . . .	Upper-street, Islington.	*William Lawson,*	55, *Penton-street, Islington.*
		Barnsbury-Chapel . . .	Barnsbury-street, Islington.		
		Holloway Chapel . . .	Holloway, in the parish of St. Mary, Islington.		
		Maberly Chapel . . .	Ball's Pond-road, Islington.		
		The Scotch Church . .	River-terrace, City-road, Islington.		
IVE'S, ST.	Hunts . . .	The Baptist Meeting-house	Somersham	G. G. Day . .	St. Ive's . . . .
		The Independent Chapel .	St. Ive's.	F. Parry,	Ditto.
		Baptist Chapel . . .	Bluntisham.		
		The Baptist Chapel . .	Warboys.		
		The Baptist Meeting . .	St. Ive's.		
		The Baptist Chapel . .	Bull-lane, St. Ive's.		
KEIGHLEY	York	Hall Green Chapel . .	Haworth, in the parish of Bradford.	George Spencer .	Keighley . . . .
				John Mitchell,	Ditto.
		The Independent Chapel .	Keighley.		
KENDAL	Westmoreland .	The Dissenting Chapel .	Market-place, Kendal . . .	R. Remington .	Kendal . . . .
		The Catholic Chapel . .	New-road, Kendal.		
KENSINGTON	Middlesex . .	Ranelagh Chapel . . .	George-street, Chelsea . . .	Samuel Cornell .	Smith-street, Chelsea.
		Hornton-street Chapel .	Hornton-street, Kensington.	Henry Locke,	Upper Cheyne-row, Chelsea.
		The Kensington Catholic Chapel.	Holland-street, Kensington.		
		George-yard Chapel . .	Near Brook-green, Hammersmith.		
		St. Mary's Chapel . . .	Cadogan-terrace, Sloane-street, Chelsea.		
		The Baptist Chapel . .	Hammersmith.		
		Silver-street Chapel . .	Kensington.		
		Catholic Chapel . .	King-street, Hammersmith.		
KETTERING	Northampton .	The Baptist Meeting . .	Gold-street, Kettering . . .	W. J. F. Marshall	Kettering . . . .
		The Independent Meeting	Rothwell.		
		The Wesleyan Chapel . .	Desborough.		
KEYNSHAM	Somerset . . .	Kingswood Tabernacle .	Kingswood-hill, in the parish of Bitton.	R. J. Mason . .	Keynsham. . . .
KIDDERMINSTER . . .	Worcester . .	The New Meeting-house .	Church-street, Kidderminster.	Henry Saunders .	Kidderminster. . .
		The Old Meeting-house .	Kidderminster.	A. Y. Bird,	Ditto.
		Ebenezer Chapel . . .	Dudley-street, Kidderminster.		
KINGSBRIDGE	Devon . . .	The Ebenezer Chapel . .	Fore-street, Kingsbridge . .	Thomas Harris .	Kingsbridge . . .
		The Calvinist Baptist Chapel	Modbury.	Thos. Harris, jun.,	Ditto.
		Providence Chapel . . .	Loddiswell.		
KINGSCLERE	Hants . . .	. . .	. . .	William Holding .	Kingsclere . . . .
KING'S LYNN	Norfolk . . .	The Unitarian Chapel .	King's Lynn	J. J. Coulton .	33, Austin-street, King's Lynn.
		The Independent Chapel .	New Conduit-street, King's Lynn.	J. J. Coulton, jun.,	Ditto.
KING'S NORTON . . .	Worcester, Warwick, & Stafford.	The Independent Chapel .	Smethwick, in the parish of Harborne.	Joseph Woodward	Edgbaston, Birmingham.

REGISTRARS of MARRIAGES.		Registrars' Districts.	REGISTRARS of BIRTHS and DEATHS.		Deputy Registrars of Births and Deaths.	
Name.	Address.		Name.	Address.	Name.	Address.
J. O. Francis	Ipswich	*St. Clement's*	G. J. Harmer	New-street, St. Clement's, Ipswich.		
		St. Margaret's	W. Hutchinson	Foundation-street, St. Margaret's, Ipswich.		
		St. Mathew's	Henry Watson	Norwich-road, St. Mathew's, Ipswich.		
John Watts	17, Felix-terrace, Liverpool-road, Islington	*West District*	John Watts	17, Felix-terrace, Liverpool-road, Islington.	J. K. Starling	87, Upper-street, Islington.
		East District	W. H. Butterfield	2, Halton-cottages, Halton-street, Islington.	H. B. Cowell	Lower-road, Islington.
G. L. Girling	St. Ive's	*St. Ive's*	G. L. Girling	St. Ive's, Hunts.		
James Wiles	Somersham, Hunts.	*Swavesey*	Thomas Mortlock	Swavesey, Cambridgeshire.		
John Campion	Warboys.	*Somersham*	Edward Castle	Somersham, Hunts.		
		Warboys	John Campion	Warboys, Hunts.		
Thomas Umpleby	Keighley	*Keighley*	Thomas Umpleby	Keighley.		
		Bingley	Edward Sutcliffe	Bingley.		
		Haworth	James Ogden	Lower Town, Haworth, Bradford, Yorkshire.		
James Tebay	Kendal	*Kendal*	Wm. Greenwood	Lowther-street, Kendal	Joseph Wilson	Highgate, Kendal.
		Ambleside	William Mounsey	Limefoot; Troutbeck-bridge; Ambleside.		
		Grayrigg	Wm. Atkinson	The Ashes, in Scalthwaite-rigge, Kendal.		
		Milnthorpe	J. Spier	Beethwaite Green, Levens, Milnthorpe.		
		Kirkby Lonsdale	William Cragg	Newbiggin, Kirkby Lonsdale.		
W. C. Smith	Exeter-place, Exeter-street, Sloane-street.	*Paddington, St. John's*	Robert Holloway	89, Junction-terrace, Edgeware-road.	John Holloway	89, Junction-terrace.
		Paddington, St. Mary's	Thomas Gurney	Newcastle-place.		
		Fulham	Thomas Hackman	Wimberley House, Fulham-road.	Henry Hackman	High-street, Fulham.
		Hammersmith, St. Paul's.	D. T. Roy	Broadway, Hammersmith.		
		Hammersmith, St. Peter's.	T. W. C. Perfect	Hammersmith-terrace.		
		Kensington, Town District.	Thomas Madden	2, Charles-place, Kensington.	Thomas Meadows	Silver-street.
		Kensington, Brompton District.	William Bateman	Elm-terrace.	Edward James	Elm-terrace.
		Chelsea, South	Thomas Long	3, Beaufort-place, Chelsea.	Henry Thorpe	37, Sloane-square.
		Chelsea, North-west	William Larner	16, Paradise-row, Chelsea.		
		Chelsea, North-east	W. C. Smith	Exeter-place, Exeter-street, Sloane-street.		
George Bates	Kettering	*Kettering*	P. F. Linnell	Kettering.		
		Rothwell	P. M. Gue	Rothwell, Kettering.		
R. Edwards	Keynsham	*Keynsham*	Roger Edwards	Keynsham.		
R. J. Biggs	Kingswood-hill, near Bristol.	*Newton*	A. Armstrong	Compton Dando, Pensford.		
		Bitton	William Tyler	Hanham, Bristol.		
		Oldland	H. M. Grace	Down-end, Bristol.		
William Brinton	Kidderminster	*Kidderminster*	William Brinton	Kidderminster	William Collins	Stourbridge-street, Kidderminster.
		Wolverley	William Shutt	Wolverley, Kidderminster.	Thomas Worrall	Wolverley, Kidderminster.
		Bewdley	W. N. Marcy	Bewdley		
		Chaddesley, Corbett	Thomas Glover	Stone, Kidderminster.		
		Lower Mitton, or Stourport	John Parsons	Stourport.		
F. D. Pearce	Kingsbridge	*Kingsbridge*	F. D. Pearce	Kingsbridge	W. L. Pearce	Duncombe-street, Kingsbridge.
		Westallington	Wm. Thos. Honey	Salcombe, Kingsbridge.		
		Stokenham	William Miles	Frogmore, Kingsbridge.	Richard Mullis	Frogmore, Kingsbridge.
		Blackhawton	William Bartlett Hambling.	Blackhawton, Dartmouth.		
		Modbury	S. Gillard	Modbury	A. Foster	Modbury.
Henry Dale	Kingsclere	*Kingsclere*	Henry Dale	Kingsclere.		
		Highclere	C. R. Hall	East Woodhay, Newbury.		
Thomas Cook	London-road, King's Lynn.	*King's Lynn, North*	George Bainbridge	Norfolk-st., King's Lynn.		
		King's Lynn, Middle	J. W. Chadwick	Broad-street, King's Lynn.		
		King's Lynn, South	John Murlin	All Saints'-st., King's Lynn.		
Edward Fereday	Edgbaston, Birmingham.	*Edgbaston*	W. B. Woodward	Edgbaston, Birmingham.		
		King's Norton	Isaac Clulee	King's Norton.		
		Harborne	Samuel Dugmore	Harborne, near Birmingham.		

K 2

UNION, or SUPERINTENDENT REGISTRAR'S DISTRICT.	County.	Places of Public Worship situated therein, registered for Solemnization of Marriages.		SUPERINTENDENT REGISTRARS, and Deputy Superintendent Registrars.	
		Name.	Situation.	Name.	Address.
KINGSTON-UPON-HULL	York	The Bowl-alley-lane Chapel	Bowl-alley-lane, Kingston-upon-Hull.	John Thorney .	Kingston-upon-Hull .
		Fish-street Chapel . . .	Kingston-upon-Hull.		
		Salem Chapel	Cogan-st., Kingston-upon-Hull.		
		Mill-street Chapel . . .	Kingston-upon-Hull.		
		The Independent Methodist Chapel.	Osborne-street, in Kingston-upon-Hull.		
		Providence Chapel . .	Hope-st., Kingston-upon-Hull.		
		Salthouse-lane Baptist Chapel.	Kingston-upon-Hull.		
		Trinity Chapel	Nile-street, Kingston-upon-Hull.		
KINGSTON-ON-THAMES	Surrey . . .	. . .	. . .	R. F. Bartrop .	Kingston-on-Thames.
KNARESBOROUGH . .	York	The Independent Chapel .	New-street, Wetherby, in the parish of Spofforth.	Thos. Cartwright	Knaresborough . .
		Stockeld Chapel . . .	Stockeld-park, in the parish of Spofforth.		
		St. Mary's Chapel . . .	Allerton-park, Allerton-Mauleverer.		
		St. Mary's Chapel . . .	Low Bondend, in the township of Scriven-with-Tentergate, in the parish of Knaresborough.		
		Windsor Lane Chapel . .	Knaresborough.		
		The Independent Chapel .	Green Hammerton, in the parish of Whixley.		
KNIGHTON	Radnor . . .	. . .	. . .	Edw. Mason . .	Knighton . . . .
LAMBETH	Surrey . . .	Denmark Place Chapel .	Cold Harbour-lane, Camberwell	Robt. Watmore .	7, Walcot-pl., Lambeth.
		Stockwell New Chapel .	Stockwell.	George Smith,	Park-place, Kennington.
LAMPETER	Cardigan and Carmarthen.	Aberduar	Glanduar, in the parish of Llanybyther.	D. J. Jenkins, jun.	Lampeter . . . .
		Chapel Sion	Cwrtnavydd, in the parish of Llanwenog.		
LANCASTER	Lancaster . .	High Street Chapel . .	Lancaster	Samuel Simpson.	Queen-square, Lancaster.
		The Roman Catholic Chapel	Dalton-square, Lancaster.		
LANGPORT	Somerset . . .	The Independent Chapel .	Bow-street, Langport . . .	J. F. H. Warren.	Langport . . . .
		Middle Lambrook Meeting	Kingsbury Episcopi.		
		The Independent Chapel .	Somerton.		
LAUNCESTON	Cornwall . . .	Castle Street Chapel . .	Launceston	S. R. Pattison .	Castle-street, Launceston.
		The Wesleyan Chapel .	Launceston.		
		Copthorne Chapel . . .	Copthorne, in the parish of North Petherwyn.		
LEDBURY	Hereford . .	. . .	. . .	Jesse Hughes .	Southend-street, Ledbury.
LEEDS	York	South Parade Chapel . .	South Parade, Leeds . . .	Geo. Rawson, jun.	Leeds . . . . .
		Salem Chapel	Hunslet-lane, Leeds.	Josh. Wood,	Coronation-street, Leeds.
		Mill Hill Chapel . . .	Park-row, Leeds.		
		Belgrave Chapel . . .	Leeds.		
		Call Lane Chapel . . .	Leeds.		
		Ebenezer Chapel . . .	Leeds.		
		Queen Street Chapel . .	Queen-street, Leeds.		
		St. Patrick's Chapel . .	York-road, Leeds.		
		George Street Chapel (formerly Bethel Chapel).	George's-street, Leeds.		
		Park Chapel	Caroline-street, Leeds.		
		St. Mary's Chapel . . .	Lady-lane, Leeds.		
		Gildersome Baptist Chapel	Gildersome, in the parish of Batley.		
		Holbeck Independent Chapel.	Marshall-street, Holbeck, in the parish of Leeds.		
		St. Ann's Church . . .	Park-lane, Leeds.		

REGISTRARS of MARRIAGES.		Registrars' Districts.	REGISTRARS of BIRTHS and DEATHS.		Deputy Registrars of Births and Deaths.	
Name.	Address.		Name.	Address.	Name.	Address.
John Hill . .	Kingston-upon-Hull .	*Humber*	Edward Wallis .	Whitefriars-gate, Hull.		
Joseph H. Hill .	7, Parliament-street, Hull.	*St. Mary's*	Henry Wm. Lee .	Bishop-lane, Hull.		
		Myton	Richard Jackson	22, Prospect-street, North Myton, Hull.	Wm Cocker . .	Kingston-gardens.
Riley Barnes .	Hampton Wick . .	*Kingston*	George Taylor .	Kingston, Surrey.		
		Esher	Thomas Mercer .	Thames Ditton.		
		Hampton	R. Barnes . .	Hampton Wick.		
		Wimbledon . . .	John Kelly . .	Wimbledon, Surrey.		
Thomas Taylor .	Knaresborough . .	*Knaresborough* .	Joseph Wilson .	Scriven-cum-Tentergate, Knaresborough.		
Thos. Whitehouse	Wetherby.	*Wetherby*	Thos. Whitehouse	Wetherby.		
Wm. Potter . .	Whixley, Green Hammerton.	*Whixley*	William Potter .	Whixley, Green Hammerton.		
		Harrogate . . .	Wm. Ridsdale .	High Harrogate.		
		Boroughbridge . .	John Newsam .	Boroughbridge.		
. . .	. . .	*Knighton*	James Davies .	Knucklass, Knighton.		
		Brampton, Brian .	James Edwards .	Knighton.		
		Llanbister . . .	A. Hamer . .	Llananno, Newtown.		
W. T. Logan .	2, St. Ann's-road, Brixton.	*Waterloo-road, 1st Part*	Charles Mears .	86, Cornwall-road . . .	C. J. F. Mears .	86, Cornwall-road.
W. H. Wheatley	115, Elizabeth-place, Lambeth.	*Waterloo-road, 2nd Part*	James Green .	York-road.		
		Lambeth Church, 1st Part.	J. L. Gawler .	Cambridge-place, near the Asylum.	Edward Powell .	1, North-street.
		Lambeth Church, 2nd Part.	W. H. Wheatley	115, Elizabeth-place, Lambeth.	George Wood .	144, Elizabeth-place.
		Kennington, 1st Part .	William Easter .	Upper Dorset-place, Clapham-road.		
		Kennington, 2nd Part .	J. R. Unwin .	6, Alfred-place, North Brixton.	John Abbey . .	1, Russell-street, Brixton-road.
		Brixton	John Plummer .	Brixton-place.		
		Norwood	C. J. J. Child .	Norwood.		
J. Evans . . .	Glandur, Lampeter .	*Llanybyther* . . .	David Evans .	Cilgell-Ucha, Lampeter.		
		Lampeter	Samuel Davies .	Lampeter.		
William Procter.	Lancaster	*Lancaster* . . .	William Procter .	Moor-lane, Lancaster.		
		Ellel	George Blezard .	Galgate, Lancaster.		
		Heaton	John Foxcroft .	Heysham, Lancaster.		
		Warton	Richard Whormby	Warton, Lancaster.		
		Arkholme . . .	Wm. Herdman .	Arkholme, Lancaster.		
		Tunstall . . .	T. Wright . .	Leck, Kirkby Lonsdale.		
		Wray	Robert Ripley .	Wray, Lancaster . . .	Robert Parker .	Wray, Lancaster.
		Caton	Richard Nicholson	Caton, Lancaster.		
Jno. Prankerd .	Langport	*Langport*	Jno. Prankerd .	Langport	Thos. Viney . .	Langport.
Stephen England	West Lambrook, Kingsbury Episcopi, near South Petherton.	*Somerton* . . .	T. H. Davies .	Somerton	Elias Oram . .	Somerton.
George Chant .	Somerton.	*Curry Rivell* . . .	H. P. Hurman .	Curry Rivell, Langport .	George Weaver .	Curry Rivell, Langport.
John Geake, jun.	St. Stephens, by Launceston.	*Launceston* . . .	William Philp .	Launceston	Edward Philp .	Launceston.
		St. Stephen . . .	W. J. Palmer .	Yeolmbridge, Launceston .	Thomas Searle .	Yeolmbridge, Launceston.
		Northpetherwin . .	John Bennet .	Egloskerry, Launceston	William Turner.	Egloskerry, Launceston.
. . .	. . .	*Altarnun* . . .	John Sandercock	Altarnun, Launceston .	Robert Sandercock	Altarnun, Launceston.
		Northill . . .	F. Whitford . .	Lezant, Launceston .	John Husband .	Lezant, Launceston.
. . .	. . .	*Ledbury*	William Thomas	Coddington, Ledbury.		
		Yarkhill . . .	R. Freeman . .	Post-Office, Ledbury.		
Edward Bolton .	15, Benson-buildings, Basinghall-street, Leeds.	*North District* .	G. M. Bingley .	Darley-street, Leeds.		
		West District . .	Thomas Taylor .	Princes-street, Pack-lane, Leeds.	W. B. Legg . .	19, Rockingham-street, Leeds.
Edwin Moore .	7, Infirmary-street, Leeds.	*Kirkgate*	Edward Cooke .	6, Richmond-terrace, Richmond-road, Leeds.		
		Hunslet	John Yewdall .	Glasshouse-street, Hunslet, Leeds.	James Yewdall .	Glasshouse-street, Hunslet.
		Holbeck	R. G. Horton .	57, Marshall street, Holbeck, Leeds.		
		Wortley	R. L. Armstrong.	Moor Cottage, Upper Wortley, Leeds.	C. Robinson . .	Agnes Royd, Wortley-lane-end, Leeds.
		Kirkstall . . .	Thomas Trickett	Town-street, Bramley, Leeds	William Dickinson	Kirkstall, Leeds.
		Chapeltown . . .	John Wilcock .	Newton-grove, Potternewton, Leeds.	Wm. Neal . .	Potternewton, Leeds.
		Whitkirk . . .	William Green .	Whitkirk, Leeds . . .	J. Rollisson . .	Halton, Leeds.
		Rothwell . . .	Thos. Stephenson	Rothwell, Leeds.		

UNION, or SUPERINTENDENT REGISTRAR'S DISTRICT.	County.	Places of Public Worship situated therein, registered for Solemnization of Marriages.		SUPERINTENDENT REGISTRARS, and *Deputy Superintendent Registrars.*	
		Name.	Situation.	Name.	Address.
LEEK	Stafford . . .	. . .	. . .	F. Cruso . . .	Leek . . . . .
LEICESTER	Leicester . . .	The Great Meeting . .	Bond-street, Leicester . . .	Thos. Burbidge .	New-street, Leicester.
		Bond Street Chapel . .	Bond-street, Leicester.		
		Harvey Lane Chapel .	Harvey-lane, Leicester.		
		The Friar Lane Chapel .	Friar-lane, Leicester.		
		The Archdeacon Lane Chapel.	Archdeacon-lane, Leicester.		
		Holy Cross Chapel .	Wellington-street, Leicester.		
		The Upper Charles Street Chapel.	Leicester.		
		The Dover Street Chapel .	Leicester.		
		The Gallowtree Gate Chapel	Leicester.		
		The Wesleyan Chapel .	Bishop-street, Leicester.		
LEIGH	Lancaster .	Presbyterian Chapel . .	Chowbent, within Atherton, in the parish of Leigh.	James Smith . *J. Bunney,*	Leigh, near Manchester *Church-street, Leigh.*
		The Bedford Catholic Chapel	Bedford, in the parish of Leigh.		
		Tyldesley Chapel . . .	Tyldesley, in the parish of Leigh.		
LEIGHTON-BUZZARD .	Beds	The Baptist Chapel . .	Lake-street, Leighton-Buzzard	Joseph Woodman	Leighton-Buzzard .
		The Wesleyan Methodist Chapel.	Jeff's-lane, Leighton-Buzzard.		
LEOMINSTER	Hereford. . .	The Baptist Meeting . .	Leominster	James Husbands	Church-street, Leominster.
LEWES, CHAILEY, WESTFIRLE, and NEWHAVEN	Sussex . . .	The Tabernacle . .	Lewes	W. P. Kell . .	St. Michael, Lewes .
		The Baptist Chapel .	Little East-street, Lewes.		
		The Westgate Meeting .	Lewes.		
		Zion Chapel	Newick Common, Newick.		
		General Baptist, or Unitarian Baptist Chapel .	Eastend, in the parish of Ditchling.		
LEWISHAM	Kent	Union Chapel	Lewisham	Thomas Parker .	Lewisham . . . .
LEXDEN and WINSTREE.	Essex. . . .	The New Jerusalem Church	Waterside-lane, Brightlingsea.	William Howard	Colchester . . . .
		The Baptist Meeting-house.	Langham.		
LEYBURN	York	The Roman Catholic Chapel	Leyburn	H. T. Robinson .	Leyburn . . . .
LICHFIELD	Stafford . . .	St. Francis Chapel .	Wood-lane, in the parish of Yoxall	J. P. Dyott, jun. *William Gifford,*	Lichfield . . . . *Ditto.*
		Salem Chapel	Wade-street, Lichfield.		
LINCOLN	Lincoln . .	The Independent Chapel .	High-street, Lincoln . .	Robert Cooke *R. Finley,*	Lincoln . . . . . *Union Workhouse.*
		The Catholic Chapel . .	Silver-street, Lincoln.		
		The Baptist Chapel . .	Mint-lane, Lincoln.		
LINTON	Cambridge .	Duxford Chapel . . .	Duxford	Daniel Potter .	Linton . . . . .
		Meeting-house	Linton.		
LISKEARD	Cornwall . .	Darley Chapel	Darley, in the parish of Linkinhorne.	Peter Glubb . .	Liskeard . . . .
		The Wesleyan Association.	Polperro, in the parish of Talland.		. *.*
		Trelawny Chapel . . .	Trelawny, in the parish of Pelynt.		
LIVERPOOL	Lancaster . .	St. Peter's Chapel . .	Seel-street, Liverpool . . .	James Boardman *Alfred Higginson,*	Liverpool . . . . *Ditto.*
		St. Andrew's (Scots) Church	Rodney-street, Liverpool.		
		Renshaw-street Chapel .	Liverpool.		
		Scotch Church	Oldham-street, Liverpool.		
		Bold-street Chapel . .	Liverpool.		
		St. Mary's Chapel . .	Edmund-street, Liverpool.		
		St. Anthony's Chapel . .	Scotland-road, Liverpool.		
		Great George's-street Chapel.	Great George-street, Liverpool.		
		Paradise-street Chapel .	Paradise-street, Liverpool.		
		St. Nicholas Chapel . .	Copperas-hill, Liverpool.		
		The Scotch Secession Church	Mount Pleasant, Liverpool		
		Newington Chapel . .	Renshaw-street, Liverpool.		
		Lime-street Chapel .	Liverpool.		
		The Seamen's Church . .	Rathbone-street, Liverpool.		
		The Baptist Chapel . .	Byrom-street, Liverpool.		
		Baptist Chapel . . .	Great Crosshall-st., Liverpool.		
		The Tabernacle . . .	Great Crosshall-st., Liverpool.		

REGISTRARS of MARRIAGES.		Registrars' Districts.	REGISTRARS of BIRTHS and DEATHS.		Deputy Registrars of Births and Deaths.	
Name.	Address.		Name.	Address.	Name.	Address.
Thomas Griffin	Leek	Leek	George Rider	Leek.		
		Leek-frith	Robert Pimlot	Leek-frith, Leek.		
		Longnor	J. Millward, jun.	Longnor, Leek.		
		Norton and Endon	C. Heaton, jun.	Endon, Leek.		
Thomas Cape	Bowling-green-hill, Leicester.	East	Thomas Yates	Charles-street, Leicester.		
J. H. Davis	Market-place, Leicester.	West	Wm. Mitchell	High Cross-street, Leicester		
Thomas Sale	Chowbent, within Atherton, Manchester.	Atherton and Tyldesley	Thomas Sale	Atherton, Manchester.		
Richard Knowles	Bedford, Leigh, Manchester.	Cutcheck	Samuel Moscrop.	Bedford, Manchester.		
T. Bridge	Tyldesley, with Shackerley, Manchester.	Lowton	Samuel Whittle	Westleigh, Manchester.		
Samuel Whittle	Westleigh, Manchester.					
Richard Doggett	Leighton-Buzzard	Leighton-Buzzard	Richard Doggett	Leighton-Buzzard.		
		Wing	Wm. Mortimer	Wing, Leighton-Buzzard.		
		Edlesborough	Josh. Mead	Edlesborough, Dunstable.		
		Ivinghoe	Wm. Collyer	Ivinghoe, Hemel-Hempstead, Herts.		
John Taylor	Broad-street, Leominster.	Leominster	John Taylor	Broad-street, Leominster.		
		Bodenham	Wm. Holyoak	Docklow, Leominster.		
		Kingsland	Richard Powell	Luston, Leominster.		
C. Kell	St. Michael, High-street, Lewes.	Lewes	John Cooks	St. Michael, Lewes	James Inskip	89, High-street, St. Michael, Lewes.
John Jones	High-street, All Saints, Lewes.	Chailey	T. A. Bull	Barcombe, Lewes.		
		Ditchling	George Verrall	Ditchling, Lewes.		
William Best	Chailey, Lewes.	West Firle	G. Webb	Beddingham, Lewes.		
George Webb	Beddingham, Lewes.	Newhaven	George Smith	Newhaven.		
George Smith	Newhaven.	Rottingdean	Wm. Dumbrell	Rottingdean, Lewes.		
Wm. Dumbrell	Rottingdean, Lewes.					
Robert Nunn	Lewisham	Sydenham	Dr. A. Scott, M.D.	Sydenham.		
		Lewisham Village	Robert Nunn	Lewisham.		
		Lee	C. Gemas	Blackheath-hill, Lewisham.		
		Eltham & Mottingham	C. Fry	Eltham.		
		Plumstead & Charlton	W. Carver	Charlton, Kent.		
Thomas Sanders	Stanway, Colchester	Dedham	Henry Cook	Horkesley, Colchester.		
		Fordham	T. G. Cocke	Chappel, Colchester.		
		Stanway	Thomas Sanders	Stanway, Colchester.		
		Peldon	J. S. Gonner	East Donyland, Colchester.		
		Wivenhoe	J. C. Parker	Brightlingsea, Colchester.		
Thomas Topham	Middleham	Leyburn	R. Pattinson	Wensley, Leyburn.		
		Middleham	Thomas Topham	Middleham.	Stephen Jones, jun.	Middleham.
Thomas Hall	Lichfield	Lichfield	Henry Gray	Lichfield.	William Barratt.	St. John-street, Lichfield.
		Rugeley	John Armishaw	Rugeley.		
		Yoxall	Thomas Baker	Yoxall, Lichfield	William Raworth	Yoxall, Lichfield.
Joseph Cooke	Lincoln	Home	John Wilkinson	Sheep-square, Lincoln.	George Reynolds	St. Martin's, Lincoln.
J. Dudding	Lincoln.	South-west	R. C. Moore	Harmston, Lincoln	J. Reeve	Harmston, Lincoln.
		North-east	James Gunning	Owmsby, Spittal, Lincoln.	Rob. Douglass	Owmsby.
Wm. Richardson	Linton	Linton	John Adcock	Linton.		
		Balsham	John Prince	Balsham, Linton.		
		Duxford	John Patterson	Duxford, Cambridge.		
John Barrett	Liskeard	Liskeard	John Barrett	Liskeard.		
		Looe	Wm. Wilcocks	East Looe.		
		Lerrun	John Hicks	Lerrin, Fowey.		
		Callington	William Snell	Callington.		
David Marples	Lord-street, Liverpool	St. Martin's	William Clements	36, Great Nelson-street, Liverpool.	J. McLean	Newsham-street, Scotland-road, Liverpool.
William Duxbury	Birkett-street, Liverpool.	Howard-street	John Walthew	8, Sawney Pope-street, Liverpool.		
W. F. Jones	49, Mount Pleasant, Liverpool.	Dale-street	Edward Lovatt	41, Union-street, Liverpool.	William Edisbury	41, Union-street, Liverpool
J. W. Lawson	Hunter-street, Liverpool.	St. Thomas	Thos. Blundell	42, Upper Pitt-street, Liverpool.	T. Barrow	42, Upper Pitt-street, Liverpool.
		Mount Pleasant	James Eckersley.	Brownlow-street, Liverpool.	Jno. Eckersley	Brownlow-street, Liverpool.
		Islington	William Foulkes	42, Devon-street, Liverpool.	Samuel Foulkes	42, Devon-street, Liverpool.

UNION, or SUPERINTENDENT REGISTRAR'S DISTRICT.	County.	Places of Public Worship situated therein, registered for Solemnization of Marriages.		SUPERINTENDENT REGISTRARS, and *Deputy Superintendent Registrars.*	
		Name.	Situation.	Name.	Address.
LLANDILO FAWR. . .	Carmarthen . .	Tabernacle	Ffairfach, in the parish of Llandilo Fawr.	J. P. Lewis . .	Llandilo, Carmarthenshire.
		Hermon Chapel . . .	Cefnglasfryn, in the parish of Llandilo Fawr.		
		Capel Isaac.	Mynyddbach, in the parish of Llandilo Fawr.		
		Cwmdu Chapel . . .	Cwmdu, in the parish of Talley.		
LLANDOVERY	Carmarthen . .	Salem Chapel	Queen-street, Llandovery . .	R. Williams . .	Llandovery, Carmarthenshire.
		Gelynos	Dôlycoed, in the parish of Llanwrtyd.		
		Jerusalem	Gwynfe, in the parish of Llangadock.		
		Bethlehem	Dyffryn-ceidrich, in the parish of Llangadock.		
		Tentretygwyn	Rhandyr-issaf, in the parish of Llanfairarybrin.		
		Ebenezer	Llansadwren.		
		Crygybar Chapel . .	Crygybar, in the parish of Conwil Gaio.		
LLANELLY	Carmarthen and Glamorgan.	Capel Als	Llanelly	William Rees .	Llanelly, Carmarthen
		Sion Chapel . . .	Llanelly.		
		Bethania	Near Lletty Mawr Gate, in the parish of Llannon.		
		Carmel	Cwm Firman, in the parish of Pembrey.		
		Rehoboth	Bryndy, in the parish of Pembrey.		
		Sion Chapel	Llanelly.		
LLANFYLLIN	Montgomery. .	Tabernacle	Llanrhaiadr	H. L. Williams .	Llanfyllin . . . .
		Baptist Chapel . . .	Llanfau.	*William Jones,*	*Ditto.*
		Bethesda	Llansaintffraid.		
		Penarth	Penarth, in the parish of Llanfair-caereinion.		
		Ebenezer	Penyllys, in the parish of Llanfihangel.		
		Chapel Pendre. . .	Llanfyllin.		
LLANRWST	Denbigh . . .	Nebo	Garth Garmon, in the parish of Llanrwst.	William Griffith.	Llanrwst, Denbigh .
LODDON & CLAVERING.	Norfolk . . .	. . .	. . .	James Copeman .	Loddon, near Norwich
LONDON, EAST . . .	Middlesex . .	Hare-court Chapel. . .	Hare-court, Aldersgate-street .	A. J. Baylis . .	1, Devonshire-square, Bishopsgate-street.
		Barbican Chapel . . .	Barbican.	*J. Teesdale,*	*Union Offices, Devonshire-square.*
		New Broad-street Meeting-house.	New Broad-street, Bishopsgate.		
		Devonshire-square Chapel.	Meeting-house-court, or Still-alley, in the parish of St. Botolph, Aldgate.		
		Bishopsgate Chapel . .	Bishopsgate-street.		
		The Independent . . .	Aldermanbury Postern.		
		Jewin-street Chapel . .	Jewin-street, in the parish of St. Botolph Without.		
LONDON, CITY OF . .	Middlesex . .	The Presbyterian Meeting-house.	Little Carter-lane, London . .	J. T. Rowsell .	35, Cannon-street . .
		The King's Weigh-house Meeting.	Fish-street-hill.	*C. J. Rowsell,*	*8, Philpot-lane.*
		The New Jerusalem Church	Friar-street, Shoemaker-row, Blackfriars.		
		The Poultry Chapel . .	The Poultry.		
		Silver-street Chapel . .	Silver-street, Wood-street.		
		Salters'-hall Chapel . .	Cannon-street, City.		
		St. Mary's, Moorfields . .	Finsbury-circus.		
		Finsbury Chapel . . .	Finsbury-circus.		
		Finsbury Chapel . . .	South-place, Finsbury.		
		Albion Chapel	Moorgate, Coleman-st., London.		
		The Bury-street Chapel .	Bury-street, in the parish of St. Katherine Cree.		
		Eldon-street Chapel . .	Eldon-street, in the parish of St. Stephen, Coleman-street.		
LONDON, WEST . . .	Middlesex . .	Fetter-lane Chapel . . .	Fetter-lane	John Pontifex .	5, St. Andrew's-court, Holborn.
				Wm. Chambers,	*Ditto.*
LONGTOWN.	Cumberland .	Graham-street Chapel. .	Longtown	Robert Little. .	Longtown, Cumberland
LOUGHBOROUGH. . .	Leicester . . .	The General Baptist Chapel	Baxter-gate, Loughborough .	B. Brock. . .	Loughborough . .
		St. Mary's Chapel . . .	Gracedieu, in the parish of Belton	*S. L. Jones,*	*Ditto.*
		The General Baptist Chapel	Mill-lane, Wimeswould.		
LOUTH	Lincoln . . .	Cannon-street Chapel . .	Cannon-street, Louth. . . .	J. W. Wilson .	Louth . . . . .
		The Wesleyan Methodist Chapel.	Bintrook, St. Gabriel.	*F. F. Goe,*	*Ditto.*
		The Wesleyan Chapel . .	Eastgate, Louth.		
		The Baptist Chapel . .	Maltby-le-Marsh.		

REGISTRARS of MARRIAGES.		Registrars' Districts.	REGISTRARS of BIRTHS and DEATHS.		Deputy Registrars of Births and Deaths.	
Name.	Address.		Name.	Address.	Name.	Address.
Thomas Williams	Rhosmaen-street, Llandilo, Carmarthenshire.	Llandilo	Thomas Williams	Llandilo, Carmarthenshire.	Evan Williams	Llandilo.
		Llandebie	Evan Evans	Llandebie Village, Llandilo, Carmarthenshire.	Rev. Dav. Evans	Llandebie.
		Llangathen	John Davies	Llangathen, Llandilo, Carmarthenshire.		
		Llanfynydd	Thomas Evans	Llanfynydd, Llandilo, Carmarthenshire.		
		Talley	John Davies	Talley Village, Llandilo, Carmarthenshire.		
Evan Owens	The Bellevue, Pont Rhidyberre, Llanwrtyd.	Conwil Cayo	Rees Thomas	Gwarhos, Llandovery.		
		Llangadock	John Price	Caevulche, Llangadock.		
John Price	Caevulche, Llangadock, Carmarthen.	Mydfai	John Thomas	Gorllwyn, Llandovery.	Thomas Thomas	Gorllwyn.
		Llanddausant	John Joseph	Penyrallt, Llandovery.		
David Evans	Llandovery.	Llanwrtyd and Llandulas.	Evan Owens	Llanwrtyd, Llandovery.		
Rees Thomas	Gwarhos, Llandovery.	Llanfairarybryn	Evan Jones	Crygie, Llandovery.		
		Llanwdwrn and Llanwrda.	Thomas Evans	Maesyrhiw, Llandovery.		
		Llandingat	David Evans	Llandovery.		
		Cilycwm	Evan Evans	Cilycwm, Llandovery.		
F. L. Browne	Thomas-street, Llanelly, Carmarthen.	Llanelly	D. A. Davies	Thomas-street, Llanelly.		
William Davies	Cefn Bryn, Llannon, Llanelly, Carmarthen.	Pembrey	Benj. Williams	Tyissa, Pembrey, Llanelly.		
		Llannon	William Davies	Cefn Bryn, Llannon, Llanelly, Carmarthen.		
B. Williams	Tyissa Pembrey, Llanelly.	Longhor	David H. Jones	Longhor, Glamorganshire.		
Wm. Thomas	Hall-street, Llanelly.					
Edward Evans	Rhosybrithdir Llanrhaiadr, Montgomery.	Meifod	G. Jones	Llanfyllin	Wm. Williams	Llanfyllin.
		Llansaintffraid	M. Jones	Llansaintffraid, Oswestry.		
Griffith Jones	Llanfyllin, Oswestry.	Llanrhaiadr	Edward Evans	Llanrhaiadr - yn - Mochnant; Oswestry.		
		Llanfair	G. Jones	Llanfair Caerennion; Welshpool.		
Robert Thomas	Llanrwst, Denbigh.	Llanrwst	David Davies	Wern, Llanrwst	R. Thomas	Llanrwst.
		Bettws-y-Coed.	Robert Jones	Tynyddol, Llanrwst.		
		Yspytty	G. Davies	Llanrwst.		
Wm. Hoddy	Loddon, near Norwich.	Loddon	John Dawson	Bergh Apton, by Brooke; Norwich.		
		Aldeby	J. H. Wooltorton	Hales, Loddon.		
		Woodton	J. Brigham	Seething, Loddon.		
James Reeve	24, New Broad-street	St. Botolph	T. L. Smartt	Sun-street, Bishopsgate	C. H. Smartt	25, Sun-street, Bishopgate.
		Cripplegate	J. Defries	10, Nicholl-square, Cripplegate.	G. Harrington	10, Nicholl-square, Cripplegate.
J. L. Foster	14, Fish-street-hill	North-east	T. Abraham	49, Old Broad-street	T. M. Ball	51, Coleman-street.
John Paul	35, Cannon-street, and 4, Dowgate-hill.	North-west	G. Payne, jun.	10, Bath-street, Newgate-street.		
		South-west	Thomas Hood	Bennett's-hill, Doctor's Commons.	James Burnett	216, Upper Thames-street.
		South	A. N. Wickes	8, Clement's-lane, Lombard-street.	J. R. Dunn, jun.	Nicholas-passage, Nicholas-lane.
		South-east	R. Cranch	New London-street, City.		
John Carvill	137, Salisbury-court	South District	Chas. Dunn	65, Farringdon-street.		
		North District	Wm. Fortescue	9, Smithfield-bars	Wm. Fortescue, jun.	9, Smithfield-bars.
Thos. Plenderleath	Longtown, Cumberland	High	Rev. J. Hope	Stapleton Rectory, Longtown		
		Low	T. Plenderleath	Longtown, Cumberland	Thos. Tweddle, jun.	Longtown.
Samuel Lee	Loughborough	Leake	B. W. Brown	Wimeswould, Loughborough		
		Loughborough	Samuel Lee	Loughborough.		
John Porter	Louth	Louth	Wm. Parkin	Walkergate, Louth	John Arliss	Lee-street, Louth.
W. Richardson	Binbrook, Market-Rasen.	Tetney	John Nelthorpe	Fulstow, Louth.	J. Birkitt	Grimoldby, Louth.
		Saltfleet	James Bourne	Grimoldby, Louth	T. J. Pawson	Binbrook, St. Gabriel, Market-Rasen.
T. Mager	Maltby-le-Marsh, Alford, Lincoln.	Binbrook	Wm. Richardson	Binbrook, Spital		
		Withern	John Mawer	Aby Grange, Alford	Wm. Grant	Withern, Alford.

L

UNION, or SUPERINTENDENT REGISTRAR'S DISTRICT.	County.	Places of Public Worship situated therein, registered for Solemnization of Marriages.		SUPERINTENDENT REGISTRARS, and Deputy Superintendent Registrars.	
		Name.	Situation.	Name.	Address.
LUDLOW	Salop and Hereford.	The Independent Chapel . The Primitive Methodist Chapel.	Old-street, Ludlow . Old-street, Ludlow.	Robert Thomas .	Ludlow . . . .
LUKE, ST.	Middlesex . .	. . .	. . .	Joseph Smith .	41, Chiswell-street .
LUTON	Beds	The Baptist Meeting-house Union Chapel . . . . The Baptist Meeting-house	West-street, Dunstable . . . Luton. Park-street, Dunstable.	T. E. Austin .	Luton . . . . .
LUTTERWORTH . . .	Leicester, Warwick, and Northampton.	The Independent Chapel . The Independent Chapel .	Lutterworth, Leicestershire Welford, Northamptonshire.	Stephen Mash .	Lutterworth . .
LYMINGTON	Hants . . .	Old Town Chapel . . . Baptist Chapel . . .	Lymington . . . . Lymington.	A. Guy . . .	Lymington . . .
MACCLESFIELD . . .	Chester . . .	St. Michael's Catholic Chapel. Ebenezer Independent Chapel. Roe-street Independent Chapel. Brunswick Chapel . . .	Macclesfield . . . . . Townley-street, Macclesfield. Macclesfield. Sutton, in the parish of Prestbury.	Thomas Parrott .	Macclesfield . . .
MACHYNLLETH . . .	Montgomery .	The Old Chapel . . . Capel y Graig . . . . Talywern Chapel . . . Lama Chapel . . . . Bethesda	Caenycoed Cwmcarnedd, in the parish of Llanbrynmair. Machynlleth. Talywern, in the parish of Penegoes. Cwmlline, in the parish of Cemmes. Towyn.	David Howell . J. A. Vaughan,	Machynlleth . . . Ditto.
MADELEY	Salop . . .	The Roman Catholic Chapel Brand-lee Chapel . . .	Madeley . . . . . . Dawley Green, in the parish of Dawley.	George Potts . J. W. Rowland,	Iron Bridge; Salop . Ditto.
MAIDSTONE.	Kent	The Baptist Chapel . . The Independent Chapel . The Independent Chapel .	King-street, Maidstone . . . Week-street, Maidstone. The Church Green, in the parish of Marden.	W. N. Ottaway .	Staplehurst, Maidstone
MALDON	Essex. . . .	The Independent Chapel .	Market-hill, Maldon . . .	Wm. Codd, jun. Henry Codd,	Maldon . . . . Ditto.
MALLING	Kent	. . .	. . .	J. N. Dudlow .	West Malling . . .
MALMSBURY	Wilts and Gloucester.	The Independent Chapel .	Westport, St. Mary, Malmsbury	J. T. Handy .	Malmsbury . . .
MALTON	York	Ebenezer Chapel . . .	New Malton	A. Simpson . .	Malton . . . .
MANCHESTER	Lancaster . .	Cross-street Chapel . . St. Augustine's Chapel . Christ Church . . . St. Mary's Chapel . . . The Independent Chapel . St. Chad's Chapel . . . St. Patrick's Chapel . . Grosvenor-street Chapel . Mosley-street Independent Chapel. Lloyd-street Chapel . New Jerusalem Church . York-street Chapel . . Scotch Church . . . . The Particular Baptist Chapel. Day and Sunday Schools . New Connexion Chapel . Tabernacle . . . . Strangeways Chapel . . George-street Chapel . .	Manchester . . . . . . Manchester. Ancoats, Manchester. Mulberry-street, Manchester. Cannon-street, Manchester. Rook-street, Manchester. Livesey-street, Manchester. Manchester. Mosley-street, Manchester. Lloyd-street, Manchester. Peter-street, Manchester. Manchester. St. Peter's-square, Manchester. St. George's-road, Manchester. Lower Mosley-st., Manchester. Oldham-street, Manchester. Gartside-street, Manchester. Bridge-street, Strangeways, Manchester. Manchester.	W. Johns, M.D. William Gregson,	Manchester . . Oldham-street, Manchester.

REGISTRARS of MARRIAGES.		Registrars' Districts.	REGISTRARS of BIRTHS and DEATHS.		Deputy Registrars of Births and Deaths.	
Name.	Address.		Name.	Address.	Name.	Address.
Wm. Russell . .	Ludlow	*Ludlow*	Richard Valentine	Ludlow.		
James Jennings .	Corve-street, Ludlow.	*Cainham*	Richard Bate .	Cainham, Ludlow.		
		Munslow	Charles Pothecary	Munslow, Ludlow.		
		Diddlebury . .	Edward Taylor .	Culmington, Ludlow.		
		Leintwardine . .	John Parry . .	Wigmore, Ludlow.		
R. Phillips . .	35, Chiswell-street .	*Finsbury* . . .	G. Sinclair . .	4, Finsbury-terrace.		
		Whitecross-street .	John Archer . .	22, Banner-square.		
		Old-street	Matt. Garland .	18, Ratcliffe-terrace, Goswell-road.		
		City-road	H. Hamlin . .	6, Fountain-place, City-road		
Edward Taylor .	Luton	*Luton*	William Mead .	Luton.		
		Dunstable . . .	S. Stimpson . .	Dunstable.		
Thos. Baker . .	Lutterworth . . .	*Lutterworth* . . .	Thomas Evans .	Lutterworth.		
William Short .	Lymington . . .	*Lymington.* . . .	H. Hapgood . .	Lymington	Robert King. .	Lymington.
		Milford	P. W. Jackson, jun.	Milton, Lymington.		
George Eaton . .	Macclesfield . . .	*East Macclesfield* .	Isaac Eaton . .	Macclesfield.		
		West Macclesfield .	J. Braithwaite .	Macclesfield.		
		Sutton	John Bradbury .	Sutton; Macclesfield.		
		Rainow	M. Longden . .	Rainow, Macclesfield.		
		Bollington . . .	John Taylor . .	Bollington, Macclesfield.		
		Prestbury . . .	H. R. Rice . .	Prestbury, Macclesfield.		
		Alderley	C. Baguley . .	Nether Alderley, Macclesfield.		
		Gawsworth . . .	W. Swindells . .	Gawsworth, Macclesfield.		
Edward Owen .	Machynlleth . . .	*Machynlleth* . . .	Lewis Ellis . .	Machynlleth.	J. Ellis . . .	Machynlleth.
Josiah Jones . .	Llanbrynmair, Machynlleth.	*Darowen* . . .	Edward Jones .	Darowen, Machynlleth.		
T. Edwards . .	Towyn, Merioneth.	*Pennal*	Edward Pryce .	Pennal, Machynlleth.		
Benjamin Wright	Coalbrookdale, Iron Bridge, Salop.	*Madeley*	Benjamin Wright	Coalbrookdale, Iron Bridge.		
John Barker . .	Dawley, Shiffnal.	*Dawley*	John Barker . .	Dawley, Shiffnal.		
		Broseley . . .	Richard Evans .	Broseley, Iron Bridge.		
		Much Wenlock. .	A. G. Brookes .	Much Wenlock, Iron Bridge.		
R. Holmes . .	24, High-street, Maidstone.	*East Maidstone* .	James Ruck . .	King-street, Maidstone.		
N. Walter, jun. .	Marden, Maidstone.	*West Maidstone* .	R. Holmes . .	24, High-street, Maidstone.		
		Loose	W. Streatfield .	Bearsted, Maidstone.		
		Marden . . .	N. Walter, jun. .	Marden, Maidstone.		
		Yalding . . .	John White . .	Hunton, Maidstone.		
Richard Poole .	Maldon	*All Saints* . . .	J. S. Sanders. .	Purleigh; Maldon.		
		St. Peter . . .	Edward Hance .	Maldon.		
		Bradwell . . .	G. M. Whimper .	Tillingham, Maldon . .	J. Osborne . .	Tillingham.
		Southminster . .	Isaac Rush . .	Southminster, Maldon.		
		Tollesbury . . .	Wm. Otway . .	Tolleshunt D'Arcy, Maldon.		
T. Medhurst . .	Mereworth ; Tonbridge	*Aylesford* . . .	William Gorham	Snodland, West Malling, Maidstone.	Ambrose Gorham	Snodland, Maidstone.
		Wrotham . . .	Abraham Sugden	Addington, Maidstone.		
		East Peckham	Thomas Medhurst	Mereworth, Tonbridge.		
John Lewis . .	Malmsbury . . .	*Eastern* . . .	Thomas Jones .	Malmsbury, Wilts.	H. F. Jones . .	Malmsbury.
		Western . . .	A. F. W. Jeston .	Malmsbury, Wilts.		
William Simpson	Malton	*Malton*	William Flint .	Malton	H. Spurr . . .	Malton.
		Rillington . . .	T. Allanson . .	Rillington, Malton.		
		Weston	T. Creyke . .	Burythorpe, Malton	W. Creyke . .	Burythorpe, Malton.
		Bulmer. . . .	William West .	Bulmer, Malton . . .	John Swann . .	Bulmer, Malton.
		Hovingham. . .	Wm. Chapman .	Slingsby, Malton . .	W. Bell . . .	Slingsby, Malton.
Richard Webb .	18, Brown-street, Manchester.	*Ancoats*	John Bennett .	27, Mill-street, Ancoats.		
W. V. Johns. .	Lloyd-street, Manchester.	*St. George's* . .	T. Worthington .	7, David-street, Manchester	William Cowgill.	5, Oldham-road, Manchester.
		Market-street . .	R. Webb . . .	18, Brown-street, Manchester.	R. Webb, jun. .	18, Brown-street, Manchester.
		London-road . .	J. A. Smith . .	25, Granby-row, Manchester	W. R. F. Lane .	25, Granby-row, Manchester.
		Dean's-gate . .	George Moody .	27, Cooper-street, Manchester.	W. V. Johns. .	42, Bootle-street, Manchester.
		Cheetham . . .	Thos. Robinson .	Cheetham	J. Rhodes . .	Cheetham.
		Prestwich . . .	Daniel Hope . .	Prestwich.		
		Blackley . . .	L. Smethurst .	Blackley.		
		Failsworth . . .	J. Lancashire .	Failsworth.		
		Newton. . . .	S. Lancashire .	Newton-heath.		

UNION, or SUPERINTENDENT REGISTRAR'S DISTRICT.	County.	Places of Public Worship situated therein, registered for Solemnization of Marriages.		SUPERINTENDENT REGISTRARS, and Deputy Superintendent Registrars.	
		Name.	Situation.	Name.	Address.
MANSFIELD	Nottingham . .	The Unitarian Chapel . .	Mansfield	W. Goodacre, jun.	Mansfield . . . .
		The Independent Chapel .	Mansfield.		
MARKET BOSWORTH .	Leicester . . .	The General Baptist Chapel	Barton Fabis	J. Bodin . . .	Market Bosworth .
MARKET HARBOROUGH	Leicester . . .	The General Baptist Chapel	Lubenham-lane, Market Harborough.	T. Abbott . .	Market Harborough .
		The Independent Chapel .	Market Harborough.		
		The Baptist Chapel . .	Clipston.		
MARLBOROUGH . . .	Wilts. . . .	. . .	. . .	T. B. Merriman .	Marlborough . . .
				W. C. Merriman,	Ditto.
MARTIN, ST., IN THE FIELDS.	Middlesex . .	The Adelphi Chapel . .	James-street, Adelphi . . .	P. H. Le Breton .	44, Castle-street, Leicester-square.
		The Scotch Church . .	Oxendon-street, Haymarket.		
MARTLEY	Worcester . .	. . .	. . .	C. W. Winnall .	Stourport, Worcestershire.
MARYLEBONE, ST. . .	Middlesex . .	Little Portland-street Chapel.	Marylebone	H. C. Wilson .	Register Office, Court House, St. Marylebone.
		Wells-street Chapel . .	Wells-street, Oxford-street.		
		French Catholic Chapel .	No. 1, Little George-street, King-street, Portman-square.		
		The Spanish Chapel . .	Charles-street, Marylebone.		
		The Lady's Chapel . .	Grove-road, St. John's Wood, in the parish of Marylebone.		
		Enon Chapel	New Church-street, Portman-market.		
		Paddington Chapel . .	Harcourt-street.		
MEDWAY	Kent	Ebenezer Chapel . . .	Clover-street, Chatham . .	Friend Hoar . .	Laurel Cottage, Chatham-hill.
		The Unitarian General Baptist Meeting-house.	Heaviside-lane, Chatham.		
		Zion Chapel	Clover-street, Chatham.		
MELKSHAM	Wilts. . . .	The Baptist Chapel . .	Old Broughton-lane, Melksham	John Read . .	Trowbridge, Wilts .
		The Independent Chapel .	Melksham.		
		The General Baptist Meeting.	The Conigree, in the parish of Trowbridge.		
MELTON MOWBRAY .	Leicester . . .	The Independent Chapel .	Chapel-street, Melton Mowbray	E. Batty . . .	Melton Mowbray . .
		The Wesleyan Chapel . .	Melton Mowbray.		
MERE	Wilts. . . .	Independent Chapel . .	Shaftesbury-street, Mere . .	F. Seymour . .	Castle-street, Mere .
		Bonham Catholic Chapel .	Bonham, in the parish of Stourton.		
MERIDEN	Warwick . .	. . .	. . .	J. Clarke . . .	Coleshill . . . .
MERTHYR TYDFIL . .	Glamorgan . .	Ynysgau	Merthyr Tydfil	J. W. Edwards .	Merthyr Tydfil . .
		Bethel	George-town, in the parish of Merthyr Tydfil.	Peter M'Gregor,	Ditto.
		Bethania	Dowlais, in the parish of Merthyr Tydfil.		
		Zoar	High-street, Merthyr Tydfil.		
		Tŷ Cwrdd Hengoed . .	Cefn Hengoed, in the parish of Gelligaer.		
		Bethesda	Pontystorehouse, in the parish of Merthyr Tydfil.		
		Carmel	Penypond, in the parish of Aberdare.		
		Ebenezer	Mill-street, Aberdare.		
		Tabernacle	Hirwain, in the parish of Penderyn.		
		Caer Salem	Dowlais, in the parish of Merthyr Tydfil.		
MIDHURST	Sussex . . .	. . .	. . .	R. Wardroper .	Midhurst . . . .
MILDENHALL	Suffolk . . .	. . .	. . .	W. Isaacson . .	Mildenhall . . . .
MILTON	Kent	. . .	. . .	Jno. Hinde . .	Milton, next Sittingbourne.
				J. Taylor,	Ditto.

REGISTRARS of MARRIAGES.		Registrars' Districts.	REGISTRARS of BIRTHS and DEATHS.		Deputy Registrars of Births and Deaths.	
Name.	Address.		Name.	Address.	Name.	Address.
E. G. Goodacre .	Sutton in Ashfield, Mansfield.	*Mansfield*	Rev. W. Cursham	Mansfield	A. J. Cursham .	Mansfield.
		Warsop	R. Bowler . .	Warsop, Mansfield.		
		Pleasley . . .	J. Hodgkinson .	Hardwick-park, Mansfield.		
		Sutton in Ashfield .	J. W. Valantine .	Sutton in Ashfield, Mansfield	W. Adin . . .	Upper Green, Sutton in Ashfield.
		Blackwell . . .	W. Mountany .	Blackwell, Alfreton, Derbyshire.		
		Blidworth . . .	J. Stevenson . .	Blidworth, Mansfield.		
R. Stretton . .	Carlton, Market Bosworth.	*Market Bosworth* . .	R. Stretton . .	Carlton, Hinckley.	John Myott . .	Ibstock.
		Ibstock	T. Patterson .	Ibstock, Ashby-de-la-Zouch		
J. K. Faulkner .	Market Harborough .	*Market Harborough* .	John Abbey . .	Market Harborough.		
R. Lavington .	Marlborough . . .	*Marlborough* . . .	D. P. Maurice .	Marlborough	J. Rogers . .	Marlborough.
James Kilner .	24, St. Martin's-court, Westminster.	*Charing Cross* . .	George Rawlins .	15, Salisbury-street, Strand	S. G. Rawlins .	15, Salisbury-street, Strand.
		Long Acre . . .	Edwd. Cobbett .	21, Newport-street, Long Acre.	J. N. Bainbridge	86, St. Martin's lane.
J. Wormington .	Shrawley, Stourport .	*Witley*	J. Wormington .	Shrawley, Stourport.		
		Leigh	C. Rowberry . .	Leigh, Swan-inn, Newland, near Worcester.		
		Martley	E. Lipscombe .	Martley, Worcester.		
		Holt	John Nutt . .	Hallow, Worcester.		
T. Tindall . .	13, Paradise-street, St. Marylebone.	*All Souls* . . .	T. Daniels . .	43, Great Portland-street, Marylebone.		
		Cavendish-square .	William Clapp .	62, Welbeck-street.		
		Rectory	Edwd. Joseph .	15, Great Marylebone-street.		
		St. Mary's . . .	M. Knapp . .	73, Upper Berkeley-street, Portman-square.		
		Christchurch . .	W. G. Pau . .	16, Upper Baker-street, Regent's-park.	R. Maybank . .	16, Stafford-street.
		St. John's . . .	G. H. Backhoffner	13, Aberdeen-place, St. John's Wood.	Samuel Galloway	33, Aberdeen-place.
F. Furrell . .	St. Margaret's Bank, Chatham.	*Gillingham* . . .	A. Tracey . .	High-street, Brompton, Kent.		
		Rochester . . .	F. Furrell . .	St. Margaret's Bank, Rochester.		
H. Frame . .	Trowbridge . . .	*Trowbridge* . . .	Henry Frame .	Trowbridge.		
J. H. Butterworth	Melksham.	*Melksham* . . .	George Flooks .	Melksham.		
John Towne . .	Melton Mowbray .	*Melton Mowbray* .	John Towne . .	Melton Mowbray . . .	W. Campion. .	Melton Mowbray.
		Somerby . . .	John Higgs Lee.	Twyford, Melton Mowbray.		
		Waltham . . .	J. Chamberlain .	Waltham.		
		Clawson . . .	N. Kemm . .	Eaton, Waltham.		
E. F. Maidment .	Mere	*Mere*	Wm. Godwin .	Castle-street, Mere.		
T. Harris . .	Coleshill	*Coleshill*	T. Harris. . .	Coleshill.		
		Meriden	J. H. Fretton. .	Meriden.		
M. Williams .	Aberdare, Merthyr Tydfil.	*Upper Merthyr Tydfil*	John Russell. .	Dowlais, Merthyr Tydfil.	H. P. Powell .	Dowlais, Merthyr Tydfil.
L. Williams . .	Merthyr Tydfil.	*Lower Merthyr Tydfil*	Job James . .	Merthyr Tydfil.		
R. Williams . .	Merthyr Tydfil.	*Gelligaer*	L. Edwards . .	Gelligaer, Merthyr Tydfil.		
		Aberdare	M. Williams .	Aberdare, Merthyr Tydfil.		
Daniel Moore .	Midhurst	*Midhurst*	Daniel Moore .	Midhurst.		
		Lodsworth	Charles Reed .	Lodsworth, Midhurst.		
		Trotton	William Wild .	Harting, Petersfield.		
G. C. Postans .	Mildenhall . . .	*Worlington* . . .	J. Cawston . .	Worlington, Mildenhall	W. Poulter . .	Worlington, Mildenhall.
		Lakenheath . . .	G. C. Postans .	Mildenhall	S. Playford . .	Mildenhall.
H. Hyder . .	Milton, next Sittingbourne.	*Milton*	George Ray . .	Milton, next Sittingbourne.		

UNION, or SUPERINTENDENT REGISTRAR'S DISTRICT.	County.	Places of Public Worship situated therein, registered for Solemnization of Marriages.		SUPERINTENDENT REGISTRARS, and Deputy Superintendent Registrars.	
		Name.	Situation.	Name.	Address.
MITFORD and LAUNDITCH	Norfolk . . .	The Independent Chapel .	East Dereham	Samuel King .	Litcham, Swaffham .
MONMOUTH	Monmouth . .	The Baptist Meeting-house	Coleford	W. F. Powell .	Monmouth. ' . . .
		The Catholic Chapel . .	Monmouth.		
		St. Mary's-street Chapel .	Monmouth.		
MONTGOMERY. . . .	Montgomery . .	Lord's Hill Chapel . . .	Worthin	E. Edye . . .	Montgomery . . .
		The Independent Chapel .	Welshpool.	J. Jones,	Ditto.
MORPETH	Northumberland and Durham.	The Independent Chapel .	King-street, Morpeth . . .	George Brumell .	Morpeth . . . . .
		The Presbyterian Chapel .	Morpeth.		
		The Catholic Chapel . .	Oldgate-street, Morpeth.		
		The Presbyterian Chapel .	Widdrington, in the parish of Woodhorn.		
MUTFORD and LOTHING-LAND.	Suffolk . . .	The Independent Chapel .	Lowestoft	E. Norton .	Lowestoft . . .
NANTWICH	Chester . . .	The General Baptist Chapel	Tarporley.	J. Broadhurst .	Nantwich . . .
		The Wesleyan Methodist Chapel.	Bunbury.	James Pick,	Ditto.
NARBERTH	Pembroke . .	Templeton Chapel . . .	Templeton, in the parish of Narberth.	J. Miles . . .	Narberth . . . .
		The Tabernacle . . .	Narberth.		
		Fynnon	Fynnon, in the parish of Llanwy Velfrey.		
		Hebron	Hebron, in the parish of Llanglydwen.		
		Henllan	Henllan, in the parish of Henllan, Amgoed.		
		Landilo	Landilo.		
		Bethesda	Narberth.		
		Fynnon	Fynnon, in the parish of Llandewy Velfrey.		
NEATH	Glamorgan . .	Carmel	Kaegurwen, in the parish of Llanguke.	A. Cuthbertson .	Neath . . . . .
		Pant-teg	Hamlet of Alltgrug, in the parish of Llanguke.		
		Alltwen Chapel	Alltwen, in the parish of Killybebill.		
		Zoar	Neath.		
		The Baptist Chapel . .	Neath.		
		Summersfield Chapel . .	Neath.		
		Yorath Chapel	Cwmgiedd, in the parish of Ystradgumlais.		
NEOT'S, ST..	Hunts . . .	The Old Meeting-house .	St. Neot's	George Day . .	St. Neot's . . . .
		The Dissenting Chapel .	Kimbolton.	W. Matlock,	Ditto.
NEWARK	Nottingham and Lincoln.	The Independent Chapel .	Lombard-street, Newark-upon-Trent.	G. Talleuts . .	Newark . . . : .
				J. Knight,	Ditto.
		The Wesleyan Chapel .	Balderton-gate, Newark.		
		The Roman Catholic Church of the Trinity.	Newark.		
NEWBURY	Berks. . . .	The Presbyterian Meeting-house.	Newbury . . . . . . ' .	J. Tanner . .	Speenhamland, Newbury, Berks.
		The Independent Chapel .	North-brook-street, Newbury.		
		Primitive Methodist Chapel	Bartholomew-street, Newbury.		
NEWCASTLE-IN-EMLYN	Carmarthen . .	Glandwr	Glandwr, in the parish of Llanfirnach.	T. Jones . . .	Newcastle-in-Emlyn .
		Glynarthen	Glynarthen, in the parish of Penbryn.		
		Graig	Newcastle-in-Emlyn.		
		Hawen	Rhyd Hawen, in the parish of, Troedraur.		
NEWCASTLE - UNDER - LYNE.	Stafford . . .	Ebenezer Chapel . . .	Newcastle-under-Lyne . . .	Samuel Harding.	Newcastle-under-Lyne
		The Independent Chapel .	Newcastle-under-Lyne.		
NEWCASTLE-UPON-TYNE	Northumberland	Clavering-place Chapel .	Clavering-place, Newcastle-upon-Tyne.	T. Brown. . .	Newcastle-upon-Tyne.
		Tothill-stairs, or Baptist Chapel.	Tothill-stairs, Newcastle-upon-Tyne.	Joseph Heslop,	Ditto.
		The Postern Chapel . .	Postern, Newcastle-upon-Tyne.		
		New Court Chapel. . .	New Court, Westgate-street, Newcastle-upon-Tyne.		
		The Catholic Chapel . .	Pilgrim-street, in the parish of St. Andrew.		
		Carliot-street Chapel . .	Newcastle-upon-Tyne.		
		The New Jerusalem Temple	Percy-st., Newcastle-upon-Tyne.		
		Hanover-square Chapel .	Newcastle-upon-Tyne.		
		St. James's Chapel . .	Blackett-street, Newcastle-upon-Tyne.		
		The Nelson-street Chapel.	Newcastle-upon-Tyne.		
		The Close Chapel . .	Newcastle-upon-Tyne.		
		Wall Knoll Chapel . .	Newcastle-upon-Tyne.		

REGISTRARS of MARRIAGES.		Registrars' Districts.	REGISTRARS of BIRTHS and DEATHS.		Deputy Registrars of Births and Deaths.	
Name.	Address.		Name.	Address.	Name.	Address.
W. M. Warcup	East Dereham	Litcham	C. Wallis	Litcham, Swaffham.		
		Elmham, North	T. H. Dent	North Elmham, East Dereham		
		Mittishall	H. Daveney	Mittishall, East Dereham.		
		Shipdham	J. R. Clouting	Shipdham, East Dereham.		
		East Dereham	M. Warcup	East Dereham.		
		Bawdeswell	C. Baker	Lyng, East Dereham.		
J. T. Thomas	Coleford	Monmouth	H. Thompson	Monmouth.		
		Coleford	T. Marsh	Coleford.		
		Dingeston	Edw. Farr	Rockfield, Monmouthshire.		
		Trelleck	W. Miller	Trelleck, Monmouth.		
A. Bagley	Montgomery	Montgomery	W. Blakeway	Llandysil.		
D. Gwynne	Welshpool.	Chirbury	B. Bridgwater	Chirbury.		
		Welshpool	P. Owen	Welshpool.		
E. Watson	Morpeth	Morpeth	E. Watson	Morpeth.		
		Bedlington	R. Soulaby	Bedlington, Morpeth.		
G. S. Crisp	Lowestoft	Lowestoft	John Hole	Lowestoft.		
		Gorleston	John Smith	Gorleston.		
		Kessingland	Samuel Smith	Carlton Colvile.		
W. Worthen	Wrenbury, Nantwich	Nantwich	E. H. Griffiths	Nantwich	T. Cawley	Nantwich.
		Wrenbury	W. Worthen	Wrenbury, Nantwich.		
		Wybunbury	G. Wakeman	Stapeley, Nantwich.		
		Bunbury	John Large	Bunbury, Tarporley	Peter Smith	Bunbury.
J. Griffiths	Narberth	Narberth	W. Phillips	Narberth.		
Edward Davies	Pontyrodin, Narberth.	Amroth	R. Morgan	Trenewydd, Narberth	Richard Morgan	Trenewydd.
		Begelly	J. D. Palmour	Cresselly, Narberth.		
		Slebech	H. O. Martin	Templeton, Narberth.		
		Llanboidy	R. Richards	Whitland, Narberth.		
		Llandissilo	E. Harries	Bryndissil, Narberth	John David	Llandissilio.
E. Thomas	Neath	Neath	W. P. Rees	Neath.		
		Margam	F. Cole	Taibach, Margam.		
		Ystradfelte	David Powell	Goitre, Ystradfelte, Neath.		
		Cadoxton	E. Thomas	Cadoxton Cottage, Neath.		
		Lansamlet	T. Thomas	Tirbach, Lansamlet, Neath.		
		Ystradgunlais	William Price	Yniscedwin, Swansea.		
L. Addington	St. Neot's	St. Neot's	L. Addington	St. Neot's.		
W. Ennals	Kimbolton.	Kimbolton and Eaton	W. Ennals	Kimbolton.		
John Welby	Newark	Collingham	R. Cooper	Collingham, Newark	William Woolley	Collingham.
		Bassingham	Thomas Johnson	Bassingham, Newark.		
		Bennington	Charles Poole	Long Bennington, Newark.		
		Newark	John Welby	Newark, Notts	W. Bousfield	Bargate, Newark.
		Claypole	Edw. Elston	Claypole, Newark.		
Thomas Ward	Newbury	Newbury	Thos. Ward	Newbury	W. Daniels	Newbury.
		Speen	R. R. Robison	Speen, Newbury	B. Butt	Speenhamland, Newbury.
		Thatcham	James Billing	Thatcham, Newbury	J. Wimbolt	Thatcham, Newbury.
John Morgan	Broxwyn, Troedyraur, Cardigan.	Llandissel	J. Mathias	Llandissel ; Newcastle-in-Emlyn.		
T. Thomas, jun.	Newcastle-in-Emlyn.	Kenarth	J. Jones	Newcastle-in-Emlyn.		
		Penbryn	T. Williams	Adpar-in-Emlyn	David Darres	Adpar-in-Emlyn.
J. H. Robey	Newcastle-under-Lyne	Newcastle-under-Lyne	William Howson	Newcastle-under-Lyne.		
		Whitmore	G. Fairbanks	Whitmore, Newcastle-under-Lyne.		
		Audley	Samuel Hilditch	Audley, Newcastle-under-Lyne.		
John Routledge	Newcastle-upon-Tyne.	St. Nicholas	W. Findley	Newcastle-upon-Tyne.		
D. M'Allum	Blacket-street, Newcastle-upon-Tyne.	All Saints	Joseph Pearson	Newcastle-upon-Tyne	T. Grey	The Manors, Newcastle-upon-Tyne.
		St. Andrew	D. M'Allum	Newcastle-upon-Tyne	J. Cowell	Green-court, Newgate-street, Newcastle-upon-Tyne.
		Byker	J. Findley	Stepney-field, East Byker, Newcastle.	Thomas Wailes	Ballast Hills Burying ground.
		Westgate	J. Atkinson	Blenheim-st., in Westgate, Newcastle-upon-Tyne.	G. Rutherford	Bath-lane, Newcastle-upon-Tyne.

UNION, or SUPERINTENDENT REGISTRAR'S DISTRICT.	County.	Places of Public Worship situated therein, registered for Solemnization of Marriages.		SUPERINTENDENT REGISTRARS, and *Deputy Superintendent Registrars.*	
		Name.	Situation.	Name.	Address.
NEWENT	Gloucester . .	. . .	. . .	A. Lauder . . *J. Cannock,*	Newent . . . . *Ditto.*
NEW FOREST	Hants . . .	Ebenezer Independent Chapel.	Totton, in the parish of Eling.	E. Coxwell . .	Totton, Eling, Hants.
NEWINGTON	Surrey . . .	Beresford Chapel . . York-street Chapel . . Horsley-street Chapel . Brunswick Chapel . . .	Beresford-street, Walworth . York-street, Walworth. Horsley-street, Walworth. Great Dover-road, Southwark.	John Rowbotham *William Lambe,*	55, Queen's-row, Walworth. 1, *Bolingbroke Row, Walworth-road.*
NEWMARKET	Cambridge and Suffolk.	The Baptist Meeting-house The Independent Chapel .	Clay-street, Soham . . . . High Town, in the parish of Burwell.	W. P. Isaacson .	Newmarket . . .
NEWPORT (MONMOUTH)	Monmouth . .	Tabernacle Chapel. . . Bethany . . . . . . The Welsh Baptist Chapel English Baptist Chapel . Moriah . . . . . . Bethel . . . . . Twyn Gwyn . . . . Beulah . . . . . . Bethesda . . . . Penymain . . . . Siloam . . . . . . Bethel . . . . . Hope Chapel . . . . The Baptist Chapel . . Salem . . . . . The Roman Catholic Chapel Mount Sion . . . . Zoar.	Commercial-street, Newport . Lanvaches. Charles-street, Newport. Commercial-street, Newport. Risca. Penyrhiwffranc, in the parish of Mynyddyslwyn. Ynys Ddu, in the parish of Mynyddyslwyn. Newbridge, in the parish of Mynyddyslwyn. Cefn, hamlet of Roger-stone, in the parish of Bassaleg. Penymain, in the parish of Mynyddyslwyn. Fwrwmeisdedd, in the parish of Machen. Graig, in the parish of Bassaleg. Commercial-street, Newport. Caerleon. Castletown, in the parish of Marshfield. Stow, in the parish of St. Woollos. Newport. Henllys.	H. Spratt . . *John Pollard,*	Caerleon, Monmouthshire. *Newport.*
NEWPORT (SALOP) . .	Salop	. . .	. . .	H. Heans . .	Newport, Salop . .
NEWPORT PAGNELL .	Bucks . . .	The Independent Meeting The Baptist Meeting-house Catholic Chapel . . . The Independent Chapel .	Newport Pagnell . . . . Olney. Weston Underwood. Olney.	W. Powell . . *G. Cosch.*	Newport Pagnell . . *Ditto.*
NEWTON ABBOT . . .	Devon . . .	Cross Chapel . . . . The Independent Chapel . St. Cyprian's Chapel . . Salem Chapel . . . . Zion Chapel . . . . The Wesleyan Methodist Chapel. The Wesleyan Methodist Chapel. The Old Independent Meeting-house. The Baptist Chapel . . Tor Abbey Chapel. . . The Ebenezer Baptist Chapel	Moreton-Hampstead . . . Chapel-street, Dawlish. Ugbrooke, in the parish of Chudleigh. Wolborough-st., Newton Abbot. Dawlish-road, East Teignmouth. Ipplepen. Newton Bushel, in the parish of Highweek. Ashburton. Newton Abbot. Tor Abbey, near Torquay. Torquay.	J. Alsop . . .	Newton Abbot . .
NEWTOWN and LLANIDLOES.	Montgomery . ^	The Baptist Chapel . . Zion Chapel	Shortbridge-street, Llanidloes . Shortbridge-street, Llanidloes.	D. Smith . . .	Newtown, Montgomery
NORTHALLERTON . .	York	Zion Chapel	Northallerton	E. H. Reed . .	Northallerton . . .
NORTHAMPTON . . .	Northampton .	Unitarian Chapel . . King-street Chapel . . Commercial-street Chapel. College-street Chapel . . Castle-hill Chapel . . The Wesleyan Chapel. . The Baptist Chapel . . The Baptist Chapel . . The Baptist Chapel . .	King-street, Northampton . Northampton. Commercial-st., Northampton. Northampton. Castle-hill, Northampton. Gold-street, Northampton. Kislingbury. Kingsthorpe. Rugbrook.	W. Tomalin . *George Roe,*	Northampton . . . *All Saints, Northampton.*
NORTH AYLESFORD .	Kent	The Baptist Chapel . .	Leading-street, in the parish of Meopham.	J. S. Bullard. .	Strood, Rochester . .

REGISTRARS of MARRIAGES.		Registrars' Districts.	REGISTRARS of BIRTHS and DEATHS.		Deputy Registrars of Births and Deaths.	
Name.	Address.		Name.	Address.	Name.	Address.
Wm. Bruton. .	High-street, Newent.	Newent	Wm. Bruton. .	High-street, Newent.		
W. Paine. . .	Redmarley, Newent.	Redmarley. . . .	William Paine .	Redmarley, Newent . .	J. Stephens . .	Hartpury, Gloucester.
Peter Dore . .	Totton, Southampton	Eling	T. Couchman .	Totton, Hants	C. Tozer . . .	Eling, Southampton.
		Lyndhurst . . .	Isaac Fielder .	Bramshaw, Southampton .	J. Henbest . .	Fritham, Bramshaw.
		Fawley.	T. Fry . . .	Fawley, Southampton .	E. Fry . . .	Fawley, Southampton.
G. G. Lowne. .	8, King's-row, Walworth.	St. Mary's	G. Young . .	7, Church-row, Newington	J. Packer . . .	24, Albion-place, Walworth.
C. Wilkinson .	18, Virginia-terrace, Great Dover-road.	St. Peter's, Walworth.	G. G. Lowne. .	8, King's-row, Walworth .	Wm. Buckland .	26, Camden-street, East-lane, Walworth.
		Trinity, Newington .	Chas. Wilkinson	18, Virginia-terrace, Great Dover-road.		
R. Bayley . .	St. Mary, Newmarket	Newmarket . . .	Robt. McPherson	Newmarket.		
		Bottisham . . .	J. Dilliston . .	Bottisham.		
		Cheveley	R. Faircloth . .	Newmarket.		
		Gazeley	W. Clark. . .	Gazeley.		
		Soham	E. L. Knowles .	Soham.		
C. Lewis . . .	Newport, Monmouthshire.	Newport	W. D. Evans. .	Newport, Monmouthshire	C. Lewis . . .	Newport, Monmouthshire.
E. Davies . .	Abercarn.	Mynyddyslwyn .	E. Davies . .	Abercarn, Newport, Monmouthshire.		
James Salter .	Llanhennock.	Caerleon	James Salter .	Llanhennock, Caerleon.		
		St. Woollos . . .	H. E. Hawkins .	Newport, Monmouthshire.		
J. Stanley . .	Newport, Salop . .	Newport	Joseph Wilson .	Newport, Salop.		
		Gnosall	John Hawkins .	Gnosall, Newport, Salop.		
D. Norris. . .	Newport Pagnell . .	Fenny Stratford .	T. Chew, jun. .	Great Brickhill, Fenny Stratford.		
		Newport Pagnell .	W. White . .	Newport Pagnell . . .	R. White. . .	Newport Pagnell.
		Olney	Samuel Griggs .	Sherington, Newport Pagnell	H. Hurst. . .	Olney.
Elias Ford . .	Newton Abbot . .	Newton Abbot . .	N. Walke . .	Newton Abbot	P. Major. . .	Newton Abbot.
J. Billett . . .	Moreton-Hampstead.	Moreton-Hampstead	M. W. Harvey .	Moreton-Hampstead . .	R. Tremlett . .	Moreton-Hampstead.
T. Latham . .	Chudleigh.	Chudleigh	W. Whitsway .	Chudleigh	J. Haynes . .	Chudleigh.
Wm. Yeo . .	Teignmouth.	Teignmouth . . .	W. R. Jordan .	Teignmouth.		
John Mathews .	Ashburton.	Torquay	J. S. Prowse . .	Torquay.	W. Prowse . .	Torquay.
Charles Kilby .	Torquay.	Ashburton	J. Fitze . . .	Ashburton	P. Foot . . .	Ashburton.
T. Jones . . .	China-st., Llanidloes .	Newtown	Thomas Higgins	Gas-street, Newtown.		
		Llanidloes, Upper .	T. Jones . . .	China-street, Llanidloes.		
		Llanidloes, Lower .	R. Lewis . . .	Church-street, Llanidloes.		
		Kerry	R. Pryce . .	Kerry-village, Newtown.		
		Llanmeog	C. Hughes . .	Llandinam, Newtown.		
		Tregynon	Evan Jones . .	Taullan, Llanwyddelan, Newtown.		
J. S. Walton .	Northallerton . . .	Northallerton . . .	J. S. Walton . .	Northallerton.		
		Appleton-upon-Wiske .	T. Hopton . .	Appleton-upon-Wiske, Great Smeaton.		
W. Cornfield. .	All Saints, Northampton.	Bugbrook	G. Wright . .	Nether Heyford, Northampton.		
		All Saints	W. Cornfield. .	Commercial-street, Northampton.	G. H. Law . .	Drapery, Northampton
		St. Giles	W. Sawbridge .	Abington-st., Northampton.	Geo. Barnes .	Mayorhold, St. Sepulchre, Northampton.
G. Mungeam .	Meopham, Gravesend	Northfleet	G. Mungeam .	Meopham, Gravesend .	W. Mungeam .	Meopham, Gravesend.
R. Gates . . .	Frindsbury, Rochester.	Strood	R. Gates. . .	Frindsbury, Rochester.	J. Colley. . .	High-street, Strood, Rochester.

M

UNION, or SUPERINTENDENT REGISTRAR'S DISTRICT.	County.	Places of Public Worship situated therein, registered for Solemnization of Marriages.		SUPERINTENDENT REGISTRARS, and *Deputy Superintendent Registrars.*	
		Name.	Situation.	Name.	Address.
NORTHLEACH	Gloucester . .	. . .	. . .	F. Herbert . .	Northleach . . .
NORTHWICH	Chester . . .	The Independent Chapel .	Northwich	T. R. Barker	Northwich. . . .
		The Tabernacle . . .	Witton, in the parish of Great Budworth.	*J. Carrington,*	*Northwich, Cheshire.*
		The Independent Chapel .	Over.		
		The Independent Chapel .	Queen-street, Middlewich.		
NORTH WITCHFORD .	Cambridge . .	The General Baptist Chapel	March, in the parish of Doddington.	John Sewell . .	Chatteris, Cambridgeshire.
		The Independent Chapel .	Park-street, Chatteris.		
NORWICH	Norfolk . . .	St. Mary's Chapel . . .	Norwich.	F. J. Blake . .	King-street, Norwich.
		Prince's-street Chapel . .	Norwich.	*Edward Hare,*	*Heigham, Norwich.*
		St. Peter's Wesleyan Chapel	Lady's-lane, Norwich.		
		The Octagon Chapel . .	Norwich.		
		St. Clement's Chapel . .	St. Clement's, Norwich.		
		Orford-hill Chapel . . .	In the parish of St. John, Timber-hill, Norwich.		
		The Catholic Chapel . .	Willow-lane, Norwich.		
		The Old Meeting . . .	St. Clement, Norwich.		
		The Catholic Chapel . .	Norwich, in the parish of St. John, Maddermarket.		
NOTTINGHAM	Notts.	Castle Gate Meeting-house	Castle-gate, in the parish of St. Nicholas.	A. Barnett . .	Mansfield-road, Nottingham.
		The High Pavement, or Presbyterian Chapel . .	On the High Pavement, in the parish of St. Mary, Nottingham.	*L. Hardy,*	*Derby-road, Nottingham*
		St. John's Catholic Chapel	George-street, Nottingham.		
		Mary Gate Chapel . .	Nottingham.		
		Baptist Chapel. . . .	George-street, Nottingham.		
		Bethesda Meeting . . .	Nottingham.		
		General Baptist Chapel .	Broad-street, Nottingham.		
		The General Baptist Chapel	Plumtre-place, Stoney-street, Nottingham.		
		Friar-lane Chapel . . .	Nottingham.		
		St. James's-street . . .	Nottingham.		
		Park-street Meeting-house	Nottingham.		
NUNEATON	Warwick . . .	Zion Chapel	Nuneaton	G. W. Craddock.	Nuneaton . . . .
		The Old Independent Chapel	Chilvers Coton.		
OAKHAM	Rutland . . .	. . .	. . .	H. Hough . .	Oakham . . . .
				J. R. Silver,	*Ditto.*
OKEHAMPTON	Devon . . .	Ebenezer Chapel . . .	Okehampton	H. Hawkes . .	Okehampton . . .
		Wesleyan Methodist Chapel	Sticklepath, in the parish of Sampford Courtenay.	*John James,*	*Ditto.*
OLAVE, ST., SOUTHWARK	Surrey . . .	Maze-pond Meeting-house	Maze-pond, Southwark . .	R. Slee . . .	1, Parish-street, Horselydown.
		Unicorn-yard Chapel . .	Tooley-street.		
		Union Chapel	Parish-st., St. John's, Southwark		
ONGAR	Essex. . . .	. . .	. . .	W. Baker . .	Chipping Ongar . .
				C. Mott,	*Ditto.*
ORMSKIRK	Lancaster . .	Southport Tabernacle, or Independent Chapel.	Southport, in the parish of North Meols.	L. Wright . .	Aughton, Ormskirk .
		New House Chapel . .	Aughton.		
		St. Mary's Chapel . . .	Aughton.		
		St. John's Chapel . . .	Lathom.		
		St. Mary's Chapel . . .	Scarisbrick.		
		The Independent Chapel .	Church Town, North Meols.		
ORSETT	Essex. . . .	Ockendon Chapel . . .	South Ockendon	T. Bird . . .	Orsett, Romford, Essex
OSWESTRY	Salop	Independent Chapel . .	Arthur-street, Oswestry. .	N. Minshall .	Oswestry . . . .
		Bethesda	Maesbury, in the parish of Oswestry.	*T. Minshall,*	*Ditto.*
OTLEY	York . . .	Salem Chapel	Bridge-street, Otley . . .	J. Spence. . .	Otley . . . .
		Buckstone's Chapel . .	Rawden, in the parish of Guiseley.		
		St. Maries	Middleton Lodge, Ilkley.		
		Wesley Chapel. . . .	Borough Gate, Otley.		
OUNDLE	Northampton .	The Independent Meeting-house.	West-street, Oundle. . . .	Samuel Tibbits .	Oundle. . . . .
				H. Roper,	*Ditto.*

REGISTRARS of MARRIAGES.		Registrars' Districts.	REGISTRARS of BIRTHS and DEATHS.		Deputy Registrars of Births and Deaths.	
Name.	Address.		Name.	Address.	Name.	Address.
J. Hathaway .	Coln St. Dennis, North-leach.	*Bibury and Chedworth*	J. Hathaway . .	Coln St. Dennis, Northleach	John Butlin . .	Calentt, in the parish of Coln St. Dennis, Northleach.
J. Dale . . .	Northwich. . . .	*Northwich* . . .	J. Dale . . .	Northwich.		
T. Hughes . .	Middlewich.	*Middlewich* . . .	J. Hadfield . .	Middlewich.		
		Over	Peter Plumbley .	Over Winsford.		
		Weaverham . .	Thomas Woodyer	Weaverham, Northwich.		
J. H. Wright .	Chatteris, Cambridge-shire.	*Chatteris* . . .	J. H. Wright .	Chatteris, Cambridgeshire.		
		March	C. Culledge . .	March, Cambridgeshire.		
J. O. Taylor .	St. Giles, Norwich	*East Wymer* . . .	B. H. 'Norgate .	Bank-street, Norwich.		
David Swann .	Magdalen-st., Norwich.	*Conisford* . . .	Charles Drake .	King-street, Norwich.		
		Mancroft . . .	W. P. Nichols .	Surrey-street, Norwich.		
		West Wymer . .	W. H. Taylor .	Castle Meadow, Norwich.		
		Coslany . . .	W. T. Roper. .	Colegate-street, Norwich.		
H. Wells . . .	Nottingham . . .	*St. Ann's* . . .	J. Wilcockson .	Haughton-st., Nottingham.		
George Pearson .	Nottingham.	*Byron*	John Parr . .	Warser Gate, Nottingham.		
Samuel Moore .	Nottingham.	*St. Mary's* . . .	Samuel Moore .	High Pavement, Notting-ham.		
		Exchange . . .	J. Burton . .	Bottle-lane, Nottingham.		
		Castle	Samuel Moore .	Castle-gate, Nottingham.		
		Park	W. M. Kidd .	Hound's Gate, Nottingham.		
		Sherwood . . .	C. George . .	Crown-yard, Long-row, Not-tingham.	J. Crofts . . .	Long-row, Nottingham
J. Estlin . . .	Nuneaton	*Nuneaton* . . .	T. H. Miles . .	Nuneaton	Joseph Scrivener	Nuneaton.
J. Lacey . . .	Oakham	*Oakham* . . .	E. W. Clarke .	Barleythorpe, Oakham .	J. H. Leach . .	Oakham.
H. Newton . .	Okehampton . . .	*Okehampton* . .	J. W. Thorns .	Okehampton	H. Churchward .	Okehampton.
		Chagford . . .	R. Thorn . .	Chagford	J. Thorn . . .	Chagford.
		North Tawton . .	J. Chapple . .	North Tawton . . .	J. Ellis . . .	North Tawton.
		Hatherleigh . .	J. S. Day . .	Hatherleigh	W. Edwards . .	Hatherleigh.
		Bratton Clovelly .	R. Evely . .	North Lew, Okehampton .	George Evely .	North Lew.
W. Stainer . .	2, Broadway, St. Thomas	*St. Olave & St. Thomas*	W. Stainer ?. .	Broadway, St. Thomas.		
		St. John, Horselydown	John Bensted	2, New-street, Dockhead, St. John's.	T. Powell . .	169, Tooley-street.
Jeremiah Playl .	Chipping Ongar . .	*Chipping Ongar* . .	Thomas Thompson	Stanford Rivers, Chipping Ongar.		
		Bobbingworth . .	Robert Eve . .	Fyfield, Chipping Ongar.		
H. Culshaw . .	Ormskirk . . .	*North Meols* . .	R. Wright . .	Southport, in North Meols	Wm. Mallalieu .	Southport.
John Gobin . .	Burscough, Ormskirk.	*Scarisbrick* . . .	J. Sumner . .	Burscough, Ormskirk.		
Richard Wright .	Southport, North Meols, Ormskirk.	*Ormskirk* . . .	H. Culshaw . .	Ormskirk.		
		Lathom . . .	John Rigby . .	Lathom.		
		Bickerstaffe . .	J. Fletcher . .	Bickerstaffe.		
		Aughton . . .	M. Chadwick .	Aughton.		
		Formby . . .	R. Sumner . .	Formby.		
		Tarleton . . .	G. Ascroft . .	Tarleton.		
		Halsall. . . .	T. Sumner . .	Halsall.		
D. Corbett, M.D.	Orsett, Romford, Essex	*Orsett*	D. Corbett, M.D.	Orsett, Romford, Essex.		
Thomas Woollings	North Ockendon, Rom-ford.	*Grays*	R. B. Jordison .	South Ockendon, Essex.		
J. Davies . . .	Oswestry	*Oswestry* . . .	T. Hill . . .	Oswestry	W. Pryce . .	Oswestry
		Knockin . . .	S. Briscoe . .	Long-Oak, (Ruyton-of-the-eleven-Towns) Salop.		
		St. Martin's . . .	J. Rogers. . .	Bryngwilla, St. Martin's, Oswestry.		
		Llansillin . . .	W. Mather . .	Llansilliu, Oswestry.		
W. Barret . .	Otley	*Otley*	W. Barret . .	Otley.		
		Yeadon . . .	T. Nicholson .	Yeadon.		
		Baildon . . .	W. Holmes . .	Baildon.	T. Holmes, jun. .	Baildon.
		Fewston . . .	J. Roundell . .	Norwood-cum-Clifton.		
		Harewood . . .	J. Harrison . .	Harewood.		
S. Selby . . .	Oundle	*Oundle.* . . .	S. Selby . . .	Oundle.		
J. Siddons . .	Tansor, Oundle.	*Fotheringhay* . .	J. Siddons . .	Tansor, Oundle.		
G. Webster . .	Weldon, Wansford.	*Weldon* . . .	G. Webster . .	Weldon, Wansford.		

M 2

UNION, or SUPERINTENDENT REGISTRAR'S DISTRICT.	County.	Places of Public Worship situated therein, registered for Solemnization of Marriages.		SUPERINTENDENT REGISTRARS, and *Deputy Superintendent Registrars.*	
		Name.	Situation.	Name.	Address.
OXFORD	Oxford . . .	George-street Chapel . .	Oxford	J. T. Dodney. .	Oxford.
		The Wesleyan Chapel .	New Inn, Hall-street, Oxford .	C. Y. Eldridge,	Iris-place, Oxford.
		New Road Chapel . . .	New-road, in the parish of St. Peter-le-Bailey.		
PANCRAS, ST.	Middlesex . .	St. Aloysius's Chapel . .	Clarence-square, Somers' Town.	J. Ivimey . .	13, Mornington-place, Hampstead-road.
		Tonbridge Chapel . . .	Tonbridge-place, New-road.	*Chas. Ives,*	*Ditto.*
		The Independent Chapel .	Kentish Town.		
		Bethel Chapel	Chapel-street, Somers' Town.		
PATELEY-BRIDGE . .	York	Providence Chapel. . .	Dacre, in the parish of Ripon .	R. Holgate : .	Pateley-bridge . .
		Salem Chapel	Bridgehouse-gate, near Pateley-bridge.		
PATRINGTON	York	. . .	. . .	J. Little . . .	Patrington . . .
PEMBROKE.	Pembroke . .	Bethany.	Pembroke-dock	John Jones . .	Pembroke . . . .
		Tabernacle.	Rose Market.		
PENKRIDGE.	Stafford . . .	Brewood Chapel . . .	Sandy-lane, Brewood . . .	John Hay . .	Brewood, Wolverhampton.
				S. S. Cholditch,	*Dean-street, Brewood.*
PENRITH.	Cumberland . .	Ebenezer Chapel . . .	Penrith	T. Hobson . .	Penrith . . . .
				Hm. Maychell,	*Ditto.*
PENZANCE	Cornwall .	The Jordan Baptist Chapel	Penzance.	G. D. John . .	Penzance . . . .
				E. H. Rodd . .	*Ditto.*
PERSHORE	Worcester . .	. . .	. . .	W. W. Woodward	Pershore . . . .
PETERBOROUGH . . .	Northampton .	The Independent Chapel .	Westgate-street, Peterborough.	F. J. Jenkins .	Peterborough . . .
				J. G. Atkinson,	*Ditto.*
PETERSFIELD	Hants . . .	The Independent Chapel .	College-street, Petersfield . .	W. Albery . .	Petersfield. . . .
PETWORTH	Sussex . . .	The Baptist Meeting-house	Billingshurst.	A. Dainfrey . .	Petworth . . . .
PEWSEY	Wilts	. . .	. . .	T. White . . .	Pewsey . . . .
PICKERING	York	. . .	. . .	F. D. Parkinson .	Pickering . . . .
PLOMESGATE	Suffolk . . .	The Independent Meeting	Rendham.	J. Dallenger . .	Wickham Market, Suffolk.
		The Independent Meeting-house.	New-road, Framlingham.		
		The Old Meeting-house .	Framlingham.		
		The Independent Meeting-house.	Londham-street, in the parish of Wickham Market.		
PLYMOUTH	Devon . . .	Eldad Chapel	Wyndham-place, Plymouth .	William Pridham	Plymouth . . . .
		The Presbyterian Chapel .	Higher Batter-street, Plymouth	*E. Nettleton,*	30, *Whimple-street, Plymouth.*
		Norley Chapel	Norley-street, Plymouth.		
		Salem Chapel	Salem-street, Plymouth.		
		Ebenezer Methodist Chapel	Saltash-street, Plymouth.		
		Unitarian Chapel . . .	Bilbury-street, Plymouth.		
		How-street Chapel . .	Plymouth.		
PLYMPTON ST. MARY .	Devon . . .	. . .	. . .	N. Lockyer . .	Princess-square, Plymouth.
POCKLINGTON. . . .	York	Houghton Catholic Chapel	Houghton, in the parish of Sancton.	H. Powell . .	Pocklington . . .
		Everingham, St. Mary's Catholic Church.	Everingham.		

REGISTRARS of MARRIAGES.		Registrars' Districts.	REGISTRARS of BIRTHS and DEATHS.		Deputy Registrars of Births and Deaths.	
Name.	Address.		Name.	Address.	Name.	Address.
John Cox . .	Walton-place, Oxford	*Oxford*. . . .	R. Green. . .	Pembroke-street, Oxford.	T. Green . . .	Paradise-square.
J. Worrell . .	28, Hunter-street, Brunswick-square.	*Tottenham*	J. Wells . . .	22, Percy-street, Bedford-square.	John Riley . .	23, Percy-street, Tottenham-court-road.
W. H. Matthews	44, Upper Seymour-street, Somers'-town.	*Gray's Inn-lane* . .	J. Worrell . .	28, Hunter-street, Brunswick-square.	J. Worrell . .	28, Hunter-street, Brunswick-square.
		Somers' Town . .	W. H. Matthews	44, Upper Seymour-street, Euston-square.		
		Camden Town . . .	J. Curtis . . .	12, Union-terrace, Camden Town.		
		Regent's-park . . .	C. H. Spong . .	1, Edward-street, Hampstead-road.	F. Spong . . .	1, Edward-street, Hampstead-road.
		Kentish Town . . .	Edward Hacker .	15. Bartholomew-place, Kentish Town.		
J. Gill . . .	Pateley-bridge. . .	*Pateley*	J. Gill . . .	Pateley-bridge	R. Snow . . .	Pateley-bridge.
J. Swain . . .	Summer-bridge, Pateley-bridge.	*Ramsgill* . . .	G. Warriner . .	Middlesmoor . . .	H. Lee . . .	Middlesmoor.
		Dacre Banks . .	J. Swain . . .	Summer-bridge, Pateley-bridge.	J. Burton . . .	Banks, Pateley-bridge.
		Thornthwaite . . .	J. Metcalfe . .	Thornthwaite, Pateley-bridge	W. Grange . .	Thornthwaite, Pateley-bridge.
W. Little, jun. .	Patrington. . . .	*Patrington*. . . .	W. Little . .	Patrington.		
G. Allen . .	Milton	*Pembroke* . . .	J. Russell . .	Maiden Wells, Pembroke .	T. Marychurch	Westgate, Pembroke.
J. Russell . .	Maiden Wells, Pembroke.	*Tenby* . . .	George Allen . .	Milton, Pembroke . . .	J. Llewhellin .	Milton, Pembroke.
John Lewis .	Llanstadwell, Milford.	*Roose* . . .	J. Lewis . . .	Llanstadwell, Milford.		
H. H. Bond .	Brewood, Wolverhampton.	*Brewood* . . .	H. H. Bond . .	Brewood, Wolverhampton.		
		Penkridge . . .	J. M. Lister . .	Penkridge, Wolverhampton.		
		Cannock . . .	A. Fry . . .	Cannock, Walsall . . .	Thomas Holmes	Cannock, Walsall.
T. Atkinson . .	Penrith	*Penrith* . . .	T. Atkinson . .	Penrith.	T. Smith . . .	Penrith.
		Kirkoswald . . .	Josh. Sander. . .	Ainstable, Kirkoswald, Penrith.	Edward Fisher .	Dale, Kirkoswald.
		Greystoke . . .	John Bell . .	Little Blencow, Penrith.		
John James . .	Penzance	*Penzance* . . .	John James . .	Penzance	F. Trounson . .	Clare-street, Penzance.
		St. Just . . .	John Davey . .	St. Just, Penzance.		
		St. Buryan . . .	William Thomas,	St. Buryan, Penzance . .	Wm. Thomas, jun	Church Town, St. Buryan.
		St. Ives . . .	W. Yonge . .	St. Ives.		
		Uny Lelant . . .	James Sandow .	Uny Lelant, Hayle.		
		Marazion . . .	F. Millett . .	Marazion	H. M. Praed . .	Marazion.
J. B. Baugh . .	Pershore	*Pershore* . . .	W. Wadley . .	Pershore.		
		Upton Snodsbury .	Edward Noond .	Peopleton, Pershore.		
		Eckington . . .	John Harris . .	Eckinton, Pershore.		
J. Wiggin . .	Peterborough . . .	*Peterborough* . . .	T. Southam . .	Peterborough	F. Southam . .	Peterborough.
		Stilton . . .	J. Drage . . .	Stilton	F. B. Drage. . .	Stilton.
		Crowland . . .	H. Walton . .	Crowland	John Trowell .	Crowland.
J. O. Vick . .	Petersfield. . . .	*Petersfield*. . . .	Jas. Inwood . .	Steep, Petersfield.	J. Inwood, jun.	Liss, Petersfield.
		Eastmeon . . .	W. Durman . .	Langrish, Petersfield.	G. Pink . . .	Eastmeon, Petersfield.
G. Wells . . .	Petworth . . .	*Petworth* . . .	G. Wells . .	Petworth.	J. S. Penfold .	Petworth.
		Billingshurst . .	H. Turner . .	Billingshurst, Petworth .	J. Barnes. . .	Billingshurst-street, Petworth.
S. B. Dixon . .	Pewsey	*Pewsey*. . . .	J. Beck . . .	Sunny Hill, Pewsey.		
		Netheravon . . .	J. P. Akerman .	Upavon, Pewsey.		
W. Wilsthorp .	Pickering	*Pickering* . . .	W. Wilsthorp . .	Pickering	R. Greenwood .	Pickering.
		Allerston . . .	R. Storr . . .	Farmanby, Pickering.		
		Lockton . . .	M. Taylor . .	Lockton, Pickering.		
		Lastingham . .	R. Jackson . .	Lastingham, Kirby Moorside		
		Normanby . .	J. Featherstone .	Normanby, Kirby Moorside.		
R. Welham . .	Framlingham. . .	*Earl Soham* . . .	Edward Gross .	Earl Soham.		
		Saxmundham . . .	H. L. Freeman .	Saxmundham.		
		Aldborough . . .	J. Garrod. . .	Stratford St. Andrew's, Saxmundham.		
		Orford.	R. Wigg . . .	Tunstall, Orford, Saxmundham.		
		Wickham Market . .	C. C. Minter . .	Wickham Market.		
		Framlingham . .	M. Keer . .	Framlingham.		
John West . .	23, Bilbury-street, Plymouth.	*St. Andrew* . . .	J. Wyatt . . .	27, Bedford-street, Plymouth.	Samuel Wyatt	Queen-street, Plymouth
		Charles the Martyr .	H. H. Heyden . .	1, Tavistock-street, Plymouth.		
F. C. Nettleton .	Ridgway, Plympton .	*Plympton* . . .	Thos. Southwood	Ridgway, Plympton.		
		Yealmpton. . . .	John Revell . .	Yealmpton.		
T. Scaife . . .	Pocklington . . .	*Pocklington* . . .	Edward Danson .	Pocklington.		
		Market Weighton .	R. Jefferson . .	Market Weighton.		
		East Stamford-bridge .	John Wright . .	East Stamford-bridge.		

UNION, or SUPERINTENDENT REGISTRAR'S DISTRICT.	County.	Places of Public Worship situated therein, registered for Solemnization of Marriages.		SUPERINTENDENT REGISTRARS, and *Deputy Superintendent Registrars.*	
		Name.	Situation.	Name.	Address.
PONTEFRACT	York	Halliwalls	Tanshelf, in the parish of Pontefract.	John Foster . .	Pontefract. . . .
		Ebenezer Chapel . . .	Pontefract.		
		Providence Chapel. . .	Knottingley, in the parish of Pontefract.		
PONT-Y-POOL	Monmouth . .	Pisca	Talywaine, in the parish of Trevethin.	C. T. Edwards .	Pont-y-Pool . . .
		Welsh Baptist Chapel .	Trosnant, Pont-y-Pool.		
		New-inn Chapel . . .	Panteague.		
		English Baptist Chapel .	Trosnant, Pont-y-Pool, in the parish of Trevethin.		
		The Penygarne Baptist Tabernacle.	Pont-y-Pool.		
		The English Baptist Chapel	Abersuchan, in the parish of Trevethin.		
		Sion Chapel	Pontheer, in the parish of Llanvrechva Lower.		
		Ebenezer Chapel . . .	Pontnewynidd, in the parish of Trevethin.		
		Pontrhydyyn Chapel .	Pontrhydyryn, in the parish of Llanvrechva, Lower.		
		Sardis Chapel	Garndiffaith, in the parish of Trevethin.		
POOLE	Dorset . . .	The Independent Chapel .	Skinner-street, Poole . . .	R. H. Parr . . R. W. Parr,	Fish-street, Poole. . Parkstone, Poole.
POPLAR	Middlesex . .	The Roman Catholic Chapel.	Wade-street, Poplar. . . .	John Symons .	Manor-terrace, Bromley-hall, Middlesex.
		Old Ford Chapel . . .	Bow.		
		Harley-street Chapel . .	Bow.		
PORTSEA ISLAND. . .	Hants . . .	St. Peter's Chapel . . .	Daniel-street, Portsea . . .	J. Moorman . .	2, Lion-terrace, Portsea Town.
		Independent Chapel . .	King-street, Portsea.		
		The Baptist Chapel . .	Meeting House-alley, Portsea.		
		The Catholic Chapel . . .	Prince George's-street, Portsea.		
		Buckland Chapel . .	Buckland, Portsea.		
		The Unitarian Chapel .	High-street, Portsmouth.		
		The Baptist Chapel . .	White's-row, Portsea.		
		Landport Chapel . .	Lake-lane, Landport, in the parish of Portsea.		
		Clarence-street Chapel	Landport, in the parish of Portsea.		
		Ebenezer Chapel . . .	Southsea-street, Southsea, in the parish of Portsea.		
POTTERSPURY	Northampton and Buckingham.	The Meeting-house . .	Potterspury	J. F. Congreve .	Stony Stratford . .
		Stony Stratford Chapel .	St. Mary Magdalene, Stony Stratford.		
		Protestant Meeting-house.	St. Giles, Stony Stratford.		
PRESCOT	Lancaster . .	Much Woolton Chapel .	Much Woolton, in the parish of Childwall.	J. Heyes . . .	Knowsley, Prescot .
		Low House Chapel . .	Crab-lane, within Windle, Prescot.		
		Blackbrook Chapel . .	Parr, in the parish of Prescot.		
		Portico Chapel. . . .	Eccleston, in the parish of Prescot		
		Gateacre Chapel . . .	Gateacre, in the parish of Childwall.		
		The New Chapel . . .	St. Helen's, in the parish of Prescot.		
		Ebenezer Chapel . . .	Prescot.		
PRESTEIGNE and KINGTON.	Radnor and Hereford.	. . .	. . .	Robt. Phillips, jun	Presteigne. . . .
PRESTON.	Lancaster . .	The Roman Catholic Chapel of St. Wilfrid.	Preston, in Chapel-st., Preston	J. Thackeray .	Preston . . . .
		The Roman Catholic Church of St. Ignatius.	Meadow-street, Preston.		
		Unitarian Chapel . . .	Church-street, Preston.		
		South Bank Roman Catholic Chapel.	Samlesbury, Blackburn.		
		Catholic Chapel . . .	Stydd Lodge, Ribchester.		
		Aston-lane Roman Catholic Chapel, Aston.	Ribchester. . .		
		Independent Chapel . .	Grimshaw-street, Preston.		
		Cottam Chapel	Woodplumpton.		
		The Baptist Chapel . .	Leeming street, Preston.		
		Independent Chapel . .	Cannon-street, Preston.		
		St. Mary's Catholic Chapel	Brown Edge, Walton-le-Dale, in the parish of Blackburn.		
		St. Mary's Catholic Chapel	Ferneyhalgh, in the parish of Broughton.		
PWLLHELI	Carnarvon . .	Penlan Chapel . . .	Pwllheli	D. Williams . . Owen Owen,	Pwllheli . . . . Ditto.

REGISTRARS of MARRIAGES.		Registrars' Districts.	REGISTRARS of BIRTHS and DEATHS.		Deputy Registrars of Births and Deaths.	
Name.	Address.		Name.	Address.	Name.	Address.
T. Wilmot	Pontefract.	Pontefract	E. Dyson.	Pontefract.		
		Ackworth	G. Nelstrop	Ackworth.		
		Whitley	Thos. Hogley	Whitley.		
		Knottingley	J. Crabtree	Knottingley.		
		Kippax	J. Carbut	Kippax, Pontefract.	Jno. Carbut, jun.	Kippax, Pontefract.
B. Lewis	Pont-y-Moile, Pont-y-Pool.	Llangibby	W. Davies	Llanvrechva, Pont-y-Pool.		
Isaac Hiley	Varteg, Pont-y-Pool.	Pont-y-Pool	A. Edwards	Pont-y-Pool	F. Edwards	Pont-y-Pool.
Wm. Davies	Llanvrechva.	Usk	J. Shepard	Usk.	H. C. Shepard	Usk.
H. B. Smith	High-street, Poole	Lytchet	B. Golton	Hamworthy, Poole.		
		Canford	Henry Card	Canford, Magna, Wimbourne.		
		Poole	H. B. Smith	Poole	C. G. Trowbridge	Hill-street, Poole.
T. W. Gagen	278, High-street, Poplar	Poplar	T. W. Gagen	278, High-street, Poplar	W. Welldon	246, High-st., Poplar.
		Bow and Bromley	J. Dunstan	Dyer's-lane, Bromley, Bow	D. Rutley	Four Mills-street, Bromley, Bow.
S. Reeves	Queen-street, Portsea.	Portsmouth Town	E. Luscombe.	High-street, Portsmouth	W. Mitchell	High-st., Portsmouth.
		Portsea Town	S. Reeves	Queen-street, Portsea	Wm. Hicks	Cross-street, Portsea.
		Kingston and Landport	W. Hatch	Fratten, Portsmouth	T. Ireland	Mile-end, Landport.
		Landport and Southsea	W. Ellis	Hampshire-terrace, Southsea.	W. Ellis, jun.	14, Hampshire-terrace, Southsea.
Robert Bell	St. Giles, Stony Stratford.	Potterspury	R. Chibnall, jun.	Stony Stratford.		
W. Brunskill	St. Helen's	Rainford	J. Woods	Rainford, Prescot.		
J. Scarisbrick	Prescot.	St. Helen's.	W. Brunskill	St. Helen's.		
		Prescot.	J. Scarisbrick	Prescot.		
		Farnworth	Rev. W. Jeff.	Farnworth, Prescot.		
		Huyton	P. Pendleton	Huyton, Liverpool.		
		Much Woolton	J. Baker.	Much Woolton, Liverpool.		
		Hale	Rev. W. Stewart.	Hale, Warrington.		
R. Parry	Kington	Presteigne	W. Jones.	Presteigne.		
T. A. Shewell	Weythal.	Kington	W. Blakeley	Kington.		
		Radnor	T. A. Shewell	Weythal, Old Radnor.		
		Brilley.	Wm. Davies	Huntington, Kington.		
J. Hothersall	Alston	Preston.	T. Green	Preston.		
M. Barlow	Broughton, Four-lane-ends, Preston.	Broughton	C. Hoole	Broughton, Preston.		
W. Walker	13, Chapel-street, Preston.	Alston	F. Maude	Longridge, Preston	William Halsall.	Longridge, Preston.
		Longton	T. Rowlandson	Longton, Preston.		
		Walton-le-Dale	J. Tomlinson	Walton-le-Dale, Preston.		
M. Lewis.	Rhydyclafrdu, Pwllheli, Carnarvon.	Pwllheli	T. Williams	Llannor, Pwllheli.		
		Nevin	W Jones.	Hendrebodean, Pwllheli.		
		Aberdaron	D. Griffith	Bodwrdda, Pwllheli	W. Griffith	Gegin Bodwrdda, Pwllheli.
		Criccieth	J. Jones	Glynn, Pwllheli.		

UNION, or SUPERINTENDENT REGISTRAR'S DISTRICT.	County.	Places of Public Worship situated therein, registered for Solemnization of Marriages.		SUPERINTENDENT REGISTRARS, and Deputy Superintendent Registrars.	
		Name.	Situation.	Name.	Address.
RADFORD.	Notts. . . .	The Independent Chapel .	Hyson-green, in the parish of Radford.	L. Hardy . .	Derby-road, Nottingham.
READING	Berks. . . .	Baptist Meeting-house . Broad-street Meeting . . Roman Catholic Chapel . The Congregational Chapel	King's-road, Reading . . . Broad-street, Reading. Vastern-street, Reading. Castle-street, Reading.	T. G. Curtis . . F. F. Curtis,	Albion-place, Reading 12, Albion-place, Reading.
REDRUTH	Cornwall . .	. . .	. . .	W. Davey . .	Redruth . . . . .
REETH	York	. . .	. . .	Ottiwell Tomlin, jun.	Richmond, Yorkshire
REIGATE.	Surrey . . .	The Independent Chapel .	High-street, Reigate . . .	T. Hart . . .	Reigate . . . . .
RHAYADER	Radnor . . .	. . .	. . .	E. Williams . .	Rhayader . . . . .
RICHMOND (SURREY) .	Surrey . . .	The Independent Chapel . East Sheen Chapel . .	Richmond . . . . East Sheen, in the parish of Mortlake.	W. Chapman .	Ormond-row, Richmond, Surrey.
RICHMOND (YORK). .	Yorkshire . .	The Catholic Chapel . . The Chapel of St. Paulinus	Richmond . . . . Brough-hall, in the parish of Catterick.	C. Hammond . T. Bradley .	Frenchgate, Richmond, Yorkshire. Richmond, Yorkshire.
RINGWOOD	Hants . . .	The Lower Meeting . .	Ringwood	H. St. John Neale G. Cottman,	Ringwood . . . . Ditto.
RIPON.	York	The Temple . . . . The Catholic Chapel . .	Ripon. . . . . Bishop Thornton, in the parish of Ripon.	A. Buck . . .	Ripon . . . . .
RISBRIDGE	Suffolk and Essex	Independent Chapel . . The Baptist Chapel . . Congregational Meeting-house. The Independent Chapel.	Stansfield . . . . . . Clare. Moor-green, in the parish of Wickhambrook. Steeple Bumstead.	J. H. Jardine .	Stoke, Halstead, Essex.
ROCHDALE	Lancaster . .	Providence Chapel. . . The Presbyterian Chapel . The Wesleyan Methodist Association Chapel. The Catholic Chapel . . Ebenezer Chapel . . . The Baptist Chapel . .	High-street, Rochdale . . . Blackwater-street, Rochdale . Baillie-street, Rochdale. Bell Green, Rochdale. Calderbrook, in the parish of Rochdale. Irwell-terrace, in Bacup, in the parish of Rochdale.	W. Roberts . J. Holgate,	Drake-street, Rochdale Rochdale.
ROCHFORD	Essex. . . .	Rochford Independent Chapel.	Rochford.	M. Comport . .	Rochford . . . . .
ROMFORD	Essex. . . .	Upminster Chapel. . . Barking Chapel . . .	Upminster-hill . . . . . Barking.	E. Griffin . . N. Surridge,	Ilford . . . . . Romford.
ROMNEY MARSH . . .	Kent	. . .	. . .	W. Harrison. .	New Romney . . .
ROMSEY	Hants. . . .	The Abbey Chapel. . . Ebenezer Chapel . . .	Romsey . . . . Lockerley.	J. Lordan . .	Romsey . . . . .
ROSS	Hereford . .	The Baptist Chapel . . The Independent Chapel . Ruxton Chapel . . . . Lay's Hill Chapel . . .	Ross . . . . Ross. Ruxton, in the parish of Marstow The Lays, in the parish of Walford.	E. M. Davis .	Ross . . . . .
ROTHBURY	Northumberland.	The Presbyterian Chapel .	Thropton, in the parish of Rothbury.	Robert Moody .	Rothbury, Morpeth .

REGISTRARS of MARRIAGES.		Registrars' Districts.	REGISTRARS of BIRTHS and DEATHS.		Deputy Registrars of Births and Deaths.	
Name.	Address.		Name.	Address.	Name.	Address.
J. Vessey	Denman-street, Radford	Radford	Stephen Creswell	Ilkiston-road, New Radford	J. Smith	Radford.
		Hyson Green	D. Hooke	Prospect-place, Old Radford	J. Maltby	23, Pleasant-row, Hyson-green.
		Lenton	J. Maples	Lenton	H. T. Mortimer	Lenton.
		Snenton	T. Morley	Snenton	J. Potchet	Snenton-road, Snenton.
F. West	20, Coley-street, Reading.	St. Mary's.	F. West	20, Coley-street, Reading	J. Cumber	Howard-st., Reading.
J. Rosser	Blue-coat School, Albion-street, Reading.	St. Giles's	W. West, jun.	Bath House, Reading.	W. West, sen.	2, Bath-court, Reading.
		St. Lawrence	T. Bath	Forbury, Reading	R. Bartlett	11 Friar-st., Reading.
T. Phillips	Redruth	Gwennap	C. Williams	Gwennap, Redruth.		
		Redruth	T. Phillips	Redruth.		
		Illogan	Thos. Chegwin	Lovely-cottage, Illogan, Redruth.		
		Camborne	R. Lanyon	Camborne.		
		Phillack	T. Bryant	Copperhouse, Hayle.		
J. R. M'Culloch.	Reeth, Yorkshire.	Reeth	J. R. M'Culloch.	Reeth, Yorkshire.		
		Muker	William Radd	Muker, Reuth.		
G. Doubell	Santon-cottage, Reigate	Reigate	G. Doubell	Santon-cottage, Reigate.		
		Horley	R. Wood	Hookwood-common, Charlwood, Reigate.		
. . .	. . .	Rhayader	D. Evans	Rhayader.		
		Nantmel	L. Jones	Holmes, Rhayader	E. Williams	Nantymynach, Rhayader.
J. Darnill	Richmond, Surrey	Richmond	J. Darnill.	Hill-street, Richmond, Surrey	W. Drew	Friar's-lane, Richmond
		Mortlake	H. Brown	High-street, Mortlake	J. Squire	High-street, Mortlake.
J. Hunton	Richmond, Yorkshire.	Richmond	A. Clement	Richmond, Yorkshire.		
		Catterick	W. H. Thorpe	Catterick	J. Todd	Catterick.
		Aldborough	Henry Marsh	Aldborough, Darlington.		
		Newsham	J. Graham	Newsham.		
W. Hunt.	Ringwood	Ringwood	W. Yale	Ringwood	W. Hunt.	Ringwood.
J. Chapman	Ripon	Ripon	W. Farrer	Ripon	J. Leckenby	Ripon.
		Markington	J. Neeson	Markington, Ripon.		
		Dishforth	G. Porter	Rainton, via Boroughbridge.		
		Sutton Howgrave	A. Guyll	Wath, near Ripon.		
		Kirkby Malzeard	Wm. Storry, M.D.	Kirkby Malzeard, Ripon	J. Kearton	Kirkby Malzeard, Ripon
T. B. Brooke	Haverhill, Halstead, Essex.	Haverhill	T. B. Brooke	Haverhill, Halstead.		
		Clare	T. Jolly	Clare, Sudbury.		
		Wickhambrooke	J. P. Brown	Wickhambrooke, Newmarket	G. Peacock	Wickhambrooke.
T. Spencer	Church Stile, Rochdale	Spotland, nearer side	S. Stott	St. Mary's-gate, Rochdale	F. Greenwood	St. Mary's-gate, Rochdale.
		Spotland, further side.	B. Butterworth	Caldershaw, Rochdale.	James Heap	Caldershaw, Rochdale.
		Whitworth and Brandwood.	J. Scholfield	Walmsley, Rochdale	J. Clegg	Facit, Rochdale.
		Castleton, within the Borough.	T. Spencer	Church Stile, Rochdale	W. Schofield	Caton-street, Rochdale.
		Castleton, without the Borough.	F. Clough	Balderstone, Rochdale.	Daniel Clough	Balderstone, Rochdale.
		Blotchnworth and Calderbrook.	J. Baron	Littleborough, Rochdale	John Rigg	Littleborough, Rochdale.
		Butterworth, Lordship side.	A. Schofield	Miln-row, Rochdale	C. Schofield	Stonepitfield, Rochdale
		Butterworth, Freehold side.	T. Sykes	Lawhouse, Rochdale	J. Sykes	Lawhouse, Rochdale.
		Wardleworth	J. Whitehead	St. James's-street, Rochdale	R. Crowther	Regent-st., Rochdale.
		Wuerdle and Wardle	J. Tupper	Small-bridge, Rochdale	A. Grindrod	Hollow-spell, Rochdale
C. Carter, jun.	Rochford	Rochford	J. Grabham	Rochford	G. Marsh	Rochford.
		Great Wakering	C. Miller	Great Wakering	G. Bullock	Great Wakering.
		Rayleigh	E. Digby	Rayleigh.		
		Prittlewell	M. Sheehy	Southend, Rochford.		
W. G. Beadle	Barking	Romford	R. A. Bowers	Romford	J. Parker	Romford.
		Hornchurch	R. W. Quennell	Hornchurch	W. Holmes	Hornchurch.
		Barking Town	W. G. Beadle	Barking.	W. G. Beadle, jun.	Barking.
		Great Ilford	W. Coxhead	Ilford	C. Coxhead	Ilford.
B. Wood.	New Romney.	Lydd	James Buss	Lydd, New Romney.		
		New Romney	B. Wood	New Romney.		
C. L. Lordan	Romsey	Romsey	J. Scorey	Romsey.		
T. Berry.	Romsey.	Mitchelmersh	T. Green	Awbridge, Romsey.		
James Hill	Scott's School, Ross	Ross	J. Halford	Ross.		
		St. Weonard's	J. Lodwidge	Hentland, Ross.		
		Sollarshope	W. Dobles	Upton Bishop, Ross.		
		Langarren	Samuel Garness	Langarren, Ross.		
H. Boag.	Rothbury	Rothbury	H. Boag	Rothbury.		
		Elsdon	John Pye	Elsdon.		

N

UNION, or SUPERINTENDENT REGISTRAR'S DISTRICT.	County.	Places of Public Worship situated therein, registered for Solemnization of Marriages.		SUPERINTENDENT REGISTRARS, and *Deputy Superintendent Registrars.*	
		Name.	Situation.	Name.	Address.
ROTHERHAM	York	The Independent Chapel .	Masbrough, in the parish of Rotherham.	J. Oxley . . .	Rotherham . . .
		The Independent Chapel .	West Melton, in the parish of Wath-upon-Dearne.		
		The Unitarian Chapel. .	Near the Oil Mill, Fold Rotherham.		
ROTHERHITHE . . .	Surrey . . .	. . .	. . .	M. Nottingham .	6, Paradise-row, Rotherhithe.
ROYSTON and BUNTINGFORD.	Herts, Cambridge, and Essex.	Bassingbourn Independent Meeting-house.	Bassingbourn	H. Thurnall . . Thomas Pickering,	Royston . . . John-street, Royston.
		The Unitarian Chapel. .	Royston.		
		Chishill Independent Meeting.	Little Chishill.		
		The New Meeting . . .	Royston.		
		Barkway Independent Chapel.	Barkway.		
		The Independent Meeting.	Foulmire.		
		The Old Meeting . . .	Royston.		
		The Independent Meeting.	Barrington. .		
RUGBY	Warwick. . .	The Independent Chapel .	Yelvertoft	G. V. Hefford .	Rugby . . . . .
		The Independent Chapel .	Kilsby.		
		The Baptist Chapel . .	Rugby.		
RUNCORN	Chester . . .	Bethesda Chapel . . .	Runcorn	D. Ashley . .	Frodsham . . . .
RUTHIN	Denbigh . . .	English Independent Church.	Llanrhydd	S. Jones . . .	Ruthin. . . . .
		Baptist Chapel. . . .	Mwrog-street, in the parish of Llanfwrog.		
RYE	Sussex . . .	. . .	. . .	H. E. Paine . .	Pump-street, Rye. .
SADDLEWORTH . . .	York	Ebenezer Chapel . . .	Upper Mill, in the parish of Saddleworth.	J. Harrop . . .	Saddleworth . . .
SAFFRON WALDEN . .	Essex. . . .	The Abbey-lane Chapel .	Abbey-lane, Saffron Walden .	R. D. Thurgood . Wm. Thurgood,	Saffron Walden . . Ditto.
		Clavering Meeting-house .	Hole-lane, Clavering.		
		The Baptist Chapel . .	Bailey's-lane, Saffron Walden.		
SALFORD	Lancaster . .	Independent Chapel . .	Chapel-street, Salford . . .	John Hope . .	Pendleton, near Salford
		The New Jerusalem Temple	Bolton-street, Salford.		
		New Windsor Chapel . .	New Windsor, Salford.		
		Unitarian Meeting-house .	Dawson's Croft, Green Gate, Salford.		
		Hope Chapel	Liverpool-street, Salford, in the parish of Manchester.		
SALISBURY	Wilts. . . .	The Independent Chapel .	Endless-street, Salisbury . .	C. W. Squarey . J. Toone,	Salisbury . . . . . High-street, Salisbury.
		The Baptist Chapel . .	Brown-street, Salisbury.		
		Scot's-lane Chapel . . .	Scot's-lane, Salisbury.		
SAMFORD	Suffolk . . .	Independent Chapel . .	East Bergholt	E. Lawrance. . W. Hutchinson,	Ipswich . . . . Ditto.
SAVIOUR. ST.	Surrey . . .	Surrey Chapel	Blackfriars'-road	R. C. Smith . . E. Garnett,	26, Bridge-street, Southwark. 27, Bridge-street, Southwark.
		The Baptist Chapel . .	New Park-street, Southwark.		
SCARBOROUGH . . .	York	Ebenezer Chapel . . .	Long Westgate, Scarborough	E. S. Donner . W. E. Woodall,	15, Long-room-street, Scarborough. Scarborough.
		The Roman Catholic Chapel	Scarborough.		
		Primitive Methodist Chapel	Scarborough.		
SCILLY ISLES	Cornwall . .	Wesleyan Chapel . . .	Hugh Town, St. Mary's, Scilly	W. Hoskin . . W. M. Hoskin,	St. Mary's, Scilly Isles Ditto.
SCULCOATES	York	The Catholic Chapel . .	Jarrat-street, Sculcoates . .	Wm. Chatham .	44, George-street, Hull
		Holborn-street Chapel. .	Witham, Kingston-on-Hull.		
		George-street Chapel . .	Sculcoates.		
SEDBERGH	York	The Wesleyan Methodists' Chapel,	Sedbergh	Thos. Wearing .	Sedbergh . . . .

REGISTRARS of MARRIAGES.		Registrars' Districts.	REGISTRARS of BIRTHS and DEATHS.		Deputy Registrars of Births and Deaths.	
Name.	Address.		Name.	Address.	Name.	Address.
J. Mycock . .	Crofts, Rotherham	*Rotherham* . . .	R. T. Barras . .	Rotherham.		
		Kimberworth . .	John Barras . .	Masbrough, Rotherham.		
		Wath	John Wood . .	Swinton, Rotherham.		
		Maltby	F. W. Flower .	Maltby, Rotherham.		
		Beighton	J. A. Tillotson .	Beighton, Sheffield.		
G. Pitt . . .	23, Paradise-row, Rotherhithe.	*Rotherhithe* . . .	G. Pitt	Paradise-row, Rotherhithe.		
J. Johnson . .	Barley, Royston . .	*Royston*	J. Johnson . .	Barley, Royston . . .	T. Savell . . .	Barley, Royston.
J. Trigg. . .	Barrington, Royslo n.	*Melbourn* . . .	J. Trigg . . .	Barrington, Royston.		
		Buntingford . .	C. Macklin . .	Buntingford	H. G. Macklin .	Buntingford.
W. Johnson . .	Wolston, Coventry	*Rugby*	W. Johnson . .	Black Dog, Stretton-on-Dunsmore, Wolston.		
		Crick	R. Sharp . . .	Crick, Daventry,		
		Dunchurch . . .	J. Ireson . . .	Dunchurch.		
W. Calveley . .	Frodsham	*Runcorn*	E. Lynn . . .	Runcorn.		
		Frodsham . . .	W. Calveley . .	Frodsham.		
		Budworth . . .	Peter Edgerley .	Appleton, near Warrington.		
		Groppenhall . .	J. Warburton .	Daresbury, Preston Brook.		
T. Jones . . .	Ruthin	*Ruthin*	T. Jones . . .	Ruthin	Thos. Prytherch.	Castle-street, Ruthin.
		Gyffylhog . . .	H. Davies . .	Gyffylliog, Ruthin.		
		Llanelidan . . .	J. Evans . . .	Ty'nllan Llanelidan.		
		Llanarmon . . .	E. Edwards . .	Llanarmon.		
		Llanrhaiadr . .	J. Williams . .	Pentre, Llanrhaiadr.		
		Llandyrnog . .	E. Lewis . . .	Llandyrnog.		
R. Chester . .	Rye	*Rye*	R. Chester . .	Rye.		
		Beckley	J. Richardson .	Brede, Rye.		
J. Wrigley . .	Upper Mill, Saddleworth.	*Delph*	J. Brook . . .	Delph, Saddleworth.		
		Upper Mill . .	J. Wrigley . .	Upper Mill, Saddleworth.		
Thomas Perring .	Saffron Walden . .	*Saffron Walden* .	W. Proctor . .	Saffron Walden . . .	T. Perring . .	Saffron Walden.
J. Pavitt, jun. .	Clavering.	*Newport*	C. Traylen . .	Newport, Bishop's Stortford	J. C. Day . .	Newport, Bishop's Stortford.
		Radwinter . . .	J. Benton . .	Radwinter, Saffron Walden	C. Cade . . .	Radwinter, Saffron Walden.
J. Hill . . .	33, St. Stephen's-street, Salford.	*Regent Road* . .	B. Youngman .	90, Oldfield-road, Salford.		
		Green Gate . .	J. Hill . . .	33, St. Stephen-street, Salford.		
		Pendleton . . .	Thomas Allen .	1, Chester-place, Pendleton	Wm. Chadwick .	1, Chester-place, Pendleton.
		Broughton . . .	John Tonge . .	Chapel-street, Broughton.		
G. Sidford . .	Salisbury	*Salisbury* . . .	W. Sutton, sen. .	Bedwin-street, Salisbury .	W. Sutton, jun. .	Bedwin-street, Salisbury.
John Mixer . .	Stratford St. Mary .	*Holbrook* . . .	D. Kerridge . .	Washbrook, Ipswich.		
		Capel St. Mary	G. Bickmore. .	Capel St. Mary, Ipswich.		
W. Norris . .	New-street, Southwark-bridge-road	*St. Saviour* . . .	F. Parr . . .	22, Bridge-street, Southwark	Wm. Norris . .	7, New-street, Southwark-bridge-road.
J. White . . .	Great Charlotte-street, Blackfriars'-road.	*Christchurch* . . .	J. White . . .	Great Charlotte-street, Blackfriars'-road.	William Mackie.	Charlotte-street, Christchurch, Southwark.
A. G. Tyson . .	Long Westgate, Scarborough.	*Scarborough* . .	L. Walshaw . .	3, King-street, Scarborough	J. Grice . . .	Newborough-street, Scarborough.
		Filey	W. Munro . .	Filey, Hunmanby.		
Isaac Walshaw .	3, King-street, Scarborough.	*Sherburn* . . .	Philip Hubbert .	Sherburn, Malton.		
		Hutton Bushel .	G. Smart. . .	Hutton Bushel, Scarborough.		
C. Mumford . .	St. Mary's, Scilly Isles	*Scilly Isles*. . . .	C. Mumford . .	Scilly Isles	F. Banfield . .	Hugh Town, St. Mary's, Scilly Isles.
W. C. Colbeck .	Cottingham . . .	*East Sculcoates*	C. T. West . .	North-street, Hull.		
		West Sculcoates	J. M. Fullam .	Saville-street, Hull. . .	Sam. Fulstow .	4, Christchurch-street.
		Sutton	T. Dibb . . .	Sutton, Hull.		
		Drypool . . .	Joseph Willson .	Prospect-place, Holderness-road, Hull.		
		Hedon	J. Tesseyman .	Hedon.		
		Hessle	F. B. Anderson .	Hessle.		
		Ferriby	J. Smith . . .	North Ferriby.		
		Cottingham . .	J. Waltham . .	Cottingham.		
. . .	. . .	*Sedbergh* . . .	T. Atkinson . .	Sedbergh.		
		Dent	M. Baynes . .	Dent.		
		Garsdale . . .	Jas. Buck . .	Kiln-haw, Garsdale.		

UNION, or SUPERINTENDENT REGISTRAR'S DISTRICT.	County.	Places of Public Worship situated therein, registered for Solemnization of Marriages.		SUPERINTENDENT REGISTRARS, and Deputy Superintendent Registrars.	
		Name.	Situation.	Name.	Address.
SELBY.	York	Bethesda Chapel . . . The Carlton Catholic Chapel	Selby . . . . Carlton, in the parish of Snaith.	M. Fothergill .	Selby . . . . . .
SETTLE	York	. . .	. . .	G. Dudgeon . .	Settle . . . . . .
SEVENOAKS	Kent	The Baptist Chapel . . The Old Meeting-house .	Sevenoaks . . . . . . At Bessell's Green, in the parish of Chevening.	Thomas Carnell .	Sevenoaks. . . . .
SHAFTESBURY. . . .	Dorset . . .	The Independent Chapel .	Shaftesbury	C. E. Buckland .	Shaftesbury . . .
SHARDLOW.	Derby . . .	The General Baptist Chapel. General Baptist Chapel . The New Methodist Chapel	Melbourne . . . . . . Castle Donnington. Stapleford.	S. Dumelow . .	Shardlow . . .
SHEFFIELD	York	Nether Chapel . . . The Catholic Chapel . The Upper Chapel . The Baptist Chapel . Queen-street Chapel . . The Independent Chapel . Mount Zion Chapel . The Lee Croft Chapel. Surrey-street Chapel . Scotland-street Chapel	Norfolk-street, Sheffield . Norfolk-row, Sheffield. Norfolk-street, Sheffield. Townhead-street, Sheffield. Westfield-terrace, Sheffield. Howard-street, Sheffield. Sheffield. Sheffield. Sheffield. Sheffield.	G. Crosland . .	Sheffield . . .
SHEPPEY.	Kent	Bethel Chapel . . .	Sheerness, in the parish of Minster, in the Isle of Sheppey.	E. Eastman . .	Mile Town, Sheerness
SHEPTON-MALLET . .	Somerset . .	Presbyterian Chapel . The Wesleyan Chapel. . Independent Chapel . .	Cowl-street, Shepton Mallet . Paul-street, Shepton Mallet. Shepton Mallet.	R. Norton . .	Shepton Mallet . .
SHERBORNE	Dorset . . .	Union Chapel	Long-street, Sherborne . .	J. P. Melmoth . J. Y. Melmoth,	Sherborne . . . . Ditto.
SHIFFNAL	Salop	. . .	. . .	P. Osborne . .	Shiffnal . . . .
SHIPSTON-ON-STOUR .	Worcester . .	Braile's Roman Catholic Chapel. Ebenezer Chapel . . . The Baptist Chapel . .	Lower Brailes . . . . . Blockley. Shipston-on-Stour.	J. H. Clark . .	Shipston-on-Stour .
SHOREDITCH, ST. LEONARD.	Middlesex . .	The General Baptist Meeting-house. Gloucester Chapel . . . Hoxton Academy Chapel . Holywell Mount Chapel .	Worship-street, Shoreditch. . Gloucester-street, St. Leonard, Shoreditch. Hoxton Old Town, Shoreditch. Chapel-street, Curtain-road, in the parish of St. Leonard, Shoreditch.	T. Ware . . . J. Ware,	98, Kingsland-road . 97, Kingsland-road.
SHREWSBURY	Salop	The Baptist Meeting-house The Independent Chapel . The Presbyterian Chapel . Ebenezer Chapel . . . St. Mary's Catholic Chapel	Claremont-street, Shrewsbury . Swan-hill, parish of St. Chad. High-street, Shrewsbury. St. Chad's parish. St. Chad's parish.	C. B. Teece . . Henry Pidgeon,	Shrewsbury . . . . High-street, Shrewsbury
SKIPTON	York	Zion Chapel . . . The Catholic Chapel . . The Wesleyan Chapel. .	Skipton . . . . Broughton Hall, in the parish of Broughton. Addingham.	C. Carr . . . T. Mason,	Skipton . . . . . Embsay, Skipton.
SKIRLAUGH	York	Marton Chapel. . . .	Marton, in the parish of Swine, in Holderness.	J. B. Bainton .	Beverley . . . .
SLEAFORD	Lincoln . . .	. . .	. . .	Chas. Clements .	Sleaford . . . .
SOLIHULL	Warwick . . .	. . .	. . .	G. J. Harding .	Solihull . . . .

REGISTRARS of MARRIAGES.		Registrars' Districts.	REGISTRARS of BIRTHS and DEATHS.		Deputy Registrars of Births and Deaths.	
Name.	**Address.**		**Name.**	**Address.**	**Name.**	**Address.**
George Lowther.	Selby	*Selby* . . . . *Snaith* . . . . *Riccall*	J. Fothergill, jun. T. Perkins . . R. S. Fielding .	Selby . . . . . Snaith. Riccall.	J. Fothergill, sen.	Selby.
T. D. Burrow .	Settle	*Arncliffe* . . . . *Bentham* . . . . *Kirkby Malham* . *Long Preston* . . *Settle*	J. Armistead. . Wm. Thompson. J. C. Mount . . Henry Wildman. T. Robinson . .	Litton, Settle. Ingleton, Settle. Scostrop, Settle. Wigglesworth, Settle. Settle	W. Brennand. .	Settle.
T. Parker . .	Sevenoaks . . .	*Sevenoaks* . . . . *Shoreham* . . . . *Penshurst* . . .	T. Waring . . M. D. Pryer . W. Young . .	Sundridge, Sevenoaks. Otford, Sevenoaks. Chiddingstone, Sevenoaks.		
W. Swyer . .	Shaftesbury . . .	*Shaftesbury* . . . *Fontmell* . . . . *Gillingham* . . .	G. W. Buckland. F. R. Hussey . John Meaden .	Shaftesbury. Fontmell Magna . . . Gillingham.	R. Hussey . .	Fontmell Magna.
Wm. Pegg. . . .	Melbourne. . . .	*Castle Donnington.* *Spondon* . . . . *Shardlow* . . . . *Stapleford* . . . . *Melbourne* . . .	Henry Day . . J. Cade . . . M. Jones . . . J. W. Cade . W. Pegg . .	Castle Donnington. Spondon . . . . . Shardlow. Breaston, Derby . . . Melbourne, Derby.	T. C. Cade . . W. Walker . .	Spondon. Breaston, Derby.
R. J. Gainsford .	Arundel-street, Sheffield.	*Park*	B. Skidmore. .	New Haymarket, Sheffield	J. Skidmore . .	Duke-street, Park, Sheffield.
B. Skidmore. .	New Haymarket, Sheffield.	*South* . . . . *West* . . . . *North* . . . . *Brightside* . . . *Attercliffe* . . . *Handsworth* . . .	E. Smith . . . B. Rawlins . . W. Clark . . . G. Sykes . . . G. Marshall . . J. Nicholson. .	Norfolk-street, Sheffield 4, Carver-street, Sheffield. West Bar, Sheffield . Rock-street, Sheffield . . Attercliffe, Sheffield. Handsworth, Sheffield.	A. Smith . . . G. W. Clark . John Hunt . .	Norfolk-st., Sheffield. West Bar, Sheffield. Occupation-rd., Brightside, Barlow, Sheffield.
W. Fishenden .	Mile Town, Sheerness.	*Minster* . . . . *Eastchurch*. . . .	W. Fishenden . C. Peters. . .	Mile Town, Sheerness. Eastchurch, Queenborough.		
J. Gaite . . . John Wason. .	Shepton Mallet . . . Shepton Mallet.	*Shepton Mallet* . . *Stoke-lane* . . . *Evercreech* . . .	R. Collet . . H. Nuth . . . J. Boyce . .	Shepton Mallet. Stoke-lane, Shepton Mallet. Evercreech, Shepton Mallet.		
S. Blake . . .	Blackmarsh Farm, Sherborne.	*Sherborne* . . . . *Bradford Abbas* . *Yetminster*. . . .	C. West . . . R. S. Langdon . J. Godwin . .	Sherborne . . . . . Sherborne. Longburton, Sherborne.	Thomas Hodges.	Sherborne.
C. Bennett . .	Shiffnal	*Shiffnal* . . . . *Albrighton* . . .	W. Jackson . . J. Totty . .	Shiffnal . . . . . . Albrighton, Wolverhampton	C. Bennett . . T. Thomas . .	Shiffnal. Albrighton, Wolverhampton.
Samuel Coleman.	Shipston-on-Stour	*Shipston* . . . . *Campden* . . . . *Moreton* . . . . *Halford*	S. Jarrett. . . Wm. Simcox . G. Figgures . . C. Holland . .	Shipston-on-Stour. Chipping Campden. Blockley, Chipping Campden Oxhill, Kineton.		
J. C. Edwards .	2, Whitmore-row, Hoxton.	*Hoxton New Town* *Hoxton Old Town.* .	W. H. Skegg . W. B. Kilpin .	14, Brudenell-place, Hoxton. Hoxton	H. B. Kilpin. .	39, Turner's-square, Hoxton.
		Holywell & Moorfields *St. Leonard's* . . *Haggerstone, East.* .	Edward Earls George Yarrow J. Johnson . .	4, Worship-square . . Shoreditch-church-yard. 46, Great Cambridge-street, Hackney-road.	John Hall . .	23, Paul-st., Finsbury.
		Haggerstone, West. .	N. Bowring . .	7s, Pearson-street, Kingsland-road.	W. H. Barry. .	94, Kingsland-road.
Thos. Pidduck .	Castle-gates, Shrewsbury.	*St. Chad's* . . .	T. Boyce . . .	St. Chad's, Shrewsbury	W. Boyce . .	Claremont-street, Shrewsbury.
Rich. Clarke .	Abbey Foregate, Shrewsbury.	*St. Mary's*. . .	R. Price . . .	St. Mary's, Shrewsbury	W. Blount . .	College-hill, Shrewsbury.
E. Tindal . .	Skipton	*Skipton* . . . . *Addingham* . . . *Barnoldswick* . . . *Kildwick* . . . . *Gargrave* . . . . *Grassington* . . . *Kettlewell* . . .	E. Tindal . . W. Lister . . H. Waite . . . J. Crossley . . R. Greenwood . J. Harker . . T. Marshall . .	Skipton. Addingham, Skipton. Barnoldswick, Colne . . Kildwick, Skipton. Gargrave, Skipton. Grassington, Skipton. Kettlewell, Skipton . .	R. Waite . . . A. Lupton . .	Barnoldswick, Colne. Kettlewell, Skipton.
W. Henderson .	Hornsea, Hull .	*Brandes Burton* . . *Hornsea* . . . . *Aldborough* . . . *Humbleton* . . . *North and South Skirlaugh.*	G. Poskitt, sen. W. Henderson . J. H. Clark . . T. Westoby . . C. Richardson .	Brandes Burton, Beverley. Hornsea, Hull. Aldborough, Hull. Humbleton, Hull. South Skirlaugh, Hull.		
T. Johnson . .	Scopwick, Sleaford .	*Sleaford* . . . . *Heckington* . . . *Aswarby* . . . . *Leadenham* . . . *Billinghay* . . .	J. Bissill . . . A. Briggs . . C. S. Evans . . J. Smith . . . C. W. Frend .	Sleaford. Heckington, Sleaford. Helpringham, Sleaford. Wellingore, Sleaford. Billinghay, Sleaford.		
J. B. Thomson .	Solihull	*Solihull* . . . . *Tamworth* . . . . *Knowle*	J. Grundy . . W. Kimbell . C. Kimbell . .	Solihull. Tamworth, Henley-in-Arden. Knowle.		

UNION, or SUPERINTENDENT REGISTRAR'S DISTRICT.	County.	Places of Public Worship situated therein, registered for Solemnization of Marriages.		SUPERINTENDENT REGISTRARS, and Deputy Superintendent Registrars.	
		Name.	Situation.	Name.	Address.
SOUTHAM	Warwick . . .	. . .	. . .	R. F. Welchman	Southam . . . .
SOUTHAMPTON . . .	Hants	Independent Chapel . . St. Joseph's Chapel . .	Southampton . . . . . Bugle-street, Southampton.	T. B. Nichols . W. Wakeford,	Southampton . . . All Saints'-place, Southampton.
SOUTH MOLTON . . .	Devon	Mr. Sharpe's Chapel (Independent). The Baptist Chapel . . The Independent Chapel .	Chumleigh . . . . . . Brayford, in the parish of Charles South Molton.	J. E. J. Richard .	South Molton . . .
SOUTH SHIELDS . . .	Durham . . .	Secession Chapel . . . The Scotch Church . . The Congregational Chapel	East-street, South Shields . . Savile-street, Westoe. Wallis-street, in the township of Westoe, in the parish of Jarrow	G. Spurrier . .	East King-street, South Shields.
SOUTH STONEHAM . .	Hants . . .	. . .	. . .	J. J. P. Hoare .	Bitterne, Southampton.
SOUTHWELL	Notts	. . .	. . .	T. Marriott . . J. Whittingham,	Southwell . . . . Ditto.
SPALDING	Lincoln . . .	The General Baptist Meeting-house.	Spalding	A. Maples . .	Spalding . . . .
SPILSBY	Lincoln . . .	The Methodist Chapel . . The West End Independent Chapel.	Spilsby . . . . Alford.	W. Walker, jun. .	Spilsby . . . . .
STAFFORD	Stafford . . .	St. Austin's Chapel . . Zion Chapel . . . . The Catholic Chapel . .	Forebridge, in the parish of Castle Church. St. Martin's-lane, Stafford. Tixall.	P. Lowe . . .	Marston, Stafford . .
STAINES	Middlesex . .	The Independent Chapel .	High-street, Staines. . . .	R. Horne . . .	Staines
STAMFORD	Lincoln . . .	Independent Chapel . . The Roman Catholic Chapel.	Stamford . . . . Stamford.	J. Clapton . .	St. Mary's-street, Stamford.
STEPNEY	Middlesex . .	Wycliffe Chapel . . . St. Andrew's Scotch Church Virginia-street Chapel. . Sion Chapel . . . . Stepney Meeting . . . Ebenezer Chapel . . . Queen-street Meeting . .	Philpot-street, Mile-end Oldtown. St. Vincent's-street, Stepney. Pennington-street, Wapping. Union-street, Mile-end Old-town. Garden-street, Stepney. High-street, Shadwell. In the parish of St. Anne, Middlesex.	W. Leach . .	Colet House, White-horse-street, Stepney.
STEYNING	Sussex . . .	Henfield Chapel . . . Trinity Chapel. . . . New Shoreham Chapel .	Henfield . . . . . . Jarvis Lane, Steyning. New Shoreham.	J. Tribe	Steyning . . . . .
STOCKBRIDGE	Hants	The Baptist Chapel . .	Broughton	W. Busigny .	Stockbridge . . .
STOCKPORT.	Chester . . .	The Catholic Chapel of Saints Philip and James. High-street Chapel . . Hyde-lane Chapel . . . Hyde Old Chapel . . The Orchard-street Chapel Hatherlow Chapel . . . The Ebenezer Chapel . . Mount Tabor Chapel . .	Edgeley, in the parish of Cheadle. High-street, Stockport. Hyde, in the parish of Stockport. Hyde, in the parish of Stockport. Stockport. Hatherlow, within Bredbury, in the parish of Stockport. Bosden, in Hasle Grove, in the parish of Cheadle. Stockport.	H. Coppock . .	Stockport . . . .
STOCKTON and SEDGE-FIELD.	Durham . . .	The Independent Chapel St. Mary's . . . . . (No distinguishing name.) St. Hildas	Stockton-on-Tees . . . . Stockton. Stockton. Hartlepool.	John Balmer. .	Stockton-on-Tees . .
STOKE DAMEREL . .	Devon	Mount Zion Chapel . . Prince's-street Chapel. . Mount-street Chapel . . The Morice-street Wesleyan Methodist Chapel. Morice-square Chapel . .	Ker-street, Devonport . . Prince's-street, Devonport. Devonport. At Devonport, in the parish of Stoke Damerel. Devonport.	J. Elms . . . R. Oram,	Devonport. . . . . St. Aubyn-street, Devonport.

REGISTRARS of MARRIAGES.		Registrars' Districts.	REGISTRARS of BIRTHS and DEATHS.		Deputy Registrars of Births and Deaths.	
Name.	Address.		Name.	Address.	Name.	Address.
John Montgomery	Southam	Southam	W. Taylor . .	Napton-on-the-Hill, Southam.		
R. Wakeford . .	15, Brunswick-square, Southampton.	Southampton . . .	G. B. Corfe . .	Hanover Buildings, Southampton.	T. Weeks . .	French-street, Southampton.
J. K. Cutcliffe .	South Molton . . .	Chumleigh . . .	L. Babbage . .	Chumleigh.		
		Witheridge . .	R. Melton . .	Mariansleigh, South Molton.		
		South Molton . .	J. Cole . . .	South Molton.		
G. Forsyth . .	East King-street, South Shields.	South Shields . .	T. Wilson . .	King-street, South Shields.		
		Westoe	C. Johnson . .	Catharine-street, Westoe, South Shields.		
W. Fry . . .	Bitterne, Southampton	St. Mary's Extra .	J. C. Prince . .	Pear-tree-green, St. Mary's Extra.	Geo. Matthews .	Itchen, Southampton.
		South Stoneham .	J. Anthony . .	Bitterne, Southampton .	J. Gurman .	Bitterne, Southampton.
		Millbrook . . .	R. Sharp . .	Redbridge, Millbrook.		
W. Jones. . .	Southwell . . .	Southwell . . .	J. Taylor. . .	Southwell	W. Adamson .	Westhorpe, Southwell.
		Kneesall . . .	J. Turtle . .	Kneesall	W. Turtle . .	Kneesall.
E. Storr . . .	Spalding	Spalding . . .	F. H. Mair . .	Spalding	J. Blake . .	Spalding.
		Pinchbeck . . .	T. Styles . .	Pinchbeck, Spalding . .	C. Irving. .	Pinchbeck, Spalding.
		Gosberton . . .	A. Young . .	Gosberton, Spalding . .	B. Smith .	Gosberton, Spalding.
		Donington . . .	J. Mansell . .	Donington, Spalding . .	W. Clifton .	Donington, Spalding.
		Moulton . . .	H. Clay . .	Moulton, Spalding . .	W. Smith .	Moulton, Spalding.
J. Rhoades . .	Spilsby	Spilsby . . .	J. Green . .	Spilsby	S. North . .	Spilsby.
		Alford . . .	William Burkitt .	Alford	T. S. Handsley .	Alford.
		Burgh-le-Marsh .	T. Towl . .	Burgh, Spilsby . . .	J. Wakelin .	Burgh, Spilsby.
		Wainfleet . . .	B. Pickersgill .	Wainfleet, All Saints, Boston.	W. Brooks .	Wainfleet, All Saints, Boston.
		Stickney . . .	J. Adams . .	East Kirkby, Spilsby .	J. Richardson .	East Kirkby, Spilsby.
T. Rainham . .	Foregate-street, Stafford.	Stafford . . .	J. Masfen . .	Stafford	R. Tildesley .	Stafford.
		Castle Church .	W. J. Perrin . .	Forebridge, Stafford . .	W. Tildesley .	Forebridge, Stafford.
		Colwich . . .	E. Tylecote . .	Great Haywood . . .	C. Heywood .	Great Haywood.
S. Taylor. . .	Staines	Sunbury . . .	R. Broxholm . .	Sunbury	R. G. Broxholm .	Sunbury.
		Staines	J. Baker . .	Staines	J. Wagner .	Staines.
H. Whittome . .	St. Leonard's-street, Stamford.	Stamford . . .	H. Whittome . .	St. Leonard's-street, Stamford.	T. M. Johnson .	High-street, Stamford.
		Barnack . . .	J. Wade . .	Barnack, Stamford. . .	J. Glazier .	Ryhall, Stamford.
A. Barnett . .	19, Warkworth-terrace, Limehouse.	Limehouse . . .	A. Barnett . .	19, Warkworth-terrace, Limehouse.		
Thomas Barnes .	167, High-st., Shadwell	Ratcliffe . . .	G. Wells . .	5, York-ter., Commercial-rd.		
T. Baddeley . .	21, Gloucester-terrace, Commercial-road, Mile-end Old-town.	Shadwell and Wapping	T. Barnes . .	167, High-street, Shadwell.		
		Mile-end Old-town, Upper.	T. Baddeley .	21, Gloucester-terrace, Commercial-road, Mile-end Old-town.		
Samuel Castleden	1, Beaumont-square, Mile-end Old-town.	Mile-end Old-town, Lower.	Samuel Castleden	1, Beaumont-square, Mile-end Old-town.		
J. Puttock . .	Henfield	Steyning . . .	J. Puttock . .	Henfield.		
W. Walker . .	Coppera's Gap, New Shoreham.	Shoreham . . .	W. Walker . .	Coppera's Gap, New Shoreham.		
W. Gutch . .	Broughton, Hants	Stockbridge . .	J. Pursell . .	Stockbridge	J. Nicholson .	Stockbridge.
		Broughton . .	Luther Owen Fox	Broughton, Stockbridge	H. Smith . .	Broughton, Stockbridge
H. Coddington .	Stockport	Stockport, First .	J. Shawcross. .	Lower Hillgate, Stockport.		
R. Mann . .	Stockport.	Stockport, Second .	J. Vaughan . .	Waterloo-road, Stockport.		
D. Charlton . .	Hyde, by Manchester.	Hyde	D. Charlton . .	Hyde, by Manchester.		
		Heaton Norris .	A. R. Blake . .	Heaton Norris, Stockport.		
		Marple . . .	J. Ernill . .	Marple, Stockport.		
		Cheadle . . .	T. N. Beever .	Cheadle Moseley, Stockport.		
		Hazle Grove . .	S. Healey . .	Hazle Grove, Stockport.		
J. Nesbit . .	Stockton	Stockton . . .	J. Nesbit . .	Stockton.		
		Hartlepool . . .	E. Spence . .	Hartlepool.		
		Yarm . . .	T. Taylor. .	Egglescliffe, Yarm.		
		Sedgefield . . .	W. Eeles . .	Sedgefield	J. Tasker . .	Sedgefield.
H. Granville . .	Devonport	Stoke . . .	Rivoire de Carteret	6, Home Park-buildings, Stoke.		
		St. Aubyn . . .	P. Pascoe . .	25, Cumberland-street, Devonport.		
		Morice . . .	A. Granville . .	Tavistock-street, Devonport.		
		Clowance . . .	J. Gedye . .	60, Monument-street, Devonport.	C. Gedye . .	29, Mount-street, Devonport.
		Tamar	T. Howard . .	3, Union-terrace, Morice-town, Devonport.		

UNION, or SUPERINTENDENT REGISTRAR'S DISTRICT.	County.	Places of Public Worship situated therein, registered for Solemnisation of Marriages.		SUPERINTENDENT REGISTRARS, and *Deputy Superintendent Registrars.*	
		Name.	Situation.	Name.	Address.
STOKESLEY	York	St. Mary's Catholic Chapel	Crathorne	J. P. Sowerby . *T. Coates,*	Stokesley . . . . *Ditto.*
STOKE-UPON-TRENT .	Stafford . . .	Tabernacle	Hanley. in the parish of Stoke-upon-Trent.	T. Griffin, jun. .	Shelton, Stoke-upon-Trent.
		The Independent Chapel .	Caroline-street, Lane-end, Stoke-upon-Trent.	*T. Griffin, sen. .*	*Shelton.*
		Hope Chapel	Shelton. in the parish of Stoke-upon-Trent.		
		Bethesda Chapel . . .	Shelton. in the parish of Stoke-upon-Trent.		
		St. Gregory's Catholic Chapel.	Lane-end, in the parish of Stoke-upon-Trent.		
STONE	Stafford . .	St. Mary's Chapel . . .	Swynnerton	J. S. Joule . . *W. Joule,*	Stone, Staffordshire . *Ditto.*
		Aston Chapel	Aston, Stone.		
STOURBRIDGE	Worcester . .	Presbyterian Meeting-house	High-street, Stourbridge . .	W. B. Collis . .	High-street, Stourbridge.
		Park-lane Chapel . . .	Netherend, Cradley, in the parish of Halesowen.	*W. Parrott,*	*Stourbridge.*
		Ebenezer Wesleyan Chapel	Cradley, Halesowen.		
		All Saints' Chapel . . .	New-road, Stourbridge.		
		Independent Chapel . .	Halesowen.		
STOW	Suffolk . . .	The Independent Meeting-house.	Ipswich-street, Stowmarket.	K. R. Buchanan .	Stowmarket . . .
		Independent Meeting . .	Pound-lane. in the parish of Wattisfield.		
		Bethesda Chapel . . .	Bury-street, in Stowmarket.		
		The Baptist Chapel . .	Rattlesden.		
		The Primitive Methodist Chapel.	Regent-street, Stowmarket.		
		The Baptist Chapel . .	Cranmer-green, in the parish of Walsham-le-Willow.		
STOW-ON-THE-WOLD .	Gloucester . .	. . .	. . .	G. Pearce . .	Stow-on-the-Wold
STRAND	Middlesex . .	Essex-street Chapel . .	Essex-street, Strand. . . .	J. Corder. . . .	23, Surrey-street, Strand
		New-court Chapel . .	New-court, Carey-street.	*Wm. Fitch,*	49, Carey-street.
		St. Patrick's Chapel . .	Sutton-street, Soho-square.		
		The Independent Chapel .	Little Chapel-street, Soho.		
		St. Mary's German Lutheran Church or Chapel.	Savoy.		
STRATFORD-ON-AVON .	Warwick . . .	The Independent Chapel .	Stratford-on-Avon	R. H. Hobbes .	Stratford-on-Avon .
		Payton-street Chapel . .	Old Stratford.		
STRATTON	Cornwall . .	. . .	. . .	E. Shearm . .	Stratton, Cornwall .
STROUD	Gloucester . .	France Chapel	Chalford-hill, Bisley . . .	T. Bond . . .	Stroud . . . . .
		The Baptist Chapel . .	Eastcombs, Bisley.		
		Rodborough Tabernacle .	Rodborough.		
		Shortwood Meeting-house	Shortwood, in Horsley.		
		Corps Meeting	Chalford, in Bisley.		
		The Old Meeting . . .	Stroud.		
		The Baptist Chapel . .	Chapel-street, Stroud.		
		New Baptist Meeting . .	Minchinhampton.		
		The Independent Chapel .	Bedford-street, Stroud.		
		The Congregational Chapel	Stonehouse.		
STURMINSTER. . . .	Dorset . . .	Catholic Chapel . . .	Old Mill, in the parish of Marnhull.	C. C. Foot . .	Sturminster-Newton, Blandford.
		Independent Chapel . .	Stalbridge.		
SUDBURY	Suffolk . . .	The Old Meeting-house .	Sudbury	R. Stedman . .	Sudbury . . . .
SUNDERLAND	Durham . .	Spring Garden-lane Chapel	Sunderland	N. C. Reed . .	Bishop Wearmouth .
		Bethel Chapel	Villiers-st., Bishop Wearmouth	*T. Brunton,*	*Ditto.*
		Union Chapel	Coronation-street, Bishop Wearmouth.		
		St. Mary's Catholic Chapel	Bridge-st., Bishop Wearmouth.		
		The Independent Chapel .	Dundas-street, Monkwearmouth Shore.		
		The Tabernacle . . .	South Durham-street, Bishop Wearmouth.		

REGISTRARS of MARRIAGES.		Registrars' Districts.	REGISTRARS of BIRTHS and DEATHS.		Deputy Registrars of Births and Deaths.	
Name.	Address.		Name.	Address.	Name.	Address.
R. Neasham . .	Stokesley	Stokesley	R. Neasham . .	Stokesley.		
		Hutton	T. Harker . .	Hutton, Stokesley . . .	W. Routledge .	Hutton, Stokesley.
William Palmer.	Shelton, Stoke-upon-Trent.	Fenton	R. Cordon . .	Fenton.		
E. H. Miller. .	Lane-end, Stoke-upon-Trent.	Stoke-upon-Trent . .	H. Duffort . .	Stoke-upon-Trent.		
		Lane-end	T. Goddard . .	Church-street, Lane-end, Staffordshire.		
		Hanley	R. Harding . .	Old Hall-street, Hanley.		
		Shelton	J. B. Davis . .	Albion-street, Shelton . .	E. Y. Haslam .	Eastwood, Shelton.
F. Shelley . .	Aston, Stone . . .	Stone	J. Akroyd . .	Stone	J. Nickisson . .	Stone.
		Eccleshall	J. Bradshaw . .	Eccleshall.		
		Trentham	I. Swift . . .	Blurton, Stone.		
G. D. Haslewood	Cradley, Stourbridge.	Stourbridge . . .	R. Hopkins . .	Stourbridge. . . .	R. Hopkins, jun.	Stourbridge.
R. Hopkins . .	Stourbridge.	Kingswinford . . .	R. Mills . . .	Wordsley, Stourbridge.		
		Halesowen	G. D. Haslewood	Cradley, Stourbridge .	S. Smith . . .	Cradley, Stourbridge.
H. Crabb. . .	Stowmarket . . .	Rattlesden	G. J. Bridges .	Woolpit.		
C. M. Burcham .	Wattisfield, Ixworth.	Stowmarket . . .	S. Freeman . .	Stowmarket.		
		Walsham le-Willows .	C. M. Burcham .	Wattisfield, Ixworth.		
T. Palmer . .	Bourton-on-the-Water, Stow-on-the-Wold.	Stow-on-the-Wold .	G. Hayward . .	Stow-on-the-Wold.		
		Bourton-on-the-Water	W. Wells . .	Bourton-on-the-Water; Stow-on-the-Wold.		
W. Boswood . .	23, Surrey-street . .	St. Clement Danes .	P. Cosgreave .	34, Norfolk-street, Strand .	J. J. Ford . . .	29, Surrey-street.
Wm. Fearn . .	Lyon's Inn.	St. Anne's	H. D. Jones . .	23, Soho-square . . .	T. H. Pettitt . .	Old Compton-street, Soho.
		St. Mary's	W. Fearn . .	5, Lyon's-inn	R. A. Kirby . .	23, Surrey-street, Strand.
E. Ashwin . .	Stratford-on-Avon	Stratford-on-Avon .	D. Rice . . .	Stratford-on-Avon . . .	R. T. Tasker . .	Stratford-on-Avon.
		Old Stratford . . .	J. Pritchard . .	Stratford-on-Avon . .	T. Pritchard . .	Stratford-on-Avon.
		Wellesbourne . . .	J. C. Pritchard .	Wellesbourne, Stratford-on-Avon.	John Cherry .	Wellesbourne.
		Kineton	J. M. Brown. .	Kineton	Henry Hobbes .	Kineton.
		Wootton Wawen . .	W. Wiggins. .	Wootton Wawen; Henley-in-Arden.		
H. James, jun. .	Stratton, Cornwall	Stratton	H. James, jun. .	Stratton, Cornwall.		
		Kilkhampton . . .	W. Trewin . .	Kilkhampton; Stratton, Cornwall.		
		Week St. Mary . .	J. S. Cobbledick.	Whitstone, Stratton, Cornwall.		
S. R. Clissold .	Stroud	Stroud	J. S. Howell. .	Stroud.		
J. P. Ross . .	Chalford Hill.	Painswick	W. Gardner . .	Painswick.		
E. Barnard . .	Nailsworth, Minchinhampton.	Bisley	J. P. Ross . .	Chalford	W. Long . . .	Chalford Hill.
		Minchinhampton . .	S. Butler . .	Minchinhampton . . .	B. Dudbridge .	Brimscombe.
		Horsley	J. C. Tabram .	Nailsworth, Minchinhampton.		
		Rodborough . . .	J. Stephens . .	Rodborough, Stroud . .	J. Stephens, jun.	King's-court, Rodborough.
		Stonehouse . . .	J. C. Grimes. .	Stonehouse, Stroud . .	Henry Grimes .	Stonehouse, Stroud.
J. Goodridge. .	Sturminster-Newton, Blandford.	Sturminster . . .	J. Goodridge .	Sturminster, Newton, Blandford.		
Thos. Hunt . .	Marnhull, Shaftesbury	Stalbridge	Thomas Hunt .	Marnhull, Shaftesbury.		
J. Durrell . .	Boreham-gate-street, Sudbury.	Sudbury	W. Steggles . .	Ballingdon, Sudbury . .	W. Hart . . .	Ballingdon, Sudbury.
		Hartest	W. King . . .	Shimpling, Bury St. Edmunds.	J. Kimmis . .	Hartest, Bury St. Edmunds.
		Melford	G Green. . .	Melford, Sudbury.		
		Bures	R. Pratt . . .	Bures St. Mary, Sudbury.	T. Potter . . .	Nayland, Colchester.
		Bulmer	S. Ramscar . .	Bulmer, Sudbury . . .	J. Carter . . .	Gestingthorpe, Castle Hedingham.
W. Allison . .	Monkwearmouth . .	Sunderland, East . .	G. Lord . . .	Sunderland.		
W. Richardson .	43, Upper Nile-street, Bishop Wearmouth.	Sunderland, West . .	R. Hodgson . .	Bishop Wearmouth.		
		Bishop Wearmouth, North.	J. Dunn . . .	Bishop Wearmouth.		
		Bishop Wearmouth, South.	W. Bailes . .	Bishop Wearmouth.		
		Monkwearmouth . .	J. C. Hare . .	Monkwearmouth . . .	William Greig .	Hall-garth-square, Monkwearmouth.

UNION, or SUPERINTENDENT REGISTRAR'S DISTRICT.	County.	Places of Public Worship situated therein, registered for Solemnization of Marriages.		SUPERINTENDENT REGISTRARS, and *Deputy Superintendent Registrars*.	
		Name.	Situation.	Name.	Address.
SWAFFHAM	Norfolk . . .	. . .	. . .	R. Sewell . . .	Swaffham . . . .
SWANSEA	Glamorgan . .	The Presbyterian Chapel . The late Countess of Huntingdon's Chapel. Mount Pleasant Meeting . The Three Crosses Chapel Hebron Chapel . . . Libanus. . . . . . Brynteg, otherwise Fair-hill Meeting-house. Castle-street Chapel . . Ebenezer Chapel . . . Silo . . . . The Roman Catholic Chapel	High-street, Swansea . . . The Burrows, Swansea. Mount Pleasant, Swansea. Three Crosses, Llanrhidian. Clydach, in the parish of Llangafelach. Morriston, in the parish of Llangafelach. Brynteg, in the parish of Llandilo-talybont. Castle-street, Swansea. Ebenezer-street, Swansea. Glandwr, in the parish of Llangafelach. Nelson-terrace, Swansea.	C. Collins . . *R. H. Attwood,*	Wind-street, Swansea. *Rutland-place, Swansea.*
TADCASTER. . . .	York	St. Leonard's Chapel . . The Aberford Catholic Chapel.	Hazelwood, in the parish of Tadcaster. Lotherton-cum-Aberford, in the parish of Sherburn.	R. Baillie . . *W. Backhouse,*	Tadcaster . . . Ditto.
TAMWORTH. . . .	Stafford . . .	Aldergate Chapel . . St. John's Chapel . .	Aldergate-lane, Tamworth . . Tamworth.	F. J. Hamel . .	Tamworth. . . .
TAUNTON	Somerset . .	Independent Chapel . . Paul's Meeting . . . The Mary-street Chapel . The Baptist Meeting-house The Wesleyan Chapel or Temple. St. George's Chapel . . The Baptist Chapel . .	Bishop's Hull . . . . . Paul's-street, Taunton. Mary-street, Taunton. Hatch Beauchamp. Shuttern, Taunton. The Crescent, Taunton. Silver-street, Taunton.	John Chorley .	Middle-street, Taunton
TAVISTOCK. . . .	Devon . . .	Brook-street Chapel . . The Abbey Chapel . .	Tavistock . . . . . Tavistock.	John Physick .	Tavistock . . . .
TEESDALE	Durham . . .	The Independent Chapel . The Catholic Chapel . . The Primitive Methodist Chapel. Hall-street Chapel . .	Staindrop . . . . . . Lartington, in the parish of Romaldkirk. Barnard Castle. Barnard Castle.	G. Brown . . *William Bell,*	Barnard Castle . . Ditto.
TENBURY	Worcester . .	. . .	. . .	Matthias Trumper	Teme-street, Tenbury
TENDRING	Essex. . . .	. . .	. . .	W. Angell . . *W. Rayner,*	Mistley . . . . *Manningtree.*
TENTERDEN	Kent . . .	The Presbyterian Chapel . Salem Chapel	Tenterden . . . . . . Tenterden.	J. Exall . . .	Tenterden . . . .
TETBURY	Gloucester . .	. . .	. . .	W. Maskelyne .	Tetbury . . . .
TEWKESBURY. . . .	Gloucester . .	The Baptist Chapel . .	Barton-street, Tewkesbury . .	S. Ricketts . .	Tewkesbury . . .
THAKEHAM	Sussex . . .	. . .	. . .	A. Mant . . .	Storrington . . .
THAME	Oxford . . .	The Independent Chapel .	Thame	J. Hollier . .	Thame. . . . .
THANET, ISLE OF . .	Kent	The Baptist Chapel . . St. Augustine's Catholic Chapel. Ebenezer Chapel . . . Beulah Chapel . . . . Ebenezer Chapel . . . Hawley-square Chapel .	St. Peter's, Isle of Thanet. Prospect-place, Margate. New-street, Margate. Ramsgate. Ramsgate. Margate.	W. Freeman . .	Minster, Margate .
THETFORD	Norfolk and Suffolk.	The Catholic Chapel . .	Thetford	W. Clarke . . *D. Daly,*	Thetford . . . . Ditto.
THINGOE	Suffolk . . .	. . .	. . .	S. Nunn . . . *T. Cook,*	Ixworth, Bury t. Edmunds. Ditto.

REGISTRARS OF MARRIAGES.		Registrars' Districts.	REGISTRARS of BIRTHS and DEATHS.		Deputy Registrars of Births and Deaths.	
Name.	Address.		Name.	Address.	Name.	Address.
J. Philo	Swaffham	Swaffham	C. B. Rose	Swaffham.		
		Saham Toney	G. Whitby	Swaffham.		
W. Bevan	Swansea	Swansea	W. Bevan	3, York-place, Swansea	W. Strick	Castle-street, Swansea.
M. Morgan	Rhyanvaur, Llanrhidian, Swansea.	Gower	J. Gordon	Berry Llandewy, Swansea.	W. Tucker	Berry-hall, Swansea.
		Llangafelach	D. Oliver	Morriston, Swansea	D. Jones	Morriston, Swansea.
		Llansito-talybont	P. Cook	Clydach, Swansea.		
J. Cameron	Tadcaster, West	Tadcaster	J. Cameron	Tadcaster, West.		
		Aberford	C. Simpson	Aberford, Wetherby.		
		Bramham	J. Thomson	Clifford, Wetherby.		
		Bilton	J. Fletcher	Bilton, Wetherby.		
		Appleton Roebuck	A. M'Master	Appleton Roebuck, Tadcaster.		
A. A. Hamel	Tamworth	Tamworth	J. Wright	Tamworth	J. Grundy	Austrey, Tamworth.
		Fazeley	J. Mead	Fazeley.		
W. Warren	East Reach, Taunton	St. Mary Magdalen	Henry Alford	5, Hammet-street, Taunton	S. S. Alford	5,Hammet-st., Taunton
		St. James	H. Norris	Canon-street, Taunton	Robert Dinham	North-town, Taunton.
		Bishop's Lydeard	Charles Gibbs	Cotford, Bishop's Lydeard, Taunton.		
		North Curry	H. W. Mead	North Curry, Taunton.		
		Pitminster	F. W. Ling	Pitminster, Taunton.		
F. A. Davis	Tavistock	Tavistock	F. A. Davis	West-street, Tavistock	R. Luxton	West-street, Tavistock.
J. Percy	Lamerton.	Buckland	R. Toop	Horrabridge.		
		Milton Abbot	J. Percy	Lamerton.		
		Lifton	J. J. Palmer	Lifton.		
H. Atkinson	Barnard Castle	Barnard Castle	G. Middleton	Barnard Castle.	Enos Metcalf	Barnard Castle.
		Staindrop	J. Nichols	Staindrop.		
		Middleton	W. Lind	Romaldkirk, Barnard Castle	L. Holme	Romaldkirk, Barnard Castle.
George Green	Tenbury	Tenbury	S. Collins	Burford Cottage, Tenbury.		
		Buckleton	J. Wainwright	Broad Heath, Hanley William, Tenbury.		
S. Hitchcock	Mistley	Thorpe	H. Spurling	Thorpe.		
		St. Osyth	G. Pudney	Thorington.		
		Ardleigh	S. Wymark	Elmstead, Colchester.		
		Harwich	H. Harris	Dovercourt, Essex.		
		Manningtree	S. Hitchcock	Mistley.		
T. B. Greenhill	Tenterden	Rolvenden	J. Winser	Rolvenden, Tenterden	J. Morris	Biddenden.
		Tenterden	J. Longley, jun.	Tenterden	W. Smeeth	Woodchurch, Tenterden.
Geo. Lloyd	Tetbury	Tetbury	J. B. Williams	Tetbury.		
		Didmarton	G. Hooper	Leighterton, Tetbury.		
W. Dee	Tewkesbury	Tewkesbury	W. Dee	Tewkesbury.	R. Castle	Twyning, Tewkesbury.
		Overbury	J. Martin	Overbury, Tewkesbury.		
		Deerhust	W. Lane	Deerhurst, Tewkesbury.	W. Cox	Deerhurst,Tewkesbury.
G. Lear	Storrington	Pulborough	H. R. Hurst	Pulborough, Petworth.		
		Washington	H. Hill	Washington, Shoreham.		
W. Scadding	Thame	Thame	E. White	Thame.	G. Mead	Thame.
		Brill	S. Caporn	Long Crendon, Thame	J. Shrimpton	Long Crendon, Thame.
		Lewknor	V. Fletcher	Little Milton, Tetsworth.		
T. T. Sadler	Ramsgate	Margate	G. Y. Hunter	Margate	W. Cobb, jun.	Margate,
G. Y. Hunter	Margate.	Ramsgate	J. Powell.	Ramsgate	J. Powell, jun.	Ramsgate.
		Minster	R. Freeman	Minster	T. Freeman	Minster.
D. Smith	Thetford	Thetford	D. Smith	Thetford	W. Whistler.	Thetford.
J. Sharpe	Methwold, Brandon.	Methwold	J. Sharpe	Methwold, Brandon	W. Sharpe.	Brandon.
T. E. Robinson	Nowton	Fornham	G. Wiseman	Fornham St. Martin, Bury St. Edmunds.		
		Barrow	F. Adams	Whipstead, Bury St. Edmunds.		
		Rougham	T. E. Robinson	Nowton, Bury St. Edmunds		
		Ixworth	J. Clark	Ixworth, Bury St. Edmunds.		

UNION, or SUPERINTENDENT REGISTRAR'S DISTRICT.	County.	Places of Public Worship situated therein, registered for Solemnization of Marriages.		SUPERINTENDENT REGISTRARS, and *Deputy Superintendent Registrars.*	
		Name.	Situation.	Name.	Address.
THIRSK	York	The Catholic Chapel . .	North Kilvington, in the parish of Thoraton-le-Street.	J. Rider . . .	Thirsk . . . . .
		The Wesleyan Chapel . .	Thirsk.		
THOMAS, ST.	Devon . . .	Glenorchy Chapel . . .	Exmouth	J. G. Bidwill .	St. Thomas the Apostle, Exeter.
		Salem Chapel	East Budleigh.	*J. Bowring,*	*Ditto.*
THORNBURY	Gloucester . .	The Baptist Meeting-house	Thornbury	R. Scarlett . .	Thornbury . . .
THORNE	York	The Unitarian Chapel .	School Bridge-road, Thorne .	W. Thorpe . .	Thorne . . . .
				W. Lister,	*Ditto.*
THRAPSTON	Northampton .	The Baptist Meeting-house	Thrapston	J. Archbould. .	Thrapston. . . .
TICEHURST	Sussex . . .	. . .	. . .	R. Tournay . .	Ticehurst, Lamberhurst
TISBURY	Wilts	Wardour Chapel . . .	Wardour Castle	E. V. Clarke .	Linley, Hindon, Wilts
		Baptist Chapel	Semley.		
		Birdbush Chapel . . .	Ludwell, in the parish of Donhead St. Mary.		
TIVERTON & DULVERTON	Devon & Somerset	The Presbyterian Meeting	Collumpton	T. L. T. Rendell	Bampton-street, Tiverton.
		The Independent Chapel .	St. Peter-street, Tiverton.		
		The Baptist Chapel . .	The Mill-way, Bradninch.		
		The Independent Chapel .	Cold Harbour, in the parish of Uffculm.		
TODMORDEN	Lancaster and York.	Heptonstall Slack Chapel.	Stone Slack, Heptonstall, in the parish of Halifax.	J. Stansfield . .	Ewood, Todmorden .
		The Wesleyan Methodist Association Chapel.	Todmorden, in the parish of Halifax.		
		Eastwood Chapel . . .	Stansfield, in the parish of Halifax.		
TONBRIDGE	Kent	Independent Chapel . .	Tonbridge	E. Stidolph . .	Tonbridge . . .
		Mount Zion Chapel . .	Tonbridge Wells.		
TORRINGTON	Devon . . .	The Independent Meeting	Great Torrington	W. G. Glubb .	Great Torrington . .
		Baptist Chapel . . .	Great Torrington.	*W. Perry,*	*Langtree, Torrington.*
TOTNES	Devon . . .	Presbyterian Meeting-house	Near the Foss, Dartmouth . .	G. Hannaford .	Totnes . . . .
		The Totnes Chapel . .	Totnes.		
		The Baptist Meeting . .	Atkins'-lane, South Town, Dartmouth.		
TOWCESTER	Northampton .	The Baptist Meeting . .	Towcester	J. H. Sheppard .	Towcester . . . .
		The Independent Chapel .	Towcester.	*W. Sheppard,*	*Ditto.*
		The Baptist Meeting-house	Weston, in the parish of Loys, Weedon.		
TREGARON	Cardigan . . .	. . .	. . .	Jas. Jones . .	Tregaron, Lampeter .
TRURO	Cornwall . . .	Bethesda Chapel . . .	River-street, Truro	R. M. Hodge .	Truro . . . .
				William Hockin,	*Ditto.*

REGISTRARS of MARRIAGES.		Registrars' Districts.	REGISTRARS of BIRTHS and DEATHS.		Deputy Registrars of Births and Deaths.	
Name.	Address.		Name.	Address.	Name.	Address.
R. Peat	Thirsk	Knayton	T. Newton	Knayton, Thirsk.		
		Thirsk	R. Peat	Thirsk.		
		Sutton	N. Edwards	Thirkleby, Thirsk.		
		Topcliffe	R. Hirst	Topcliffe, Thirsk.		
		Pickhall	J. Routledge	Pickhill, Thirsk.		
W. M. Benison	St. Thomas	St. Thomas	W. M. Benison	Exe-bridge, St. Thomas	T. Dyer	Cowick-street, St. Thomas.
J. Treuchard, jun.	Exmouth.					
		Exmouth	W. H. Land	Exmouth	G. Blackmore	Exmouth.
		Kenton	W. Collyns	Kenton, St. Thomas	W. W. Collyns	Kenton, St. Thomas.
		Topsham	T. C. Tothill	Topsham	J. M. Byrom	Topsham.
		East Budleigh	W. Kendall	Budleigh, Salterton	S. Teed	East Budleigh.
		Heavitree	J. M. Madden	Heavitree.		
		Alphington	C. N. Cheeseworth	New-buildings, Dunsford, Morton Hampstead.	J. Seward	Dunsford.
		Woodbury	J. S. Lindsey	Woodbury	T. G. Skinner	Woodbury.
		Broadclist	G. R. Ayshford	Broadclist	C. Francis	Broadclist.
		Christow	J. Hamlyn	Christow	G. Amery	Christow.
T. J. Councell	Thornbury	Almondsbury	C. Powell	Ridgeway, Thornbury.	E. O. Robertson	Thornbury.
		Berkeley	J. Darke	Berkeley	A. J. Griffiths	Berkeley.
		Thornbury	E. Salmon	Thornbury	P. Salmon	Thornbury.
John Goodworth	Thorne	Thorne	J. Goodworth	Thorne	J. Mason	Thorne.
		Crowle	W. Chapman	Crowle, Bawtry	W. Blunt	Crowle, Bawtry.
		Epsworth	R. Pullan	Epsworth, Bawtry.		
W. Whiteman	Titchmarsh, Thrapston	Thrapston	W. Whiteman	Titchmarsh, Thrapston.		
		Rounds	Jonas Hill	Rounds, Higham Ferrers.		
T. B. Wiles	Ticehurst, Lamberhurst	Ticehurst	T. A. Evans	Burwash, Lamberhurst	T. B. Wiles	Ticehurst, Lamberhurst
		Wadhurst	J. Micklefield	Lamberhurst	E. W. Gilbert	Frant, Tombridge.
		Salehurst	A. Matthews	Salehurst, Robertsbridge.		
W. Jeffery	Old Wardour, Donhead St. Andrew.	Tisbury	T. Jukes	Tisbury.		
J. H. Brothers	Cumbe, Donhead St. Mary.	Donhead	J. Wills	Donhead St. Andrew, Shaftesbury.	John Wills, jun.	Donhead St. Andrew, Shaftesbury.
		Hindon	T. Harrison	Hindon.		
W. H. Maunder	Collumpton	Tiverton	J. J. Owen	St. Peter-street, Tiverton	W. R. Hooper	St. Andrew-street, Tiverton.
F. S. Gervis	Tiverton.	Bampton	J. Edwards	Bampton.		
		Uffculm	W. F. Merson	Sampford Peverell, Tiverton.	C. Hutchings	Sampford Peverell, Tiverton.
		Collumpton	W. H. Maunder	Collumpton.		
		Silverton	F. A. Cleeve	Bradninch, Collumpton	T. C. Squire	Bradninch, Collumpton
		Washfield	W. Jordan	Stoodley, Bampton.		
		Dulverton	C. P. Collyns	Dulverton, Somerset.		
J. Sutcliffe	Heptonstall, Halifax.	Todmorden	J. Oliver	Todmorden.		
W. Halstead	Horsfall, Todmorden.	Hebdenbridge	J. Thomas	Hebdenbridge, Halifax.		
Thos. Waterman	Tonbridge	Tonbridge Wells	H. L. Sopwith	Tonbridge Wells	F. Sopwith	Tonbridge Wells.
		Tonbridge	J. Smith	Hadlow, Tonbridge.		
		Brenchley	J. Monckton	Brenchley	G. Joy	Matfield, in Brenchley.
T. Fowler	Great Torrington.	Great Torrington	J. C. Hole	Great Torrington	R. L. Hole	Great Torrington.
		High Bickington	J. Cocks	High Bickington, Great Torrington.	G. Davey	High Bickington, Great Torrington.
		Shebbear	J. Mallet	Buckland, Filleigh, Okehampton.	S. Heard	Buckland, Filleigh, Okehampton.
		Winkleigh	A. Friend	Winkleigh, Crediton	T. Collihole	Winkleigh, Crediton.
		Dolton	W. Risdon	Dolton, Crediton	R. Budd	Dolton, Crediton.
S. Huxham	Totnes	Totnes	R. Harris	Totnes	R. Martyn	Totnes.
S. Follet	Dartmouth.	Buckfastleigh	J. Whiteway, jun.	Hole Staverton	J. W. Whiteway, jun.	Staverton.
		Brixham	T. Lakeman	Brixham	R. Turner	Brixham.
		Paington	J. Rossiter	Paington	E. P. Fletcher	Paignton.
		Harberton		Harberton	J. Fairweather, jun.	Harberton.
		Dartmouth	S. Follet	Dartmouth	H. Follett	Townstall, Dartmouth.
		Ugborough	R. Jeffery	Ugborough	W. Mabin	Ugborough.
T. Watkins	Towcester	Towcester	T. Watkins	Towcester	E. T. Watkins	Towcester.
		Abthorpe	George Wagstaffe	Blakesley, Towcester.		
J. Williams	Maasbannaleg, Tregaron, Lampeter.	Tregaron	M. Jones	Tregaron, Lampeter.		
		Llangeitho	D. Jones	Tynddulanbach, Llangeitho, Lampeter.		
		Gwnnee	John Jones	Tydreinees, Lampeter.		
R. Chapman	Rosewin-row, Truro	St. Clement	J. Barrett	Truro.		
		Kenwyn	T. G. Hicks	Truro.		
		Kea	J. Michell	Feock, Truro.		
		St. Agnes	J. Newton	St. Agnes, Truro	R. Newton	St. Agnes, Truro.
		St. Just	S. Libby	Veryan, Tregony.		
		Probus	S. Treemens	Probus, Truro.		

UNION, or SUPERINTENDENT REGISTRAR'S DISTRICT.	County.	Places of Public Worship situated therein, registered for Solemnization of Marriages.		SUPERINTENDENT REGISTRARS, and *Deputy Superintendent Registrars*.	
		Name.	Situation.	Name.	Address.
TUNSTEAD & HAPPING.	Norfolk . . .	Ingham Baptist Chapel . The Baptist Meeting-house	Ingham . . . . Meeting-hill, Worsted.	Washington Smith	Smallburgh, Norfolk.
TYNEMOUTH	Northumberland.	St. Andrew's Chapel . . Roman Catholic Chapel . The United Secession Church. Ebenezer Chapel . . . Baptist Chapel . . . Secession Chapel . . Primitive Methodist Chapel Scotch Church	Camden-street, Tynemouth. Bedford-street, Tynemouth. Waterloo; Blyth. South Blyth, in the parish of Earsdon. Stephenson-street, Tynemouth. Norfolk-street, Tynemouth. Union-street, Tynemouth. Howard-street, Tynemouth.	J. L. Barker . . *R. Barker, sen.,*	Howard-street, Tyne- mouth. *Ditto.*
UCKFIELD	Sussex . . .	The Baptist Chapel .	Uckfield	W. A. Rooke . .	Uckfield . . . .
ULVERSTONE	Lancaster . .	Tottlebank Chapel. . The Independent Chapel . St. Mary's Catholic Chapel	Tottlebank, in the parish of Colton. Ulverstone. Ulverstone.	John Syke . .	Ulverstone . . .
UPPINGHAM	Rutland . . .	The Independent Chapel .	Uppingham	W. Gilson . . *J. Wilmot,*	Uppingham . . . *Ditto.*
UPTON-ON-SEVERN . .	Worcester . .	. . .	. . .	J. Skey . . .	Upton-on-Severn . .
UTTOXETER	Stafford . . .	The Independent Chapel.	Carter-street, Uttoxeter. . .	C. V. W. Bedson *Tho. Rushton,*	Uttoxeter . . . . *Ditto.*
UXBRIDGE	Middlesex . .	Providence Chapel. . .	Uxbridge	C. Woodbridge .	Uxbridge . . . .
WAKEFIELD	York	Zion Chapel . . . . St. Austin's Chapel . Westgate Chapel . . . Salem Chapel . . .	Rodney Yard, Wakefield . . Wakefield. Westgate, in Wakefield. George-street, Wakefield.	J. W. Berry . . *John Berry,*	York-street, Wakefield. *Wood-street, Wakefield.*
WALLINGFORD . . .	Berks and Oxford	. . .	. . .	George Sharwood	Wallingford . .
WALSALL	Stafford . . .	St. Mary's Chapel . St. Thomas's Chapel . The Independent Chapel . Bell-street Primitive Me- thodist Chapel.	St. Mary's Mount, Walsall. . Bloxwich, in the parish of Walsall Bridge-street, Walsall. Darlaston.	H. Duignan . .	Walsall . . . .
WALSINGHAM. . . .	Norfolk . . .	The Independent Chapel . The Independent Chapel .	Fakenham . . . . . . Wells-next-the-Sea.	J. Overton . .	Fakenham . . .
WANDSWORTH and CLAP- HAM.	Surrey .	Wandsworth Chapel . . Park-road Chapel . . . Tooting Chapel . . . Baptist Chapel. . . . Union Chapel	High-street, Wandsworth . . Park-road, Clapham. Lower Tooting. Clapham. Brixton-hill, in the parish of Streatham.	B. Field . . . *G. F. Merriman,*	Clapham Common . 5, *St. Paul's-place, Wandsworth-road.*
WANGFORD.	Suffolk . . .	The Independent Chapel . Independent Chapel . . The Roman Catholic Chapel The Particular Baptist Chapel.	Beccles . . . . Bungay. Bungay. Beccles.	R. Beales . .	Beccles . . . .
WANTAGE	Berks. . . .	. . .	. . .	W. Ormond . .	Wantage . . . .
WARE	Herts . . .	The New Independent Cha- pel. Old Hall Green Chapel . The Old Independent Chapel.	Ware. . . . . Old Hall, in the parish of Standon Dead-lane, in the parish of Ware	C. R. N. Palmer.	Hoddesdon . .

REGISTRARS of MARRIAGES.		Registrars' Districts.	REGISTRARS of BIRTHS and DEATHS.		Deputy Registrars of Births and Deaths.	
Name.	Address.		Name.	Address.	Name.	Address.
W. Clowes . .	Stalham	*Smallburgh* . . .	J. Dix . . .	Smallburgh.		
		North Walsham . .	H. Bidwell . .	North Walsham.		
		Stalham	W. Clowes . .	Stalham.		
		Ludham	S. T. Huke . .	Ludham.		
R. Barker, jun. .	King-street,Tynemouth	*Tynemouth* . . .	W. Harrison . .	Dockwray-square, Tynemouth.	S. W. Harrison .	20, Dockwray-square, Tynemouth.
G. Ward . . .	Bridge-street, Blyth.	*North Shields* . .	S. J. Tibbs . .	North Shields . . .	R. Davison . .	North Shields.
		Earsdon	Stephen Aynsley.	Earsdon, Newcastle-on-Tyne.		
		Blyth	G. Ward . . .	Blyth.	J. Thoburn . .	Blyth.
		Wallsend	J. Mordue . .	Wallsend, Newcastle-on-Tyne.	Thomas Johnson	Wallsend - bank - top, Newcastle-on-Tyne.
		Longbenton	E. Lamb . . .	Longbenton, Newcastle-on-Tyne.	T. Shaw . . .	Longbenton, Newcastle-on-Tyne.
C. Prince. . .	Uckfield	*Rotherfield*	M. Wallis . .	Mayfield	G. Holman . .	Mayfield.
		Maresfield . . .	J. Jones . . .	Fletching	C. Wood, jun. .	Fletching.
		Isfield	C. Prince. . .	Uckfield.	C. L. Prince . .	Uckfield.
		Fromfield . . .	H. Holman . .	East Hothly	R. Colgate . .	East Hothly.
W. Briggs . .	Ulverstone. . . .	*Broughton, West* .	J. Hudson . .	Broughton-in-Furness.		
E. Harbottle. .	Oxen Park.	*Cartmel*	J. Rawlinson. .	Newton-in-Cartmel.		
		Colton	B. Coward . .	Greenodd.		
		Dalton	G. Simpson . .	Ulverick.		
		Hawkshead . . .	R. Lodge. . .	Hawkshead.	C. Watson, jun. .	Hawkshead.
		Ulverstone. . .	J. Barnes. . .	Ulverstone.		
N. W. Wortley .	Ridlington, Uppingham.	*Uppingham* . . .	C. Benson . .	Uppingham	R. Wignell . .	Uppingham.
		Barrowden . . .	T. Price . . .	Barrowden, Uppingham.	John Johnson .	Barrowden, Uppingham.
		Great Easton . .	J. A. Laxton. .	Great Easton, Rockingham.	J. Everitt . .	Great Easton, Rockingham.
T. W. Walker .	Upton-on-Severn .	*Upton-on-Severn* .	G. Sheward . .	Upton-on-Severn . . .	H. Cowley . .	Upton-on-Severn.
J. Dancocks . .	Powick, Worcester.	*Hanley Castle* . .	J. Dancocks . .	Powick, Worcestershire.		
B. Treeton . .	Bushley, Tewkesbury.	*Kempsey*	J. Evans . . .	Severn-Stoke, Worcestershire		
W. D. Evarard .	Uttoxeter	*Uttoxeter*	R. Lassetter . .	Uttoxeter.		
		Sudbury	Thomas Mould .	Sudbury, Derbyshire .	John Mould . .	Sudbury.
		Abbots Bromley . .	W. L. Sutton .	Abbots Bromley . . .	F, Cope . . .	Bromley Hurst, Rugeley.
W. Nash . . .	Uxbridge	*Uxbridge*	T. Collet . .	Ickenham.		
		Hillingdon	F. Stockwell . .	Hillingdon.		
		Hayes	F. Sherley . .	Hayes.		
J. Holdsworth .	Pincheon-street, Wakefield.	*Wakefield*	J. Holdsworth . .	Pincheon-street, Wakefield	R. Holdsworth .	Pincheon-street.
		Stanley	M. Jordan . .	Lake Lock, Stanley-cum-Wrenthorpe, Wakefield.	J. Morton . .	Lake Lock, Wakefield.
		Alverthorpe . . .	W. Stewart . .	Horbury, Wakefield .	S. Berry . . .	Horbury.
		Bretton	T. Prest . . .	Bretton, West, Wakefield.		
		Sandall	Thos. Schorey .	Sandall, Wakefield.		
		Ardsley	T. Flockton . .	Ardsley, East, Wakefield.		
		Oulton	Rev. J. Muncaster	Oulton, Leeds	J. Morton . .	Oulton, Leeds.
Jas. Sherwood .	High-street, Wallingford.	*Wallingford* . . .	Thos. Wells . .	Wallingford	W. Godley . .	Wallingford.
		Cholsey	J. Bennett . .	Wallingford	W. Moore . .	Cholsey.
J. Cotterell . .	Walsall	*Walsall*	W. Sleigh . .	Walsall.		
John Porter . .	Little London, Walsall	*Bloxwich*	W. Totty. . .	Bloxwich.		
W. Whitehouse .	Walsall.	*Darlaston*	J. Lowe . .	Darlaston.		
		Aldridge	J. D. Proffitt. .	Aldridge.		
G. Damant . .	Fakenham. . . .	*Wells*	J. Young. . .	Wells, Norfolk.		
		Walsingham . . .	C. Adcock . .	Walsingham.		
		Fakenham . . .	G. Damant . .	Fakenham.		
C. Mills . . .	North-street, Clapham	*Wandsworth* . . .	W. Foster . .	Wandsworth	J. Nugent . .	Wandsworth.
		Clapham	C. Mills . . .	Clapham	T. Brown. . .	Clapham.
		Putney. . . .	W. Hull . .	Putney	J. Roseblade. .	Putney.
		Streatham and Tooting	H. Withall . .	Streatham	T. Gammon . .	Streatham.
		Battersea	T. Chapman. .	Battersea	R. Lee . . .	Battersea.
J. C. Webster .	Beccles	*Beccles*	W. Stanford . .	Beccles.		
		Bungay	B. Sewell . .	Bungay.		
W. Davies . .	Wantage	*Wantage*	W. Davies . .	Wantage.		
		Ilsley	Edwin Crapper .	Farnborough, Wantage, Abingdon.		
		Hendred	J. Crapper . .	East Hendred, Abingdon.		
J. Harradence .	High-street, Ware .	*Hoddesdon*. . . .	W. Horley . .	Hoddesdon	W. Gosse . .	Hoddesdon.
		Ware	J. H. Judson . .	Ware	C. B. Judson . .	Ware.
		Standon	C. W. Carter . .	Puckeridge, Ware . .	J. Judd . . .	Puckeridge, Ware.
		Stanstead	R. Perkins . .	Stanstead, Ware . . .	C. W. Perkins .	Stanstead, Ware.

UNION, or SUPERINTENDENT REGISTRAR'S DISTRICT.	County.	Places of Public Worship situated therein, registered for Solemnization of Marriages.		SUPERINTENDENT REGISTRARS, and *Deputy Superintendent Registrars.*	
		Name.	Situation.	Name.	Address.
WAREHAM and PURBECK	Dorset	Unitarian Chapel	South-street, Wareham.	F. Filliter	Wareham
		The Catholic Chapel	Lulworth Castle Park.		
		Independent Chapel	Corfe Castle.		
		West-street Meeting	West-street, Wareham.		
		The Old Meeting	Meeting-house-lane, Wareham.		
		Congregational Chapel	Church-hill, in the parish of Swanage.		
WARMINSTER	Wilts	The Independent Chapel	Common Close, Warminster	J. Boor	Warminster
		The Independent Chapel	Codford, St. Mary.		
WARRINGTON	Lancaster	St. Alban's Chapel	Warrington	W. Wagstaff.	Warrington
		The Croft Town Catholic Chapel.	Southworth with Croft, in the parish of Winwick.	J. F. Marsh,	Fairfield House, Warrington.
		The Presbyterian Chapel	Warrington.		
		Salem Chapel	Warrington.		
		St. John's Chapel	Warrington.		
WARWICK	Warwick	Independent Chapel	Brook-street, Warwick.	E. Draper	Warwick
		Catholic Chapel	Hampton-on-the-Hill, in the parish of Budbrooke.		
		Catholic Chapel	Leamington Priors.		
		Mill-street Chapel	Leamington Priors.		
		The High-street Chapel, Warwick.	High-street, Warwick.		
		Spencer-street Chapel	Leamington Priors.		
WATFORD	Herts	Bushey Chapel.	Bushey	R. Pugh, jun.	Watford
		The Baptist Chapel	Watford.		
WAYLAND	Norfolk	The Baptist Chapel	Attleborough	S. Caley	Attleborough
WEARDALE	Durham	The Primitive Methodist Chapel.	West Gate, Stanhope.	T. H. Bates	Wolsingham
		High House Chapel	The Holts, in the parish of Stanhope.		
WELLINGBOROUGH	Northampton	Salem Chapel	Wellingborough.	H. M. Hodson	Wellingborough
		The Baptist Meeting	Irthlingborough.		
		The Old Baptist Meeting	Little-street, Rushden.		
WELLINGTON	Salop	Baptist Chapel.	Wellington	G. Marcy	Wellington, Salop
WELLINGTON	Somerset	The Baptist Chapel	South-street, Wellington	W. Rodham	Wellington, Somerset
		The Independent Chapel	Wellington.		
WELLS	Somerset			J. S. Churchill	Wells, Somerset
WEM and WHITCHURCH	Salop	Chapel-street Chapel	Wem.	W. Owen, jun.	Wem
WEOBLY	Hereford			P. S. Parker	Weobly
WESTBOURNE	Sussex			D. Smart	Emsworth, Hants.
WEST BROMWICH	Stafford	St. Michael's Chapel	West Bromwich Heath.	J. Marshall	West Bromwich
		Union Chapel	Near Grove-lane, Handsworth.		
		The Old Meeting	Black-lake, West Bromwich.		
WESTBURY-ON-SEVERN	Gloucester	Blakeney Baptist Chapel	Blakeney, in the parish of Awre	S. R. Strode	Newnham
WESTBURY and WHORWELLSDOWN.	Wilts	The Baptist Chapel	Westbury Leigh.	H. Pinniger	Westbury, Wilts
		Providence Chapel.	Penknap, Dilton Marsh, in the parish of Westbury.		
		The Baptist Chapel	Cook's Stile, Westbury.		
		The Old Independent Chapel	Warminster-road, Westbury.		

REGISTRARS of MARRIAGES.		Registrars' Districts.	REGISTRARS of BIRTHS and DEATHS.		Deputy Registrars of Births and Deaths.	
Name.	Address.		Name.	Address.	Name.	Address.
C. Filliter	Wareham	Wareham	G. Stent	Wareham.		
		Bere Regis.	T. Carter.	Bere Regis.		
		Corfe Castle	W. Florance	Corfe Castle.		
		Swanage	H. D. C. Delamotte	Swanage, Isle of Purbeck.		
W. Daniell	Portway, Warminster	Warminster	W. Daniell	Warminster.		
		Longbridge, Deverell	R. Payne.	Longbridge, Deverell.		
		Heylesbury.	Isaac Flower.	Codford St. Peter, Warminster.		
J. Cruikshank	Church-place, Warrington.	Warrington	W. Harrison	Warrington.	Isaac Andrews	Bridge-st., Warrington.
		Sankey.	J. L. Smith	Sankey, Warrington	H. S. Smith	Sankey, Warrington.
		Rixton.	J. Clarke	Rixton, Warrington.		
		Newton	William Morley	Newton. Warrington.		
		Winwick	R. Owen	Croft, Warrington.		
T. Rose	Warwick	Warwick	M. R. Margetts	Warwick.		
		Leamington	R. Croydon	Leamington.		
		Kenilworth	J. Linforth	Kenilworth.		
		Radford	T. Price	Cubbington, Leamington.		
		Budbrooke	W. Dunn	Hatton, Warwick.		
J. Adcock	Watford	Watford	N. Poulton	Watford	J. Chester	Watford.
		Rickmansworth	T. Wilson	Rickmansworth.		
		Bushey	J. Beeson	Aldenham, Watford.		
		Abbot's Langley	H. Godman	Abbot's Langley, King's Langley.		
George Kent	Attleborough	Attleborough	George Kent	Attleborough.		
		Watton	H. Stebbings	Carbrooke, Watton.		
R. Moses	Wolsingham	Stanhope	J. Benson	Stanhope.		
		St. John's	C. Harrison	Ireshope Burn, in Weardale, Stanhope.		
		Wolsingham	R. Moses	Wolsingham.		
T. Clark	Wellingborough.	Wellingborough	T. Clark	Wellingborough	D. K. Hawkins	Wellingborough.
George Arnsby	Irthlingborough, Higham Ferrers.	Earl's Barton.	E. Sanderson	Wollaston, Wellingborough.		
		Higham Ferrers	J. N. Goodhall	Irthlingborough, Higham Ferrers.		
W. Nock	Wellington, Salop	Wellington	R. Weston	Wellington, Salop.		
		Wombridge	T. Cranage	Wrockwardine-wood, Wellington, Salop.		
		Ercall Magna	H. Harris	High Ercall.		
A. Langley	Wellington, Somerset	Wellington	A. Langley	Wellington, Somerset.		
		Milverton	H. W. Randolph	Milverton.		
		Wiveliscombe	A. F. Edwards	Wiveliscombe	J. A. Edwards	Wiveliscombe.
		Culmstock	A. Dunsford	Culmstock, Wellington, Somerset.		
T. Barnes	Wells	Wells	H. Badcocke.	Wells.		
		Glastonbury	J. Harvey	Glastonbury.		
George Harris	Wem	Wem	G. Harris.	Wem	T. Parker	Wem.
W. Ikin	Prees, Wem.	Prees	W. Ikin	Prees, Wem	Thomas Hatton	Prees, Wem.
G. Gretton	Whitchurch.	Whitchurch	G. Gretton	Whitchurch, Salop	W. A. Cartwright	Whitchurch, Salop.
J. Whiting	Weobly	Weobly	T. Williams	Weobly.		
		Dilwyn	W. Starr	Dilwyn, Weobly.		
S. Cousens	Prinsted; Emsworth, Hants.	Westbourne.	W. White	Nutbourne, Emsworth, Hants.		
		Funtington	T. White.	Woodmancot, Emsworth, Hants.		
J. B. Clarke	High-street, West Bromwich.	South West.	Samuel Reeves	George-street, West Bromwich.		
		North East	J. B. Clarke	High-street, West Bromwich.		
		Wednesbury	T. Parkes	Wednesbury.		
		Handsworth and Perry Barr.	W. Price.	Handsworth Birmingham.		
		Oldbury and Warley	H. Parish	Oldbury, Salop.	O. Johnson	Oldbury.
J. Playstead	Newnham	Huntley	J. Constance	Westbury-on-Severn.		
		Newnham and Dean Forest.	J. Ross	Littledean, Newnham.		
J. Wilkins	Westbury, Wilts	Westbury	G. Shoreland.	Westbury, Wilts.		
		Edington	J. White.	Edington; Westbury, Wilts.		
		Bradley	S. Singer.	North Bradley, Trowbridge.		

P

UNION, or SUPERINTENDENT REGISTRAR'S DISTRICT.	County.	Places of Public Worship situated therein, registered for Solemnization of Marriages.		SUPERINTENDENT REGISTRARS, and Deputy Superintendent Registrars.	
		Name.	Situation.	Name.	Address.
WEST DERBY	Lancaster . .	Toxteth Chapel . . .	South Hill-place, Toxteth-park.	J. Pennell . .	West Derby, Liverpool
		Little Crosby Chapel . .	Little Crosby, in the parish of Sefton.		
		St. Patrick's Chapel . .	Park-place, Toxteth-park.		
		St. Peter's Catholic Chapel	Great Crosby, in the parish of Sefton.		
		St. Swithin's Catholic Chapel.	Gill Moss, in the parish of Walton-on-the-Hill.		
		The Ancient Chapel of Toxteth-park.	Park-road, Toxteth-park.		
		St. Bennett's Chapel . .	Netherton, in the parish of Sefton.		
		Crescent Chapel . . .	Everton Brow, in the parish of Walton-on-the-Hill.		
WEST HAM	Essex	Stratford Catholic Chapel.	Stratford, in the parish of West Ham.	S. Richardson .	Low Leyton, Essex .
		Plaistow Chapel . . .	Plaistow, in the parish of West Ham.		
		Marsh-street Chapel . .	Walthamstow.		
WEST HAMPNETT . .	Sussex . . .	. . .	. . .	R. Raper . . .	Chichester . . . .
WESTMINSTER. . . .	Middlesex . .	Trevor Chapel	Trevor-square, Knightsbridge	J. P. Makeham .	Council Office, Downing-street.
		St. Mary's	Romney-terrace, Westminster.	G. Pearse, jun.,	5, Regent-street, Westminster.
		Buckingham Chapel . .	Palace-street, Pimlico.		
WEST WARD	Westmorland	. . .	. . .	J. Atkinson . .	Hackthorpe, Penrith .
WEYMOUTH	Dorset . . .	St. Nicholas-street Chapel	Melcombe Regis	J. Henning . .	Weymouth . . . .
		Fortuneswell Chapel . .	Fortuneswell, in the parish of Portland.	R. C. Phillips,	Ditto.
		Hope Chapel	High-street, Weymouth.		
		Bank Buildings Chapel .	Melcombe Regis.		
WHEATENHURST. . .	Gloucester . .	Brethren Chapel . . .	Frampton-on-Severn . . .	R. Weight . .	Frampton-on-Severn .
WHITBY	York	Silver-street Chapel . .	Ruswarp, in the parish of Whitby.	R. Breckon . .	Whitby
		Cliff-lane Chapel . . .	Cliff-lane, Whitby.		
		St. Hilda Chapel . . .	Bagdale, in the township of Ruswarp, in the parish of Whitby.		
		(No distinguishing Name)	Egton-bridge, in the township of Egton, in the parish of Lythe.		
		St. Ann's Chapel . . .	Ugthorpe, in the parish of Lythe.		
WHITCHURCH . . .	Hants . . .	. . .	. . .	J. Jordan. . .	Whitchurch, Hants .
WHITEHAVEN	Cumberland .	St. Gregory's Catholic Chapel.	Whitehaven	J. B. Postlethwaite	Whitehaven . . .
		Providence Chapel . .	Whitehaven.	J. Robinson,	61, Lowther-street, Whitehaven.
WHITECHAPEL . . .	Middlesex . .	Wesleyan Chapel . . .	Church-street, Spitalfields . .	J. Smith . . .	23, Leman-street, Whitechapel.
		St. George's German Lutheran Church.	Little Alie-street, Whitechapel.		
WHITTLESEY	Cambridge . .	Zion Chapel	Whittlesey	J. Peed . . .	Whittlesey, Isle of Ely
WIGAN	Lancaster . .	St. John's Chapel . . .	Standishgate, Wigan . . .	H. Gaskell . .	Wigan . . . .
		Hope Chapel	Hope-street, Wigan.	H. Gaskell,	Ditto.
		St. Mary's Chapel . .	Standishgate, Wigan.		
		St. Oswald's Catholic Chapel.	Ashton within Makerfield, in the parish of Winwick.		
		Park-lane Chapel . . .	Ashton in Makerfield, in the parish of Winwick.		
		Birchley New Chapel. .	Billinge Chapel End, in the parish of Wigan.		

REGISTRARS of MARRIAGES.		Registrars' Districts.	REGISTRARS of BIRTHS and DEATHS.		Deputy Registrars of Births and Deaths.	
Name.	Address.		Name.	Address.	Name.	Address.
G. Edgar . .	1, Park-street, Park-road, Toxteth-park.	*West Derby* . . .	J. Homer . . .	West Derby, Liverpool .	J. B. Homer . .	Fairclough-lane, West Derby ; Liverpool.
Hugh Spencer .	Thornton, Liverpool.	*Everton*	W. Shaw . . .	Everton village, Liverpool	D. Griffiths . .	Mill-road, Everton.
		Walton-on-the-Hill	J. Musker . . .	Walton-on-the-Hill, Liverpool		
		Litherland . . .	J. Webster . . .	Litherland, Liverpool.		
		Crosby	S. Shearson . .	Crosby, Liverpool . .	Jno. Shearson . .	Moor-lane, Crosby.
		Wavertree . . .	W. Andrews . .	Wavertree, Liverpool.		
		Toxteth-park . .	J. F. Meyers . .	Toxteth-park, Liverpool .	G. Edgar . . .	1, Park-street, Park-road, Toxteth-park.
A. Lancaster. .	Stratford, West-Ham, Essex.	*West Ham* . . .	J. E. Beale . .	Plaistow, Essex . . .	F. H. O'Flaherty	Plaistow, Essex.
		Stratford . . .	J. T. Vallance .	Stratford, Essex.		
		Leyton	R. Collins . . .	Leyton, Essex.		
		Walthamstow . .	D. Dorward . .	Woodford, Essex . . .	T. H. Scarlett . .	Woodford, Essex.
. . .	. . .	*Manhood* . . .	Jas. Randall . .	East Wittering, Chichester		
		Whyke	J. Heath . . .	Rumbold's Whyke, Chichester.	E. Hackman . .	Rumbold's Whyke, Chichester.
		Singleton . . .	J. Adams . . .	Singleton, Midhurst.		
		Yapton	J. Yorke . . .	Walberton, Arundel.		
		Boxgrove . . .	S. Evans . . .	Maudling, Chichester.		
T. Binge . . .	76, York-street, Westminster.	*St. John's* . . .	G. Pearse . . .	46, Marsham-st., Westminster	W. Pearse . .	46, Marsham-street.
		St. Margaret's .	W. Martin . .	50, King-street, Westminster	J. Martin . . .	50, King-street, Westminster.
T. Abbot . . .	Morland, Penrith, Cumberland.	*Lowther*	W. Brown . . .	Askham, Penrith . . .	W. Brown. jun.	Helton, Penrith.
		Morland	T. Abbott . . .	Morland, Penrith . . .	J. Abbott. . .	Morland, Penrith.
W. Richards. .	Weymouth . . .	*Weymouth* . . .	W. Richards . .	Weymouth	T. Macklin . .	18, St. Mary-street, Melcombe Regus, Weymouth.
H. Hine . . .	Upway, Weymouth.	*Upway*	H. Hine . . .	Upway, Weymouth.		
W. White . . .	Portland, Weymouth.	*Portland* . . .	F. S. Frost . .	Portland, Weymouth.		
W. Sweeting. .	Abbotsbury, Weymouth	*Abbotsbury* . . .	W. Sweeting . .	Abbotsbury, Weymouth .	J. Tullidge . .	Abbotsbury, Weymouth
G. Reynolds. .	Frampton-on-Severn .	*Frampton* . . .	T. Spire . . .	Eastington, Stroud.		
		Haresfield . . .	J. Crump . . .	Wheatenhurst, Dursley.		
R. Kirby . . .	Whitby	*Whitby*	R. Kirby . . .	Church-street, Whitby.		
		Lythe	J. Pearson . .	Ugthorpe, Lythe, Whitby.		
		Egton	B. Richardson .	Egton-bridge, Whitby.		
J. Evans . . .	Church-street Whitchurch, Hants.	*Whitchurch* . . .	J. Evans . . .	Church-street, Whitchurch, Hants.	R. Parker . .	Whitchurch.
Charles Bell . .	Whitehaven . . .	*Whitehaven* . . .	Josh. Banks . .	Whitehaven.		
		St. Bees . . .	A. J. Braithwaite	Mountpleasant, Whitehaven.		
		Egremont . . .	W. Rook . . .	Egremont, Whitehaven.		
		Harrington . . .	T. Harrison . .	Distington, Whitehaven.		
T. Evitt . . .	40, Haydon-square .	*Spitalfields* . . .	G. Deboos . .	183, Brick-lane, Spitalfields.	Jno. Deboos . .	183, Brick-lane.
		Artillery . . .	T. Mason . .	7, High-street, Norton Folgate.		
		Mile-end New-town	C. H. Rich . .	70, Church-street, Mile-end New-town.	W. Horne, jun. .	34, New Montague-st., Spitalfields.
		Whitechapel, North	H. Chapman .	16, Osborn-street, Whitechapel.	W. Moseley . .	17, Whitechapel-road.
		Whitechapel Church	W. Field . . .	42, High-street, Whitechapel.	G. Byron . .	50, High-street, Whitechapel.
		Goodman's-fields .	W. Kerby . .	40, Leman-street, Whitechapel.	G. F. Reynolds .	53, Mansell-street, Goodman's-fields.
		Aldgate . . .	J. J. Harris . .	11, Upper East Smithfield, Aldgate.	W. S. Harris .	12, Upper East Smithfield, Aldgate.
J. Baker . . .	Whittlesey, Isle of Ely	*Whittlesey* . . .	J. Baker . . .	Whittlesey, Isle of Ely	J. Baker, jun. .	Whittlesey, Peterborough.
		Thorney Abbey .	Thos. Peach . .	Thorney Abbey, Isle of Ely.		
J. Fairhurst . .	Wigan	*Wigan*	J. Fairhurst . .	Wigan	W. Bancks . .	Wigan.
W. Lea . . .	Haigh ; Wigan.	*Standish* . . .	W. Darbyshire .	Standish with Langtree	Josh. Bailey . .	Standish.
		Aspull . . .	W. Lea . . .	Haigh, Wigan . . .	T. Lea . . .	Aspull.
		Hindley . . .	John Grime . .	Hindley, Wigan . . .	Jno. Greene . .	Hindley.
		Pemberton . . .	T. Windus . .	Orrell, Wigan.		
		Ashton . . .	Geo. Byrom . .	Ashton, Wigan.		
		Upholland . . .	J. Barlow . . .	Upholland, Wigan.		

UNION, or SUPERINTENDENT REGISTRAR'S DISTRICT.	County.	Places of Public Worship situated therein, registered for Solemnization of Marriages.		SUPERINTENDENT REGISTRARS, and *Deputy Superintendent Registrars.*	
		Name.	Situation.	Name.	Address.
WIGHT, ISLE OF . . .	Hants . . .	Unitarian Chapel . . .	High-st., Newport, Isle of Wight	W. Hearn . .	Newport, Isle of Wight
		Independent Chapel . .	George-street, Ryde.	J. H. Hearn,	Ditto.
		Chapel of St. Thomas of Canterbury.	West Cowes.		
		St. James-street Chapel .	St. James-street, Newport, in the Isle of Wight.		
		The Wesleyan Chapel. .	Pyle-st., Newport, Isle of Wight.		
		The Congregational Chapel	Node Hill, Carisbrook.		
		The Baptist Chapel . .	Newport.		
		The Independent Chapel .	Union-road, West Cowes.		
		The Chapel of St. Thomas of Canterbury.	Pyle-street, Newport.		
		Ebenezer Chapel . . .	Holyrood-street, Newport.		
WIGTON	Cumberland . .	. . .	. . .	J. Studholme .	Wigton . . . . .
WILLITON	Somerset . . .	The Baptist Chapel . .	Watchet, in the parish of St. Decumans.	H. White. . .	Williton, Taunton .
		Wesleyan Chapel . . .	Dunster.		
WILTON	Wilts. . . .	The Independent Chapel .	Crow-lane, Wilton	T. Thring . .	Wilton, Wilts . . .
WIMBORNE and CRANBORNE.	Dorset . . .	The Independent Chapel .	Meeting-house-lane, Wimborne Minster.	H. Rowden . .	Wimborne Minster .
		Stape Hill Catholic Chapel	Stape Hill, in the parish of Hampreston.	I. Bryant,	Ditto.
WINCANTON	Somerset . . .	The Baptist Chapel . .	Mill-street, Wincanton . . .	R. Clarke . .	Wincanton . . . .
		The Old, or Independent Meeting-house.	Chapel-lane, Milborne Port.		
		Zion Chapel	South Cary, in the parish of Castle Cary.		
		The Independent Chapel .	Henstridge.		
WINCHCOMBE	Gloucester . .	. . .	. . .	D. Trenfield . .	Winchcombe . . .
WINCHESTER and HURSLEY.	Hants. . . .	The Independent Chapel .	Parchment-street, Winchester .	J. Ventham . .	Winchester . . . .
		St. Peter's Catholic Chapel	St. Peter's-street, Winchester.		
WINDSOR	Berks and Surrey	William-street, Chapel .	William-street, New Windsor .	W. C. Long . .	Windsor . . . . .
		The Catholic Chapel . .	Clewer.	G. H. Long,	Ditto.
WINSLOW	Bucks . . .	. . .	. . .	D. T. Willis . .	Winslow . . . .
WIRRAL	Chester . . .	St. Werebugh	Grange-lane, Birkenhead . .	J. Mallaby . .	Woodside, Chester .
WISBECH	Cambridge . .	General Baptist Chapel .	Ely-place, Wisbech	W. G. Jackson .	Wisbech St. Peter's .
		The Unitarian Meeting-house.	Church-lane, otherwise Deadman's-lane, Wisbech St. Peter's.		
		The Independent Chapel .	Wisbech.		
WITHAM	Essex. . . .	Witham Meeting . . .	Newland-street, Witham . .	J. H. Blood . .	Witham . . . .
		Independent Meeting-house	Great Coggleshall.		
		The Independent Meeting-house.	Terling.		
		The Independent Chapel .	Kelvedon.		
WITNEY	Oxon . . .	The Baptist Meeting-house	Coate, in the parish of Bampton	Fras. Hunt . .	Witney, Oxon . .
WOBURN.	Bedford . . .	The Baptist Meeting-house.	Ridgmount	W. Cole . . .	Husborne Crawley, Woburn.
WOKINGHAM	Berks. . . .	The Meeting-house . .	Nonsuch-lane, in the town of Wokingham.	J. R. Wheeler .	Wokingham . . .
WOLSTANTON and BURSLEM.	Stafford . . .	St. Peter's Catholic Chapel	Cobridge, in the parish of Burslem.	J. Lowndes . .	Marsh-Cottage, Wolstanton.
		The Independent Chapel .	Queen-street, Burslem.		

REGISTRARS of MARRIAGES.		Registrars' Districts.	REGISTRARS of BIRTHS and DEATHS.		Deputy Registrars of Births and Deaths.	
Name.	Address.		Name.	Address.	Name.	Address.
J. Sayer	Newport, Isle of Wight	Newport	J. Moore	Newport, Isle of Wight	W. Etheridge	Newport.Isle of Wight.
S. Young	Ryde, Isle of Wight.	Cowes	T. Thorold	Medina-road, West Cowes	W. Hillyer	High street, West
		Ryde	R. Ellman	Ryde.		Cowes.
		Godshill	J. Jolliffe	Dungewood, Newport, Isle of Wight.		
		Calbourne	J. Woodford	Shalfleet, Isle of Wight	J. Woodford, jun.	Shalfleet, Isle of Wight.
W. Buttery	Wigton	Wigton	W. Buttery	Wigton.		
		Abbey Holm	D. Pape	Abbey-town, Wigton.		
		Caldbeck	J. Woof	Hesket New-market, Wigton.		
J. Williams	Williton, Taunton	Williton	F. W. Rossiter	Williton, Taunton.		
T. Grindon	Dunster, Taunton.	Minehead	W. Gaye	Minehead, Taunton.		
		Stogursey	D. Howse	Kilve, Bridgwater.		
		Stogumber	Jas. Anning	Monksilver, Taunton.		
		Dunster	J. Paul	Dunster, Taunton.		
T. W. Randall	Wilton, Wilts.	Wilton	W. J. French	Wilton, Wilts	J. Howell	Wilton, Wilts.
		Bishopston	J. E. Beckingsale	Fovant, Wilts.		
G. Langer	Wimborne, Minster	Wimborne	T. Dowding	Wimborne Minster	J. Smith	West-street, Wimborne.
W. Butt	Cranborne.	Witchampton	J. Keeping	Colehill, Wimborne Minster	W. Sargeant	Holt, Wimborne.
		Cranborne	J. Hunt	Cranborne	H. Hayter	Cranborne.
Samuel Game	Milborne Port, Shaftesbury.	Wincanton	H. Legg	Wincanton.		
Albin Close	Castle Cary.	Milborne Port	J. Cox	Henstridge, Shaftesbury.		
J. Coombs	Henstridge, Shaftesbury	Castle Cary	R. Bord	North Cadbury, Castle Cary.		
S. Trowbridge	Wincanton.	Bruton	J. G. Bord	Bruton, Wincanton.		
		Guiting	J. Mason	Winchcombe.	G. Timbrell	Winchcombe.
		Cleeve	B. Slack	Bishop'sCleeve, Cheltenham		
A. Davy	Parchment-street, Winchester.	Winchester	C. Mayo	St. Peter's-street, Winchester.	F. Caiger.	St. Peter-street, Winchester.
N. Warren	22, High-street, Winchester	Worthys	G. Smith	Stratton, Winchester.		
T. Dennis	Hursley.	Mitcheldever	J. Wickham	Sutton Scotney, Winchester	J. Andrews	Sutton Scotney, Winchester.
		Twyford	James Young	Twyford, Winchester.		
		Hursley	Theo. Dennis	Hursley, Winchester.		
G. Bailey	Old Windsor	Windsor	W. Towers	New Windsor	J. Cobbett	New Windsor.
		Egham	C. Brown	Egham	J. Dodd	Egham.
J. Cowley	Winslow	Winslow	J. Cowley	Winslow.	G. Cowley	Winslow.
S. T. Robinson	Birkenhead, Chester	Birkenhead	J. Blaylock	Tranmere, Chester.	A. Blaylock	Tranmere, Chester.
		Woodchurch	S. Olive	Woodchurch, Upton.		
		Wallasey	W. Peers	Liscard, Seacombe.		
		Neston	T. Cottingham	Little Neston, Chester.		
		Eastham	J. Jones	Great Sutton, Eastham.		
W. Adams	Wisbech St. Peter's	Wisbech	W. Adams	Wisbech St. Peter's.		
		Leverington, Parson Drove.	J. Burman, jun.	Wisbech St. Mary.		
		Walsoken	J. Gapp	Elm, Wisbech.		
		Upwell	J. Atkins	Upwell, Wisbech.		
		Walpole St. Peter's	J. Bridgman	Walpole St. Peter's, Lynn.		
		Terrington St. Clement's	J. Egarr	Terrington St. John's	W. R. Goodrick	Terrington St. John's.
J. Eeley	Kelvedon	Witham	Wm. Nash	Witham.	M. Colk	Witham.
W. Nash.	Witham.	Coggleshall	H. Giles	Coggleshall.		
		Kelvedon	J. Eley	Kelvedon.		
J. Shayler	Witney	Witney	E. A. Batt	Witney.		
Joseph Dutton	Bampton.	Bampton	E. F. Whitaker	Bampton	S. Hudson	Bampton.
		Burford	T. Cheatle	Burford.		
		Ensham	W. Green	Ensham.	J. Jeffrey.	Ensham.
G. Bird	Aspley Guise, Woburn	Woburn	J. Dexter	Eversholt, Woburn	G. Bird	Aspley Guise, Woburn.
		Toddingham	Charles Wagstaff	Toddington, Dunstable	J. Cotchings.	Toddington, Dunstable.
W. W. Wheeler	Wokingham	Wargrave	J. Davis	Wargrave	T. House.	Wargrave.
		Wokingham	E. Weight	Wokingham	Geo. Newnham	Broad-st., Wokingham.
R. Timmis	Burslem	Wolstanton	J. Ball	Wolstanton.		
		Tunstall	S. Adams	Queen-st. North, Tunstall.		
		Burslem	J. W. Powell.	Moorland-road, Burslem.		

UNION, or SUPERINTENDENT REGISTRAR'S DISTRICT.	County.	Places of Public Worship situated therein, registered for Solemnization of Marriages.		SUPERINTENDENT REGISTRARS, and Deputy Superintendent Registrars.	
		Name.	Situation.	Name.	Address.
WOLVERHAMPTON and SEISDON.	Stafford	Queen-street Chapel	Queen-street, Wolverhampton.	H. N. Payne	Register-office, the Union-house, Wolverhampton.
		Independent Chapel	Oxford-street, Bilston.		
		The Wesleyan Chapel	Darlington-st., Wolverhampton.		
		The Catholic Chapel of Saints Peter and Paul, named The Great House.	Wolverhampton.		
		Baptist Chapel	Little London, in the parish of Wolverhampton.		
		A Catholic Chapel	Oxford-street, Bilston, in the parish of Wolverhampton.		
		The Unitarian Chapel	Snow Hill, Wolverhampton.		
		Temple-street Chapel	Wolverhampton.		
WOODBRIDGE.	Suffolk	The Baptist Meeting-house.	Grundisburgh	T. Carthew	Woodbridge
		The Quay Meeting	Woodbridge.	C. C. Brooks,	Ditto.
WOODSTOCK	Oxford	. . .	. . .	B Hollaway	Woodstock
				George Hall,	Ditto.
WORCESTER	Worcester	Angel-street Chapel	Worcester	W. Thomason	Tallow-hill, Worcester
		Catholic Chapel	Sansom-place.	Thomas Pugh,	London-road, Worcester.
		The Baptist Chapel	Silver-street, Worcester.		
WORKSOP	Notts.	. . .	. . .	J. Whall	Worksop
WORTHING.	Sussex	The Independent Chapel.	Tarrant-street, Arundel.	R. Edmunds	Worthing
		Trinity Chapel.	Tarrant-street, Arundel.		
WORTLEY	York	Netherfield Independent Chapel.	Netherfield, in the Township of Thurlstone, in the parish of Penistone.	John Dransfield	Penistone, near Barnsley.
WREXHAM	Denbigh	The Old Meeting, or Baptist Chapel.	Chester-street, Wrexham	T. Edgworth	Wrexham
		The Presbyterian Chapel.	Chester-street, Wrexham.		
		Baptist Chapel.	Cefn Mawr, in the parish of Ruabon.		
		The Independent Chapel.	Rhos y Medro, in the parish of Ruabon.		
		Bethlehem	Rhos-Llanerchrigog, in the parish of Ruabon.		
		The Independent Chapel.	Penybryn, Wrexham.		
WYCOMBE	Bucks	Stokenchurch Chapel	Stokenchurch	C. Harman	High Wycombe
		Independent Chapel	Chinnor.	William Jackson,	Ditto.
		Crendon-lane Chapel	Crendon-lane, Chepping Wycombe.		
		Bethel Chapel	Core's End, in the parish of Woburn.		
YARMOUTH, GREAT.	Norfolk	The New Meeting-house	Gaol-street, Great Yarmouth	H. Palmer	Quay, Great Yarmouth
		The Old Meeting-house	Gaol-street, Great Yarmouth.		
		The Catholic Chapel	George-street, Great Yarmouth.		
		The Primitive Methodist Tabernacle.	Great Yarmouth.		
		The Particular Baptist Chapel	Great Yarmouth.		
YEOVIL	Somerset	Providence Chapel.	Ilchester	R. Whisby	Yeovil
		South-street Chapel	South-street, Yeovil.		
		Independent Chapel	Henford, in the parish of Yeovil.		
		Ebenezer Chapel	Bower Hinton, in the parish of Martock.		
		The Independent Chapel	Roundwell-st., South Petherton.		
		Baptist Chapel.	Montacute.		
		The Tabernacle	Yeovil.		
YORK	York	The Presbyterian Meeting-house.	St. Saviour-gate, York	Henry Brearey	York
		The Catholic Chapel	Little Blake-street, York.	Henry Hillerby,	Hope-street, York.
		Lendal Chapel.	Lendal-street, York.		

REGISTRARS of MARRIAGES.		Registrars' Districts.	REGISTRARS of BIRTHS and DEATHS.		Deputy Registrars of Births and Deaths.	
Name.	Address.		Name.	Address.	Name.	Address.
G. Young	Wolverhampton	Wolverhampton, Eastern	G. Young	Market-st., Wolverhampton.	J. Barnett	Smithfield, Wolverhampton.
W. Walters	Wolverhampton.	Wolverhampton, Western	W. Walters	North-street, Wolverhampton.	J. Moore, jun.	North-street, Wolverhampton.
J. Fellows	Bilston.	Bilston	J. Fellows	Oxford-street, Bilston.		
Richard Foster	Willenhall.	Willenhall	R. Foster	Little-London, Willenhall.	A. Thompson	Little London, Willenhall.
		Wombourne	G. Prior	Wombourne.	W. Combe	Kinfare.
		Trittenhall	J. Smith	Tettenhall	J. Lyett	Pattingham.
		Kinfare	James Bennett	Kinfare.		
W. Kemp	Woodbridge	Woodbridge and Wilford Town.	J. Thurton	Woodbridge.		
		Woodbridge, Out	J. Kent	Dallingho.		
		Carlford	J. Sheppard	Rushmere, Ipswich.		
		Colneis	T. Miles	Trimley St. Martin.		
J. Churchill	Deddington	Woodstock	G. Coles, jun.	Woodstock.		
		Deddington	J. Churchill	Deddington.		
S. Daniell	High-street, Worcester.	Worcester, North	T. H. Wheeler	Foregate-street, Worcester.		
		Worcester, West	R. Hill	Foregate-street, Worcester.		
		Worcester, South	J. R. Woodward	Sidbury, Worcester.		
. . .	. . .	Carberton	H. Turner	Whitwell, Worksop.		
		Carlton	G. Hill	Blyth, Bawtry.		
		Anston	J. Airey	Anston, Worksop.		
		Worksop	H. Hase	Worksop.		
W. Duke	Arundel	Broadwater	C. Hide	Worthing	Wm. Patching	Worthing.
		Arundel	W. Wardroper	Arundel.		
		Little Hampton	G. Grant	Angmering, Sussex.		
J. Bedford	Penistone	Wortley	Luke Moorhouse	Wortley, Sheffield.		
		Penistone	John Bedford	Penistone, Barnsley.		
		Ecclesfield	James Machon	Ecclesfield, Sheffield.		
		Bradfield	W. Guelder	Bradfield, Sheffield.		
R. Hughes	Wrexham.	Ruabon	J. Roberts	Havody Buch, Ruabon.		
E. Morris	Ruabon.	Hope	G. Jones	Caergwrle, Wrexham.		
		Malpas	J. Smith	Holt, Wrexham.		
		Wrexham	J. Hughes	York-street, Wrexham.		
J. Harman	High Wycombe	High Wycombe	R. Turner	High Wycombe	M. E. Brown	High Wycombe.
T. B. Allnutt	Chinnor.	West Wycombe	R. Holmes	Stokenchurch	J. Veary	West Wycombe.
		Great Marlow	J. Reading	Great Marlow	H. Salmon	Great Marlow.
		Wendover	J. Cox	Monk's Risborough, Princes' Risborough.	W. Croxford	Wendover.
		Princes Risborough	H. Curtis	Princes Risborough	R. Turner	Bledlow, Princes Risborough.
J. P. Poppy	Great Yarmouth	Northern	H. Worship	Regent-st., Great Yarmouth.		
		Southern	J. Bayly	King-st., Great Yarmouth.		
W. Porter	Yeovil	Yeovil	W. Tomkins	Yeovil	E. J. Latham	Hendford, Yeovil.
J. H. Nicholls	South Petherton.	Martock	G. Stuckey	Martock.		
		Ilchester	W. Francis	Ilchester.		
		South Petherton	W. Harvey	South Petherton.		
		Coker	C. A. Highmore	East Coker.		
J. Lockey	86, Micklegate, York	Micklegate	W. Paver	2, St. Martin's-court, York	J. Thackray	Micklegate, York.
		Bootham	T. Peters	Petergate, York	W. Peters	Gillygate, York.
		Walmgate	G. Watson	Walmgate, York.		
		Escrick	Thos. Duckles	Escrick, York.		
		Dunnington	J. Bell	Dunnington, York	W. Nelson	Dunnington.
		Flaxton	W. Matthew	Harton, York	John Pearson	Harton, York
		Skelton	A. Hume	Skelton, York.		

LONDON:
Printed by W. Clowes and Sons, 14, Charing Cross,
For Her Majesty's Stationery Office.